Hello Korean

Volume 1

A Language Study Guide for K-pop & K-drama Fans

Jiyoung Park
Soyoung Yoo
Lee Joon-gi

TUTTLE Publishing

Tokyo │ Rutland, Vermont │ Singapore

Contents

A Message from the Authors

Writing this book took us three years, and finally we're proud that it is finally out in the world. We didn't anticipate it taking so long as we'd had its blueprint ready for some time, but we wanted to take the time needed to make the best book possible.

This is the final product of rigorous hands-on practice in live classroom settings. When something didn't work, we changed it; so what you have before you is our most polished version. Finally we added beautiful illustrations and, of course, the voice of our celebrated star, Lee Joon-gi.

Hello Korean aims to equip language learners with a basic grasp of spoken Korean. This book utilizes authentic colloquial expressions along with clear and concise explanations of the Korean Hangul alphabet, and basic grammar. Moreover, our guide to pronunciation will help you acquire a natural speaking voice from day one. Without paying careful attention to pronunciation from the beginning, you risk adopting bad habits that will prove hard to break later.

We wish to express our gratitude to Lee Joon-gi, for not only graciously recording the listening activities, but also endorsing our book as "a well-made Korean text book for beginning language learners."

Are you ready to take the first step to learn the Korean language? It's time to study Korean with the celebrated star of *The King and the Clown*, Lee Joon-gi!

—Jiyoung Park and Soyoung Yoo

A Message from Lee Joon-gi

It took three years for this book to see the light. My initial response to the proposal to take part in this book was vaguely lukewarm. Now that I see this book published, it's a surreal feeling and I am deeply moved.

I sometimes go on tour to meet fans around the world, and every time people who are not native speakers of Korean talk to me in Korean, I am flattered. I decided to take part in writing this book, hoping I could be helpful to those who want to learn the Korean language.

While participating in the project, I learned that it takes a lot of effort to publish one book. The night before an audio recording session I would go to bed feeling excited. Recording with professional voice actors taught me the importance of articulate pronunciation and making the audio tracks for this book was a fresh experience for me, even though I am using my voice every day in my acting.

Writing the **Lee Joon-gi's Guide to Seoul** sections of this book gave me a great chance to revisit many corners of Seoul I had not seen for a while. I am grateful for this opportunity to stop and acknowledge the beauty of a city I am often too busy to appreciate. I hope you will enjoy reading about and maybe even visiting the places I have chosen.

Hello Korean is not a photo album of a celebrity called Lee Joon-gi. This is a basic Korean language textbook written over a three-year period by two professors who are specialists in teaching the Korean language and have devoted their careers to becoming experts in their field. This book is more about them than about me.

To those who are taking the first step to learn the Korean language, I hope *Hello Korean* becomes a book that you cherish. This will put your Korean linguistic skills on a firm ground. Who knows? We might have a chance to strike up a conversation in Korean together one day. Thank you.

—Lee Joon-gi

How to Use This Book

A lot of effort was made to ensure that explanations are easy enough for self-study students while focusing on basic vocabulary and expressions, challenging grammar points, as well as pronunciation rules.

- We abbreviated nouns to N, adjectives to A, and verbs to V in the text.
- Lee Joon-gi himself recorded all of his parts in the soundtrack.
- The rules of Korean pronunciation are covered comprehensively in the opening section on pages 20–43, and there regular Pronunciation Rules sections in the main lessons.
- Answers for all grammar exercises, conversation practice exercises and listening practice exercises can be found at the back of the book.
- Online audio files for this book can be found at the link below. Each chapter of this book has its own audio file, labeled with the chapter number. All exercises and dialogues in the book that have audio files are marked with a logo of a student wearing headphones. The number underneath the logo indicates the point (in minutes and seconds) where that particular exercise or dialogue begins.

To Access the Online Materials:

1. Check to be sure you have an internet connection.
2. Type the URL below into your web browser.

https://www.tuttlepublishing.com/hello-korean-v1

For support, you can email us at info@tuttlepublishing.com

The Strengths of This Book

1. Easy for self-study students

A lot of effort was made to ensure that explanations are easy enough for self-study students while focusing on basic vocabulary and expressions, challenging grammar points, as well as pronunciation rules.

2. Clear explanations to help form solid understanding

The authors have put many years of their expertise in teaching Korean effectively to foreigners into this book. Exercises, charts and explanations have all been tried and tested in the classroom and have all been proven to be effective teaching methods.

3. Contemporary language that Koreans use in everyday situations

The book has frequently used expressions that beginners can easily understand. These expressions are presented in context, along with opportunities to practice applying these expressions in various everyday situations. Learn these expressions and try them with Koreans you meet!

4. Enjoy studying Korean with Lee Joon-gi, a Korean Wave celebrity

Learning becomes more meaningful and exciting when you practice listening and speaking using audio files recorded by your favorite actor. Being able to have conversations in Korean with Lee Joon-gi is fun and rewarding.

5. Learn vocabulary and expressions systematically with illustrations

Illustrated "Special" sections at the end of many lessons in this book will help you review and consolidate the language you have learned. Many of these pages lend themselves well to being photocopied and used as flash cards.

How This Book Is Organized

❶ How to Read, Write and Pronounce the Hangul Alphabet

Consonants and vowels, which are the building blocks of each syllable in the Korean writing system, are covered in this section. You will learn all the letters of the Hangul alphabet and how to read, write and pronounce them. This section also becomes a useful reference guide as you build up your fluency.

❷ Dialogue

Each of the main fifteen lessons begins with a dialogue using everyday expressions, woven together around a grammatical theme. Use the accompanying audio file to practice reading the conversations aloud, to build your confidence.

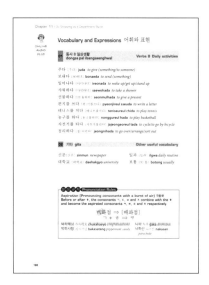

❸ Vocabulary and Expressions

New words and expressions that appear in the lesson are listed for your convenience. Relevant words are grouped together for more effective learning. Pronunciation rules for challenging words are explained separately within this section.

❹ Grammar

Essential Korean grammar points appear here. The choice of which verb form to use is an especially challenging concept for learners of Korean, and this is explained in a straightforward manner. The book contains verb charts and exercises to help you practice and gain confidence.

❺ Conversation

The conversation section presents newly learned words and grammar points in the context of an everyday situation and encourages you to practice using them. Illustrations are included to help you visualize the situation.

❻ Listening Practice

This section gives you the chance to develop your understanding of spoken Korean, by using the online audio files to do the listening comprehension exercises. Once you have completed the exercises and checked your answers in the answer key at the back of the book, you can practice reading aloud the correct sentences. This is a great way to improve your Korean proficiency quickly.

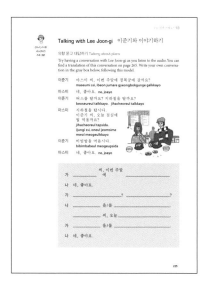

❼ Talking with Lee Joon-gi

This section of the lesson is based around an audio file of a conversation recorded by Lee Joon-gi. Listen to the audio and practice each conversation as if you were talking directly with Lee Joon-gi.

❽ Special

Many lessons end with a collection of useful illustrated expressions, based on the lesson theme. You can use these to help you review and memorize key language from that lesson. You can also photocopy and use these images as flash cards.

Characters in the Book

1 Jiyoung Choi

최지영 choejiyeong

Korea

university student

2 Lee Joon-gi

이준기 ijungi

Korea

movie actor

3 Lili

리리 riri

China

reporter

4 Wangshaowei

왕샤위 wangsyawi

China

police officer

5 Vivien

비비엔 bibien

Germany

exchange student

6 Ferdy

퍼디 peodi

Philippines

university student

7 **Stephanie**

스테파니 **seutepani**

Australia

office worker

8 **Roberto**

로베르토 **robereuto**

Spain

researcher

9 **Diana**

다이애나 **daiaena**

Côte d'Ivoire

university student

10 **Roy**

로이 **roi**

Hong Kong

doctor

11 **Masumi**

마스미 **maseumi**

Japan

chef

12 **Benson**

벤슨 **benseun**

Kenya

soccer player

Summary of Lesson Content

	Lessons	Key Points	Grammar
	Introduction: How to Read, Write and Pronounce the Hangul Alphabet	한글의 자음과 모음 *The Consonants and Vowels of Hangul* 한글의 발음 규칙 *Hangul Pronunciation Rules*	
1과	안녕하세요? *Hello!*	자기소개하기 *Introducing Yourself*	• *Particles* • *Nationalities and Occupations* • *Forms of address*
2과	이것은 무엇입니까? *What's This?*	사물 묻고 답하기 *Asking and Answering Questions about Objects*	• *This / that / what?* • *Is this / that a _____?* • *Yes, it's a ____ ./No, it isn't a ____ .*
3과	이 라면은 한 개에 얼마예요? *How Much Is This Packet of Noodles?*	물건 사기 *Shopping*	• *This / that / that* • *It is / It is not* • *____ and ____* • *Per ____* • *Numbers*
4과	오늘은 며칠이에요? *What's the Date Today?*	날짜와 요일 말하기 *Dates and Days of the Week*	• *What's the date?* • *When is (special day)?* • *What kind of N is N?*
5과	지금 몇 시예요? *What Time Is It Now?*	시간 묻고 답하기 *Asking and Telling the Time*	• *Telling the time* • *From ____ until ____*
6과	우리 집은 신촌에 있어요 *I live in Sinchon*	위치 말하기 *Describing a Location*	• *Here / there / where* • *Where is ____?* • *____ is (in this location)*
7과	저는 오늘 영화를 봅니다 *I'm Watching a Movie Today*	일정 묻고 답하기 *Talking about Schedules*	• *Asking questions* • *Answering questions* • *Time particles* • *Also / as well*

Vocabulary and Expressions	Pronunciation Rules	Special
인사 *Greetings* 나라 *Countries* 직업 *Occupations* 취미 *Hobbies*	비음화 *Nasalization*	인사하기 *Greetings*
생활필수품 *Daily necessities* 음식 이름 *Food names*	연음 법칙 *Liaison (Linking)*	지시 대명사 (이~/그~/저~/어느~) *Demonstrative pronouns* *This / That / That / Which*
생활필수품 *Daily necessities* 식품 *Food* 단위 *Counting units*	경음화 *Tense consonants*	돈 *Money*
날짜 *Year, months and days* 요일 *Days of the week*	연음 법칙 *Liaison (Linking)*	달력읽기 *Reading the calendar*
시간 *Times of day* 장소 *Places around town*	경음화 *Tense consonants*	
위치 *Location* 장소 *Places*		
기본 동사 *Basic verbs*	비음화 *Nasalization*	

Vocabulary and Expressions	Pronunciation Rules	Special
동사 – 오고 가는 것 *Verbs: Leaving and arriving* 동사 – 물건 사기 *Verbs: Shopping*	연음 법칙 *Liaison (Linking)*	동사 *Verbs*
동사 – 날씨 *Verbs: Weather* 형용사 – 날씨 *Adjectives: Weather* 기본 형용사 *Basic adjectives*	격음화 *Aspiration*	형용사 *Adjectives*
서울 근교의 유명한 장소 *Famous places in Seoul* 동사 – 놀이 *Verbs: Hanging out*	구개음화 *Palatalization* 경음화 *Tense consonants*	동사·형용사 활용표 *Verb and adjective conjugation table*
동사 – 일상생활 *Verbs: Daily activities*	격음화 *Aspiration*	'으' 불규칙 으 'ㄷ' 불규칙 ㄷ *Irregular verbs and adjectives*
음식 *Food* 여행지 *Tourist destinations* 동사 – 취미 *Verbs: Hobbies*	'의' 의 발음 *Pronunciation of the syllable* 의	취미 *Hobbies*
동사 – 약속 *Verbs: Appointments*	'ㅎ' 탈락 *Omission of* ㅎ	조사 *Particles*
동사 – 진행, 습관 *Verbs: Daily habits*	연음 법칙 *Liaison (Linking)*	장소 *Places*
교통수단 *Public transportation* 장소 *Places* 교통표지 *Traffic*		금지와 명령의 표현 *Commands*

INTRODUCTION

HOW TO READ, WRITE AND PRONOUNCE THE HANGUL ALPHABET

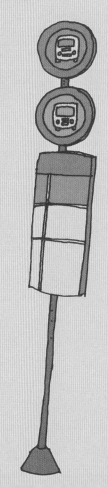

The Consonants and Vowels of Hangul
한글의 자음과 모음

The Korean language is written using the Hangul writing system, which consists of consonants and vowels that each have their own characteristic sound. Consonants and vowels are combined to make syllables, and all Korean words are composed of syllables. The charts on these pages give approximations of Korean sounds using the English alphabet. Readers who are familiar with the International Phonetic Alphabet (IPA) can find phonetic transcriptions of each Korean sound on page 45.

ONLINE AUDIO
00:22

모음 Vowels

Letter	ㅏ	ㅓ	ㅗ	ㅜ	ㅡ	ㅣ	ㅔ	ㅐ
Sound	a	eo	o	u	eu	i	e	ae
Letter	ㅑ	ㅕ	ㅛ	ㅠ			ㅖ	ㅒ
Sound	ya	yeo	yo	yu			ye	yae
Letter	ㅘ	ㅝ	ㅚ	ㅟ	ㅢ		ㅞ	ㅙ
Sound	wa	wo	oe	wi	ui		we	wae

ONLINE AUDIO
01:45

자음 Consonants

Letter	ㄱ	ㄴ	ㄷ	ㄹ	ㅁ	ㅂ	ㅅ	ㅇ	ㅈ	ㅎ
Sound	g/k	n	d	l/r	m	b	s	ng	j	h
Letter	ㅋ		ㅌ			ㅍ			ㅊ	
Sound	k		t			p			ch	
Letter	ㄲ		ㄸ			ㅃ	ㅆ		ㅉ	
Sound	kk		tt			pp	ss		jj	

한글의 모음도 Vowel diagram

In Hangul, there are eight basic short vowels: ㅏ, ㅓ, ㅗ, ㅜ, ㅡ, ㅣ, ㅔ and ㅐ, and thirteen double vowels: ㅑ, ㅕ, ㅛ, ㅠ, ㅒ, ㅖ, ㅘ, ㅙ, ㅚ, ㅝ, ㅞ, ㅟ and ㅢ. The diagram below shows the location of the tongue when articulating each of the short vowels.

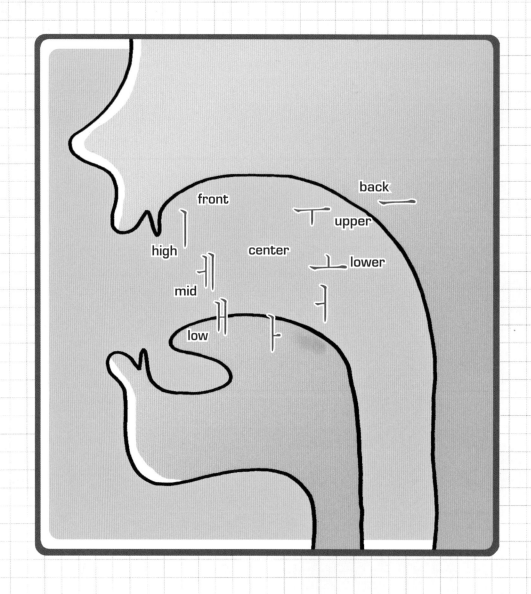

ONLINE AUDIO
03:12

(1) 발음하기 Pronunciation

Listen and repeat.

Vowel	Sound	Shape of the mouth	How to pronounce
ㅏ	a		Open your mouth wide and vocalize.
ㅓ	eo		Relax your mouth more than when pronouncing the sound ㅗ and vocalize. The gap between your upper and lower lips should be about one inch (2.5 cm).
ㅗ	o		Shrink your mouth as much as possible and vocalize.
ㅜ	u		Shrink your mouth as much as possible and vocalize.
ㅡ	eu		Pull your lips to the both sides of your mouth (the opposite as for ㅜ) and vocalize.
ㅣ	i		Flatten and widen your lips and vocalize.
ㅔ	e		Make the gap between your upper and lower lips half an inch (1cm) and vocalize.
ㅐ	ae		Open your mouth wider than as for ㅔ and vocalize.

(2) 쓰기 Writing

Write each of the following vowels in the correct stroke order.

ㅏ	ㅏ	ㅏ				
ㅓ	ㅓ	ㅓ				
ㅗ	ㅗ	ㅗ				
ㅜ	ㅜ	ㅜ				
ㅡ	ㅡ					
ㅣ	ㅣ					
ㅖ	ㅖ	ㅖ	ㅖ			
ㅒ	ㅒ	ㅒ	ㅒ			

ONLINE AUDIO
03:50

(3) 연습 Practice

Listen and repeat the words out loud.

1) 아이 [아이/ai] *child/kid*   오이 [오이/oi] *cucumber*

2) 아우 [아우/au] *younger brother/sister*   애 [애:/ae] *the shortened form of* 아이

24

ONLINE AUDIO
04:10

1) 자음 1 Consonants 1

(1) 발음하기 Pronunciation

Listen and repeat.

ㅏ		가구 〔가구/gagu〕 *furniture*		고기 〔고기/gogi〕 *meat*		가다 〔가다/gada〕 *to go*
ㅓ		나 〔나/na〕 *I/my/me*		노루 〔노루/noru〕 *roe deer*		노래 〔노래/norae〕 *song*
ㅗ		다리 〔다리dari〕 *leg/bridge*		구두 〔구두/gudu〕 *shoe*		두 개 〔두:개/du gae〕 *two pieces*
ㅐ		오리 〔오:리/ori〕 *duck*		라디오 〔라디오/radio〕 *radio*		우리 〔우리/uri〕 *we/our/us*

(2) 쓰기 Writing

Write each of the following vowels in the correct stroke order.

ㄱ	ㄱ				
ㄴ	ㄴ				
ㄷ	ㄷ	ㄷ			
ㄹ	ㄹ	ㄹ	ㄹ		

(3) 음절 Syllables

Combine vowels and consonants to construct syllables in the following chart. For the syllables below, consonants are located on the left or the top, and vowels are either on the right or below.

Vowels / Consonants	ㅏ	ㅓ	ㅗ	ㅜ	ㅡ	ㅣ	ㅔ	ㅐ
ㄱ			고				게	
ㄴ	나				느			
ㄷ		더					디	
ㄹ				루				래

A single vowel can constitute a syllable by itself but then its shape does not qualify as a valid syllable. The solution is to append ㅇ in front of the vowel. This ㅇ signifies that syllable has no consonant, as in the word 오이, and when used in this way it is silent.

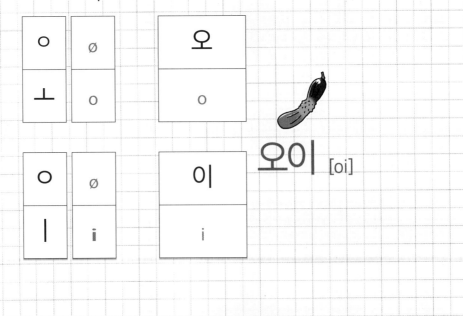

오이 [oi]

26

(4) 연습 Practice

Listen and repeat the words below.

1) 거기〔거기/geogi〕 *there*

2) 어디〔어디/eodi〕 *where*

3) 나라〔나라/nara〕 *country*

누나〔누나/nuna〕 *older sister*

나가다〔나가다/nagada〕 *to go out (from a place)*

내리다〔내리다/naerida〕 *to get off (a vehicle)*

2) 자음1 Consonants 2

(1) 발음하기 Pronunciation

Listen and repeat.

ㅁ		머리〔머리/meori〕 *head*		모자〔모자/moja〕 *hat*			무〔무:/mu〕 *radish*
ㅂ		배〔배/bae〕 *ship*		바다〔바다/bada〕 *sea*			비누〔비누/binu〕 *soap*
ㅅ		소〔소/so〕 *cow*		사다〔사다/sada〕 *to buy*			새〔새:/sae〕 *bird*
ㅈ		자〔자:/ja〕 *ruler*		아주머니〔아주머니/ ajumeoni〕 *middle-aged woman*			지도〔지도/jido〕 *map*
ㅎ		해〔해/hae〕 *the sun*		지하〔지하/jiha〕 *basement*			허리〔허리/heori〕 *waist*

(2) 쓰기 Writing

Write each of the following consonants in the correct stroke order.

ㅁ	ㅁ	ㅁ	ㅁ				
ㅂ	ㅂ	ㅂ	ㅂ	ㅂ			
ㅅ	ㅅ	ㅅ					
ㅈ	ㅈ	ㅈ					
ㅎ	ㅎ	ㅎ	ㅎ				

(3) 음절 Syllables

Combine the following consonants and vowels.

Vowels / Consonants	ㅏ	ㅑ	ㅓ	ㅕ	ㅗ	ㅛ	ㅜ	ㅠ	ㅡ	ㅣ
ㅁ				며			무			
ㅂ		뱌							브	
ㅅ	사							슈		
ㅈ					조					지
ㅎ			허			효				

ONLINE AUDIO
07:32

(4) 연습 Practice

Listen and repeat the words below.

1) 나무〔나무/namu〕 *tree*
   부부〔부부/bubu〕 *married couple*

   어머니〔어머니/eomoni〕 *mother*
   나비〔나비/nabi〕 *butterfly*

2) 사이〔사이/sai〕 *gap/between*
   서다〔서다/seoda〕 *to stand*

   소나무〔소나무/sonamu〕 *pine tree*
   수고〔수고/sugo〕 *effort*

3) 호수〔호수/hosu〕 *lake*
   휴지〔휴지/hyuji〕 *tissue*

   흐리다〔흐리다/heurida〕 *overcast*
   하마〔하마/hama〕 *hippo*

3] 자음 3 Consonants 3

ONLINE AUDIO
08:21

[1] 발음하기 Pronunciation

Listen and repeat.

ㅊ		차 〔차/cha〕 *car*		고추 〔고추/gochu〕 *chili pepper*		치마 〔치마/chima〕 *skirt*
ㅋ		코 〔코/ko〕 *nose*		키 〔키/ki〕 *height*		크다 〔크다/keuda〕 *big*
ㅌ		타조 〔타:조/tajo〕 *ostrich*		투수 〔투수/tusu〕 *pitcher*		도토리 〔도토리/dotori〕 *acorn*
ㅍ		포도 〔포도/podo〕 *grapes*		파 〔파/pa〕 *leek*		파도 〔파도/pado〕 *wave*

(2) 쓰기 Writing

Write each of the following consonants in the correct stroke order.

ㅊ	ㅊ	ㅊ	ㅊ				
ㅋ	ㅋ	ㅋ					
ㅌ	ㅌ	ㅌ					
ㅍ	ㅍ	ㅍ	ㅍ	ㅍ			

(3) 음절 Syllables

Combine the consonants and vowels below. The vowels ㅏ, ㅓ, ㅣ, ㅔ and ㅐ are positioned on the right of the consonant, and the vowels ㅗ, ㅜ and ㅡ are positioned below the consonant.

Vowels / Consonants	ㅏ	ㅑ	ㅓ	ㅕ	ㅗ	ㅛ	ㅜ	ㅠ	ㅡ	ㅣ
ㅊ			처				추			
ㅋ		캬								크
ㅌ					토					티
ㅍ	파					표				

30

(4) 연습 Practice

Listen and repeat the words below.

1) 채소 〔채:소/chaeso〕 *vegetable*

2) 커피 〔커피/keopi〕 *coffee*

3) 우표 〔우표/upyo〕 *postage stamp*

우체국 〔우체국/ucheguk〕 *post office*

카메라 〔카메라/kamera〕 *camera*

스피커 〔스피커/seupikeo〕 *speaker*

4) 자음 4 Consonants 4

[1] 발음하기 Pronunciation

Listen and repeat.

ㄲ	까치 〔까치/kkachi〕 *magpie*	토끼 〔토끼/tokki〕 *rabbit*	꼬리 〔꼬리/kkori〕 *tail*
ㄸ	띠 〔띠/tti〕 *belt*	따다 〔따다/ttada〕 *to pick/pluck*	뜨다 〔뜨다/tteuda〕 *to weave*
ㅃ	뿌리 〔뿌리/ppuri〕 *root*	뽀뽀 〔뽀뽀/ppoppo〕 *kiss*	바쁘다 〔바쁘다/ bappeuda〕 *busy*
ㅆ	쓰다 〔쓰다/sseuda〕 *to write*	비싸다 〔비싸다/bissada〕 *expensive*	아가씨 〔아가씨/agassi〕 *young woman*
ㅉ	찌개 〔찌개/jjigae〕 *Korean stew*	짜다 〔짜다/jjada〕 *to wring*	버찌 〔버찌/beojji〕 *cherry*

(2) 음절 Syllables

Combine the following consonants and vowels.

Vowels Consonants	ㅏ	ㅑ	ㅓ	ㅕ	ㅗ	ㅛ	ㅜ	ㅠ	ㅡ	ㅣ
ㄲ			꺼			꾸				
ㄸ	따									띠
ㅃ			뻐						쁘	
ㅆ			써			쑤				
ㅉ					쪼					찌

ONLINE AUDIO
11:51

(3) 연습 Practice

Listen and repeat the words below.

1) 꼬마〔꼬마/kkoma〕 *kid*
   따다〔따다/ttada〕 *to pick/pluck*

   바꾸다〔바꾸다/bakkuda〕 *to change*
   떠나다〔떠나다/tteonada〕 *to leave*

2) 아빠〔아빠/appa〕 *dad*
   쏘다〔쏘:다/ssoda〕 *to shoot*

   빠르다〔빠르다/ppareuda〕 *fast*
   쓰러지다〔쓰러지다/sseureojida〕 *to fall down*

3) 짜다〔짜다/jjada〕 *to wring*
   가짜〔가짜/gajja〕 *fake*

   찌르다〔찌르다/jjireuda〕 *to pierce*

ONLINE AUDIO
12:37

[1] 발음하기 Pronunciation

Listen and repeat.

ㅒ	 애기 〔애:기/yaegi〕 *talking*		
ㅖ	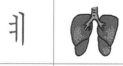 폐 〔폐/폐/pye〕 *lung*	시계 〔시계/시게/ sigye〕 *clock*	
ㅘ	사과 〔사과/sagwa〕 *apple*	화가 〔화가/hwaga〕 *painter*	
ㅙ	왜 〔왜/wae〕 *why*	 돼지 〔돼:지/dwaeji〕 *pig*	
ㅚ	외투 〔웨:투/oetu〕 *coat*	최고 〔췌:고/choego〕 *best*	회사 〔훼사/hoesa〕 *company*
ㅝ	더워요 〔더워요/deowoyo〕 *hot*	추워요 〔추워요/chuwoyo〕 *cold*	무거워요 〔무거워요/ mugeowoyo〕 *heavy*
ㅞ	궤도 〔궤:도/gwedo〕 *orbit*		
ㅟ	위 〔위/wi〕 *above*	귀 〔귀/gwi〕 *ear*	뒤 〔뒤:/dwi〕 *behind*
ㅢ	의사 〔의사/uisa〕 *doctor*	의자 〔의자/uija〕 *chair*	회의 〔훼이/hoeui〕 *conference*

(2) 쓰기 Writing

Write each of the following double vowels in the correct stroke order.

ㅒ	ㅒ	ㅒ	ㅒ	ㅒ				
ㅖ	ㅖ	ㅖ	ㅖ	ㅖ				
과	과	과	과	과				
ㅙ	ㅙ	ㅙ	ㅙ	ㅙ	ㅙ			
ㅚ	ㅚ	ㅚ	ㅚ					
ㅝ	ㅝ	ㅝ	ㅝ	ㅝ				
ㅞ	ㅞ	ㅞ	ㅞ	ㅞ	ㅞ			
ㅟ	ㅟ	ㅟ	ㅟ					
ㅢ	ㅢ	ㅢ						

ONLINE AUDIO
15:02

(3) 연습 Practice

Listen and repeat the words below.

1) 예의 〔예이 /yeui〕 *courtesy*

2) 봐요 〔봐:요 /bwayo〕 *Have a look.*

3) 쉬다 〔쉬:다 /swida〕 *to rest*

세계 〔세:계 /세:게 /segye〕 *world*

피로워요 〔페로워요 /goelowoyo〕 *I'm in agony.*

의미 〔의미 /uimi〕 *meaning*

Let's learn syllables that consist of three letters: an initial consonant, a vowel in the middle, and then a final consonant. The final consonant is called 받침 (**batchim**), and is positioned below the combined initial consonant and middle vowel.

ONLINE AUDIO
15:31

[1] 발음하기 Pronunciation

Listen and repeat.

ㄱ , ㅋ , ㄲ **[k]**		책 〔책 /chaek〕 *book*		부엌 〔부억 /bueok〕 *kitchen*		낚시 〔낙씨 /naksi〕 *fishing*
ㄴ **[n]**		눈 〔눈 /nun〕 *eye*		산 〔산 /san〕 *mountain*		돈 〔돈: /don〕 *money*
ㄷ , ㅅ , ㅈ **[t]** ㅊ , ㅌ , ㅎ		걷다 〔걷:따 /geotda〕 *to walk*		빗 〔빋 /bit〕 *comb*		낮 〔낟 /nat〕 *daytime*
		꽃 〔꼳 /kkot〕 *flower*		밭 〔받 /bat〕 *farm*		히읗 〔히읃 /hieut〕 *the letter* ㅎ
ㄹ **[l]**		달 〔달 /dal〕 *moon*		발 〔발 /bal〕 *foot*		팔 〔팔 /pal〕 *arm*

ㅁ [m]		곰 〔곰:/gom〕 *bear*		밤 〔밤/bam〕 *night*	엄마 〔엄마/eomma〕 *mom*
ㅂ ㅍ [p]		집 〔집/jip〕 *house*		앞 〔압/ap〕 *front*	무릎 〔무릅/mureup〕 *knee*
ㅇ [ng]		강 〔강/gang〕 *river*		공 〔공:/gong〕 *ball*	창문 〔창문/changmun〕 *window*

ONLINE AUDIO
17:30

[2] 연습 Practice

Listen and repeat the words below.

1) 벽〔벽/byeok〕 *wall*
   깎다〔깍따/kkakda〕 *to cut*

   남녘〔남녁/namnyeok〕 *south*
   문〔문/mun〕 *door*

2) 곧〔곧/got〕 *soon*
   벚〔벋/beot〕 *cherry blossom*
   끝〔끋/kkeut〕 *end*

   낫〔낟/nat〕 *sickle*
   빛〔빋/bit〕 *light*

3) 알다〔알:다/alda〕 *to know*
   밥〔밥/bap〕 *rice*
   공장〔공장/gongjang〕 *factory*

   몸〔몸/mom〕 *body*
   잎〔입/ip〕 *leaf*

Hangul Pronunciation Rules
한글의 발음 규칙

There are many pronunciation rules in the Korean language. Take the time to learn them by heart and so that you can perfect your pronunciation.

01 연음 법칙   Liaison (Linking)

When a syllable ends with a consonant, and the next syllable in the word begins with a vowel, then the final consonant of the first syllable is pronounced as the initial consonant of the next syllable.

Word [Pronunciation]	**Word** [Pronunciation]	**Word** [Pronunciation]
꽃이 〔꼬치/kkochi〕 *flower*	옷을 〔오슬/oseul〕 *clothes*	먹어요 〔머거요/meogeoyo〕 *eat*
밥이 〔바비/babi〕 *rice*	부엌에 〔부어케/bueokke〕*in the kitchen*	닫아요 〔다다요/dadayo〕 *close*
문어 〔무너/muneo〕 *octopus*	마음에 〔마으메/maeume〕 *in the heart*	살아요 〔사라요/sarayo〕 *live*

An obstruent sound is a consonant formed by obstructing outward airflow, hence causing increased air pressure in the vocal tract. When this obstruent sound is used as a final consonant, then it turns into a plosive, which is a speech sound made by stopping the flow of air coming out of the mouth and then suddenly releasing it, for example as in the sounds [t] and [p] in the word "top."

Obstruent sounds can also be made by placing the back of the tongue against or near the back part of the mouth, such as in ㄱ, ㄲ and ㅋ, which are articulated as ㄱ. Words such as 국〔국〕, 밖〔박〕 and 부엌〔부엌〕 are good examples.

Letter	Pronunciation	Example
ㄱ, ㅋ, ㄲ	[k]	국, 부엌, 밖
ㄷ, ㅅ, ㅆ, ㅈ, ㅊ, ㅌ, ㅎ	[t]	곧, 다섯, 갔다, 빚, 빛, 끝, 히읗
ㅂ, ㅍ	[p]	밥, 숲

03 겹받침 단순화   **Simplification of final double consonants**

The Korean language has eleven final double consonants: ㄳ, ㄵ, ㄶ, ㄺ, ㄻ, ㄼ, ㄽ, ㄾ, ㄿ, ㅀ and ㅄ. However, only seven final consonants are pronounced, which are ㄱ, ㄴ, ㄷ, ㄹ, ㅁ, ㅂ and ㅇ. Final double consonants lose either the initial consonant or the second when pronounced. The rules are as follows:

(1) 첫소리만 발음되는 경우 The first consonant is pronounced and the second is not

In the case of the final double consonants ᆪ, ᆬ, ᆰ, ᆴ and ᆹ, only the initial consonants are pronounced and the second ones are not.

Word [Pronunciation]	Word [Pronunciation]	Word [Pronunciation]
넋 〔넉/neok〕 *soul*	앉다 〔안따/anda〕 *sit*	외곬 〔웨골/oegol〕 *narrow-mindedness*
핥다 〔할따/halda〕 *lick*	값 〔갑/gap〕 *value*	몫 〔목/mok〕 *share*

(2) 첫소리는 그대로 발음되고 둘째 소리는 바뀌는 경우 The first consonant is pronounced and the second transforms

When the final consonants of a syllable are ᆭ or ᆶ, the first consonant is pronounced in the normal way. When ㅎ is the final consonant and the next syllable begins with the consonants ㄱ, ㄷ or ㅈ, both sounds merge and the pronunciation will change: ㄱ is pronounced as ㅋ; ㄷ is pronounced as ㅌ; and ㅈ is pronounced as ㅊ. ㅎ becomes silent when the next syllable begins with the consonants ㄴ or ㅅ.

Word [Pronunciation]	Word [Pronunciation]	Word [Pronunciation]
많고 〔만:코/manko〕 *many and*	많다 〔만:타/manta〕 *many*	많지 〔만:치/manchi〕 *there are a lot*
싫고 〔실코/silko〕 *dislike and*	싫다 〔실타/silta〕 *dislike*	싫지 〔실치/silchi〕 *I dislike it*
많소 〔만:쏘/mansso〕 *there are a lot*	많네 〔만:네/manne〕 *there are a lot*	
뚫소 〔뚤쏘/ttulso〕 *I pierce it*	뚫네 〔뚤레/ttulle〕 *I pierced it*	

(3) 둘째 소리만 발음되는 경우   The first consonant is not pronounced but the second consonant is

In the case of the final double consonants like ㄲ and ㄲ, the first consonants are not pronounced but the second ones are articulated.

Word [Pronunciation]	Word [Pronunciation]	Word [Pronunciation]
삶 〔삼:/sam〕 *life*	굶다 〔굼:따/gumda〕 *to starve*	젊다 〔점:따/jeomda〕 *young*
읊다 〔읍따/eupda〕 *to recite*	읊지 〔읍찌/eupji〕 *recited*	읊고 〔읍꼬/eupgo〕 *recited*

(4) 첫소리만 발음되거나 둘째 소리만 발음되는 경우 Either the first or the second consonant is pronounced (exceptions)

In the case of the final double consonant ㄼ, when a word ends in ㄼ, or when ㄼ is followed by a consonant, the first consonant ㄹ is pronounced and the second consonant ㅂ becomes silent. However, there is an exception when ㄼ is combined with 바. When 밟 is followed by a consonant, the second consonant ㅂ is pronounced and the first consonant ㄹ becomes silent.

Word [Pronunciation]	Word [Pronunciation]	Word [Pronunciation]
여덟 〔여덜/yeodeol〕 *eight*	짧다 〔짤따/jjalda〕 *short*	짧고 〔짤꼬/jjalgo〕 *short*
넓다 〔널따/neolda〕 *wide*	넓지 〔널찌/neolji〕 *wide*	넓고 〔널꼬/neolgo〕 *wide*
밟다 〔밥:따/bapda〕 *to step on*	밟지 〔밥:찌/bapji〕 *step on*	밟고 〔밥:꼬/bapgo〕 *stepped on*

According to the rules just mentioned, in the case of the double consonant ㄺ, the first consonant ㄹ is removed and the second consonant ㄱ is articulated. However, if the syllable is followed by the consonant ㄱ, then the first consonant ㄹ is articulated and the second consonant ㄱ is omitted.

Word [Pronunciation]	Word [Pronunciation]	Word [Pronunciation]	Word [Pronunciation]
읽다 〔익따/ikda〕 *to read*	읽지 〔익찌/ikji〕 *read*	읽고 〔일꼬/ilkko〕 *read*	읽게 〔일께/ilkke〕 *read it*
맑다 〔막따/makda〕 *clear*	맑지 〔막찌/makji〕 *sunny*	맑고 〔말꼬/malkko〕 *clear*	맑게 〔말께/malkke〕 *purely*

04 비음화   Nasalization

[1] 비음화   Nasalization

The consonants ㅂ, ㄷ and ㄱ are pronounced ㅁ, ㄴ and ㅇ before the nasal vowels ㄴ, ㅁ or ㅇ. The final consonants ㅂ, ㄷ and ㄱ each become ㅁ, ㄴ and ㅇ before the nasal vowels ㄴ, ㅁ or ㅇ.

Word [Pronunciation]	Word [Pronunciation]	Word [Pronunciation]
앞마당 〔암마당/ammadang〕 *forecourt*	믿는다 〔민는다/minneunda〕 *to believe*	한국말 〔한ː궁말/hangungmal〕 *Korean*
입는 〔임는/imneun〕 *worn*	있는 〔인는/inneun〕 *there is*	학년 〔항년/hangnyeon〕 *grade*

(2) 유음의 비음화 Nasalization of liquid sounds

Liquid sounds are sounds where the tongue makes a partial closure in the mouth, such as the sounds [l] and [r] in the English language. In Korean, the liquid sound ㄹ is articulated as ㄴ in front of all the consonants other than ㄴ and ㄹ.

Word [Pronunciation]	Word [Pronunciation]	Word [Pronunciation]
심리 〔심니/simni〕 *psychology*	정류장 〔정뉴/jeongnyujang〕 *station*	등록금 〔등노끔/deungnokgeum〕 *tuition*
염려 〔염녀/yeomnyeo〕 *worry*	국립 〔궁닙/gungnip〕 *national*	대학로 〔대항노/daehangno〕 *Daehangno*

05 경음화   Tense consonants

After an obstruent sound as described on page 38, the initial consonants ㄱ, ㄷ, ㅂ, ㅅ and ㅈ become the tense consonants ㄲ, ㄸ, ㅃ, ㅆ and ㅉ.

Word [Pronunciation]	Word [Pronunciation]	Word [Pronunciation]
학교 〔학꾜/hakgyo〕 *school*	받다 〔받따/batda〕 *to receive*	꽃밭 〔꼳빧/kkotbat〕 *flower garden*
국수 〔국쑤/guksu〕 *noodle*	국자 〔국짜/gukja〕 *ladle*	책상 〔책쌍/chaeksang〕 *desk*

06 격음화   Aspiration

Aspirated consonants are pronounced with a little puff of air, such as [k], [p] and [t] in English. Before or after ㅎ, the consonants ㄱ, ㄷ, ㅂ and ㅈ combine with the ㅎ and turn to the aspirated consonants ㅋ, ㅌ, ㅍ and ㅊ.

Word [Pronunciation]	**Word** [Pronunciation]	**Word** [Pronunciation]	**Word** [Pronunciation]
국화 〔구콰/gukwa〕 *chrysanthemum*	맏형 〔마텽/matyeong〕 *eldest brother*	입학 〔이팍/ipak〕 *admission*	앉히다 〔안치다/anchida〕 *to sit*
놓고 〔노코/noko〕 *put and*	놓다 〔노타/nota〕 *to put*	놓지 〔노치/nochi〕 *let go*	많다 〔만:타/manta〕 *many*

07 구개음화   Palatalization

Palatalization means to make a consonant sound harder, by putting your tongue against the roof of your mouth. The final consonants ㄷ and ㅌ turn to ㅈ and ㅊ when followed by a grammatical ending that has been added to the word that starts with 이 or 히.

Word [Pronunciation]	**Word** [Pronunciation]	**Word** [Pronunciation]
굳이 〔구지/guji〕 *unnecessarily*	맏이 〔마지/maji〕 *firstborn*	해돋이 〔해도지/haedoji〕 *sunrise*
같이 〔가치/gachi〕 *together*	끝이 〔끄치/kkeuchi〕 *the end*	굳히다 〔구치다/guchida〕 *to harden*

The final consonant ㅎ is omitted before a syllable that starts with a vowel.

Word [Pronunciation]	**Word** [Pronunciation]	**Word** [Pronunciation]
좋아요 〔조:아요/joayo〕 *good*	좋은 〔조:은/joeun〕 *good*	좋을 〔조:을/joeul〕 *will be good*
많아요 〔마:나요/manayo〕 *many*	많은 〔마:는/maneun〕 *many*	많을 〔마:늘/maneul〕 *will be many*

 사전찾기   How to use a Korean dictionary

Listing order of words in Korean Dictionary.

1	초성 Initial Consonant	ㄱ ㄲ ㄴ ㄷ ㄸ ㄹ ㅁ ㅂ ㅃ ㅅ ㅆ ㅇ ㅈ ㅉ ㅊ ㅋ ㅌ ㅍ ㅎ
2	중성 Medial Vowel	ㅏ ㅐ ㅑ ㅒ ㅓ ㅔ ㅕ ㅖ ㅗ ㅘ ㅙ ㅚ ㅛ ㅜ ㅝ ㅞ ㅟ ㅠ ㅡ ㅢ ㅣ
3	종성(받침) Final Consonant	ㄱ ㄲ ㄳ ㄴ ㄵ ㄶ ㄷ ㄹ ㄺ ㄻ ㄼ ㄽ ㄾ ㄿ ㅀ ㅁ ㅂ ㅄ ㅅ ㅆ ㅇ ㅈ ㅊ ㅋ ㅌ ㅍ ㅎ

모음 Vowels

글자 Letter	ㅏ	ㅓ	ㅗ	ㅜ	ㅡ	ㅣ	ㅔ	ㅐ
음가 Sound Value	[a]	[ʌ/ə:]	[o]	[u]	[ɯ]	[i]	[e]	[ɛ]

글자 Letter	ㅑ	ㅕ	ㅛ	ㅠ			ㅖ	ㅒ
음가 Sound Value	[ja]	[jʌ/ə:]	[jo]	[ju]			[je]	[jɛ]

글자 Letter	ㅘ	ㅝ	ㅚ	ㅟ	ㅢ		ㅞ	ㅙ
음가 Sound Value	[wa]	[wʌ]	[we]	[y/wi]	[ɯi/i]		[we]	[wɛ]

자음 Consonants

글자 Letter		ㄱ	ㄴ	ㄷ	ㄹ	ㅁ	ㅂ	ㅅ	ㅇ	ㅈ	ㅎ
음가 Sound Value	첫소리 First Phoneme	[k]	[n]	[t]	[l]	[m]	[p]	[s]	—	[ts]	[h]
	어중 Middle Phoneme	[g]	[n/ŋ]	[d]	[r/l/ʎ]	[m]	[p]	[s/ɕ/ʃ]	—	[dz]	[h]
	받침 Final Phoneme	[k]	[n]	[t]	[l]	[m]	[p]	[t]	[ŋ]	[t]	[t]

글자 Letter		ㅋ	ㅌ		ㅍ		ㅊ
음가 Sound Value	첫소리 First Phoneme	[kʰ]	[tʰ]		[pʰ]		[tsʰ]
	어중 Middle Phoneme	[kʰ]	[tʰ]		[pʰ]		[tsʰ]
	받침 Final Phoneme	[k]	[t]		[p]		[t]

글자 Letter		ㄲ	ㄸ	ㅃ	ㅆ	ㅉ
음가 Sound Value	첫소리 First Phoneme	[k']	[t']	[p']	[s'/ɕ']	[ts']
	어중 Middle Phoneme	[k']	[t']	[p']	[s'ɕ']	[ts']
	받침 Final Phoneme	[k]	—	—	[t]	

* A middle phoneme is the initial sound on the second syllable.

THE LESSONS

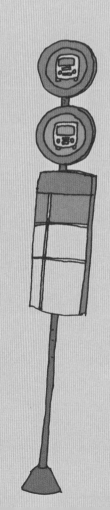

Hello! 안녕하세요?

자기소개하기
Introducing Yourself

Lesson Goals

Situation
Introducing yourself
Vocabulary
Greetings
Countries
Occupations
Hobbies
Grammar
Particles
Nationalities
Occupations
Forms of address

▼

Koreans bow their upper body by about 45 degrees when greeting people senior to them. If you only say 안녕하세요? (annyeonghaseyo *hello*) without bowing, and simply give a wave, you might be considered rude. Among closer acquaintances, phrases like 식사 하셨어요? (sigsa hasyeosseoyo *have you eaten?*) or 밥 먹었어요? (bab meogeosseoyo *did you eat?*) are frequently used.

ONLINE
AUDIO
00:10

최지영 **choejiyeong**

안녕하세요?
annyeonghaseyo
Hello.

로이 **roi**

안녕하십니까?
annyeonghasimnikka
Hello.

최지영 **choejiyeong**

제 이름은 최지영입니다.
je ireumeun choejiyeongimnida
My name is Jiyoung Choi.

로이 **roi**

제 이름은 로이입니다.
je ireumeun roiimnida
My name is Roy.

최지영 **choejiyeong**

저는 한국 사람입니다.
jeoneun hanguk saramimnida
I am Korean.

로이 씨는 어느 나라 사람입니까?
roi ssineun eoneu nara saramimnikka
Roy, what country are you from?

로이 **roi**

저는 홍콩 사람입니다.
jeoneun hongkong saramimnida
I am from Hong Kong.

최지영 **choejiyeong**

만나서 반갑습니다.
mannaseo bangapseumnida
Nice to meet you.

로이 **roi**

만나서 반갑습니다.
mannaseo bangapseumnida
Nice to meet you.

ONLINE
AUDIO
01:20

Vocabulary and Expressions 어휘와 표현

01 인사 insa   Greetings

안녕하세요? 〔안녕하세요〕 **annyeonghaseyo**
Hello.

안녕하십니까? 〔안녕하십니까〕 **annyeonghasimnikka**
Hello.

만나서 반갑습니다 〔만나서반갑씀니다〕 **mannaseo bangapseumnida**
Nice to meet you.

02 나라 nara   Countries

한국
hanguk
Korea

중국
jungguk
China

일본
ilbon
Japan

미국
miguk
United States of America

호주
hoju
Australia

프랑스
peurangseu
France

캐나다
kaenada
Canada

독일
dogil
Germany

필리핀
pillipin
Philippines

스페인
seupein
Spain

코트디부아르
koteudibuareu
Côte d'Ivoire

케냐
kenya
Kenya

홍콩
hongkong
Hong Kong

이탈리아
itallia
Italy

러시아
reosia
Russia

멕시코
meksiko
Mexico

03 직업 jigeop Occupations

선생님 [선생님] **seonsaengnim** *teacher*

학생 [학쌩] **haksaeng** *student*

의사 [의사] **uisa** *doctor*

경찰관 [경:찰관] **gyeongchalgwan** *police officer*

요리사 [요리사] **yorisa** *chef/cook*

영화배우 [영화배우] **yeonghwabaeu** *movie actor*

04 취미 chwimi Hobbies

야구 [야:구] **yagu** *baseball*

요리 [요리] **yori** *cooking*

축구 [축구] **chukgu** *soccer*

독서 [독써] **dokseo** *reading*

태권도 [태꿘도] **taegwondo** *taekwondo*

영화 감상 [영화감상] **yeonghwa gamsang** *watching movies*

05 기타 gita Other Useful Vocabulary

네 [네] **ne** *yes*

이름 [이름] **ireum** *name*

어느 나라 사람입니까? [어느나라:라밈니까] **eoneu nara saramimnikka**
What country are you from?

발음규칙 Pronunciation Rules

Nasalization of Consonants 비음화
If the consonant ㅂ is placed at the bottom of the syllable and followed by a nasal consonant such as ㄴ or ㅁ, then ㅂ becomes nasalized and is pronounced as ㅁ [m].

안녕하십니까 ⇒ 안녕하심니까]

반갑습니다 반갑씀니다 **bangapseumnida**
Nice to meet you

최지영입니다 췌지영임니다 **choejiyeongimnida**
This is Jiyoung Choi

무엇입니까 무어심니까 **mueosimnikka**
What is...

사람입니다 사 라밈니다 **saramimnida**
...is a person

Grammar 문법

01 N은 / 는 N 입니다   N eun/neun N imnida   Topic particle 은/는

A particle is a small word attached to a noun to mark it as the subject, topic or object of a sentence. Particles can also act as prepositions, meaning "with," "in," etc. Many Korean particles have just one form, while others have variant forms depending on whether the noun ends in a consonant or a vowel.

제 이름은 최지영입니다. **je ireumeun choejiyeongimnida** *My name is Jiyoung Choi.*

저는 한국 사람입니다. **jeoneun hanguk saramimnida** *I am Korean.*

저는 학생입니다. **jeoneun haksaengimnida** *I am a student.*

02 N 이 / 가 무엇입니까 ?   N i/ga mueosimnikka   Subject particle 이/가

When there is a final consonant in the last syllable of a noun, N이 is used, and N가 is used otherwise.

이름이 무엇입니까? **ireumi mueosimnikka** *What is your name?*

직업이 무엇입니까? **jigeobi mueosimnikka** *What do you do?*

취미가 무엇입니까? **chwimiga mueosimnikka** *What is your hobby?*

03 제 N je N   My N

제 **je** is a possessive pronoun meaning "my" and it is a combination of 저 meaning "I" or "me" and the possessive particle 의 **ui**.

제 이름은 스테파니입니다. **je ireumeun seutepaniimnida** *My name is Stephanie.*

제 취미는 야구입니다. **je chwimineun yaguimnida** *My hobby is playing baseball.*

제 직업은 의사입니다. **je jigeobeun uisaimnida** *I am a doctor.*

04 N 사람 N saram   Nationalities

In order to specify the nationality of a person, append the suffix ~사람 to the name of the country as in the examples below.

한국 사람 **hanguk saram** *Korean*   중국 사람 **jungguk saram** *Chinese*

일본 사람 **ilbon saram** *Japanese*   미국 사람 **miguk saram** *American*

05 N 씨 N ssi   Forms of address

최지영 씨 **choejiyeong ssi** *Ms. Jiyoung Choi*

스테파니 씨 **seutepani ssi** *Ms. Stephanie*

이준기 씨 **ijungi ssi** *Mr. Lee Joon-gi*

왕샤위 씨 **wangsyawi ssi** *Mr. Wangshaowei*

Conversation Practice 회화 연습

01 이름이 무엇입니까 ?   **ireumi mueosimnikka**   **What is your name?**

Use the example sentences to guide you as you practice. Find model sentences on page 267.

최지영
choejiyeong
Jiyoung Choi

가: 이름이 무엇입니까? **ireumi mueosimnikka**
What's your name?

나: 제 이름은 최지영입니다. **je ireumeun choejiyeongimnida**
My name's Jiyoung Choi.

로베르토
robereuto
Roberto

가: 이름이 무엇입니까?

나: 제 이름은 _____ 입니다.

리리
riri
Lili

가: _____?

나: _____.

퍼디
peodi
Ferdy

가: _____?

나: _____.

마스미
maseumi
Masumi

가: _____?

나: _____.

02 어느 나라 사람입니까? eoneu nara saramimnikka   **Where are you from?**

Use the example sentences to guide you as you practice. Find model sentences on page 267.

비비엔
bibien
Vivien

독일

가: 어느 나라 사람입니까? eoneu nara saramimnikka
Where are you from?

나: 저는 독일 사람입니다. jeoneun dogilsaramimnida
I am German.

로이
roi
Roy

홍콩

가: 어느 나라 사람입니까?

나: 저는 ＿＿＿＿＿＿＿＿＿ 사람입니다.

왕샤위
wangsyawi
Wangshaowei

중국

가: ＿＿＿＿＿＿＿＿＿＿＿＿＿＿＿＿＿ ?

나: ＿＿＿＿＿＿＿＿＿＿＿＿＿＿＿＿＿ .

마스미
maseumi
Masumi

일본

가: ＿＿＿＿＿＿＿＿＿＿＿＿＿＿＿＿＿ ?

나: ＿＿＿＿＿＿＿＿＿＿＿＿＿＿＿＿＿ .

퍼디
peodi
Ferdy

필리핀

가: ＿＿＿＿＿＿＿＿＿＿＿＿＿＿＿＿＿ ?

나: ＿＿＿＿＿＿＿＿＿＿＿＿＿＿＿＿＿ .

03 직업이 무엇입니까? jigeobi mueosimnikka **What do you do?**

Use the example sentences to guide you as you practice. Find model sentences on page 267.

비비엔
bibien
Vivien

가: 비비엔 씨 직업이 무엇입니까?
bibien ssi jigeobi mueosimnikka
Vivien, what do you do?

나: 제 직업은 학생입니다. **je jigeobeun haksaengimnida**
I am a student.

로이
roi
Roy

가: 로이 씨 직업이 무엇입니까?

나: 제 직업은 _____ 입니다.

왕샤위
wangsyawi
Wangshaowei

가: _____ ?

나: _____ .

마스미
maseumi
Masumi

가: _____ ?

나: _____ .

퍼디
peodi
Ferdy

가: _____ ?

나: _____ .

04 취미가 무엇입니까? **chwimiga mueosimnikka** **What is your hobby?**

Use the example sentences to guide you as you practice. Find model sentences on page 267.

야구
yagu
baseball

가: 취미가 무엇입니까? **chwimiga mueosimnikka**
What is your hobby?

나: 제 취미는 야구입니다. **je chwimineun yaguimnida**
My hobby is playing baseball.

요리
yori
cooking

가: 취미가 무엇입니까?

나: 제 취미는 _____ 입니다.

축구
chukgu
soccer

가: _____ ?

나: _____ .

독서
dokseo
reading

가: _____ ?

나: _____ .

태권도
taegwondo
taikwondo

가: _____ ?

나: _____ .

ONLINE
AUDIO
02:57

Talking with Lee Joon-gi 이준기와 이야기하기

자기소개하기 Introducing yourself

Try having a conversation with Lee Joon-gi as you listen to the audio. You can find a translation of this conversation on page 263.

이준기   안녕하십니까? **annyeonghasimnikka**

제 이름은 이준기입니다. **je ireumeun ijungiimnida**

저는 한국 사람입니다. **jeoneun hanguk saramimnida**

저는 영화배우입니다. **jeoneun yeonghwabaeuimnida**

제 취미는 태권도입니다. **je chwimineun taegwondoimnida**

만나서 반갑습니다. **mannaseo bangapseumnida**

비비엔   안녕하세요?
annyeonghaseyo

제 이름은 비비엔입니다.
je ireumeun bibienimnida

저는 독일 사람입니다.
jeoneun dogil saramimnida

저는 학생입니다.
jeoneun haksaengimnida

제 취미는 영화 감상입니다.
je chwimineun yeonghwa gamsangimnida

만나서 반갑습니다.
mannaseo bangapseumnida

Write a short self-introduction in Korean, following the model opposite.

안녕하십니까?

제 이름은 _____.

저는 _____.

저는 _____.

제 취미는 _____.

만나서 반갑습니다.

Greetings 인사하기

안녕하십니까?
annyeonghasimnikka
Hello. (formal)

안녕하세요?
annyeonghaseyo
Hello.

안녕히 계세요.
annyeonghi gyeseyo
Goodbye.

안녕히 가세요.
annyeonghi gaseyo
Goodbye.

잘 먹겠습니다.
jal meokgetseumnida
Thanks for the meal.
(before having meal)

잘 먹었습니다.
jal meogeotseumnida
Thanks for the meal.
(after having meal)

다녀오겠습니다.
danyeoogetseumnida
*I'm leaving,
see you later.*

잘 다녀와.
jal danyeowa
다녀오세요.
danyeooseyo
See you later.

감사합니다.
gamsahamnida
고맙습니다.
gomapseumnida
Thank you.

천만에요.
cheonmaneyo
You're welcome.

죄송합니다.
joesonghamnida
미안합니다.
mianhamnida
*I apologize.
I am sorry.*

아니에요.
anieyo
괜찮아요.
gwaenchanayo
*It's alright.
That's ok.*

실례합니다.
sillyehamnida
Excuse me.

들어오세요.
deureooseyo
Please come in.

안녕히 주무세요.
annyeonghi jumuseyo
Good night. (polite)

안녕히 주무세요.
annyeonghi jumuseyo
Good night.
(polite)

주말 잘
지내세요.
jumal jal jinaeseyo
*Have a good
weekend.*

주말 잘
보내세요.
jumal jal bonaeseyo
*Have a good
weekend.*

또 만나요.
tto mannayo
See you again.

또 봐요.
tto bwayo
See you again.

*The expressions 주말 잘 지내세요 and 주말 잘 보내세요
have the same meaning, despite their different forms.

내일 만나요.
naeil mannayo
See you tomorrow.

내일 봐요.
naeil bwayo
See you tomorrow.

축하합니다.
chukahamnida
축하해요.
chukahaeyo
Congratulations.

감사합니다
gamsahamnida
고마워요.
gomawoyo
Thank you.

*The verb 보다 (boda) means "to see with one's eyes" and "to meet someone." So, there are two
different ways you can say "see you again" and "see you tomorrow."

Myeongdong

Seoul's Busiest Shopping & Finance District

If you are shopping in Korea, check out the Myeongdong area first. You'll find a truly wide variety of clothes to buy, in all the latest styles. Other than clothes à la mode, this area is also home to many of Korea's most important financial institutions, including the Bank of Korea, the country's central bank which prints notes and coins. The historic Myeongdong Cathedral, built in 1898, can also be found in this neighborhood. The cathedral at dawn or sunset is a beautiful sight.

What's This?
이것은 무엇입니까?

Lesson Goals

Situation
Asking and answering questions about objects
Vocabulary
Daily necessities
Food names
Grammar
This / that / what?
Is this / that a _____?
What's this?
It's a _____.

▼

The most popular snacks on a Korean snack cart or 포장마차 (pojangmacha), are 떡볶이 (tteokbokki, finger-like rice cakes in red hot chili sauce), 호떡 (hotteok, Chinese stuffed pancakes) and 김밥 (gimbap, rice rolled in dried seaweed). 떡볶이 taste spicy but are popular among people from all over the world. Check out this Korean treat.

ONLINE
AUDIO
00:10

리리 **riri**
이것은 무엇입니까?
igeoseun mueosimnikka
What is this?

이준기 **ijungi**
그것은 교통카드입니다.
geugeoseun gyotongkadeuimnida
It's a transportation card.

리리 **riri**
그것은 떡볶이입니까?
geugeoseun tteokbokkiimnikka
Is that tteokbokki?

이준기 **ijungi**
네, 이것은 떡볶이입니다.
ne, igeoseun tteokbokkiimnida
Yes, it is.

리리 **riri**
저것은 김밥입니까?
jeogeoseun gimbabimnikka
Is that gimpab?

이준기 **ijungi**
아니요, 김밥이 아닙니다.
aniyo gimbabi animnida
No, it isn't.

저것은 호떡입니다.
jeogeoseun hotteogimnida
That's hotteok.

ONLINE
AUDIO
01:10

Vocabulary and Expressions 어휘와 표현

01 생활필수품 1 saenghwalpilsupum il   **Daily necessities 1**

교통카드 〔교통카드〕
gyotongkadeu
transportation card

전화카드 〔전화카드〕
jeonhwakadeu
telephone card

휴대폰 〔휴대폰〕
hyudaepon
phone

시계 〔시계/시계〕
sigye
watch/clock

구두 〔구두〕
gudu
shoe

가방 〔가방〕
gabang
bag

지갑 〔지갑〕
jigap
wallet

안경 〔안경〕
angyeong
glasses

02 생활필수품 2 saenghwalpilsupum i   **Daily necessities 2**

컵 〔컵〕
keop
cup

그릇 〔그륻〕
geureut
bowl

숟가락 〔숟까락〕
sutgarak
spoon

젓가락 〔젇까락〕
jeotgarak
chopsticks

수세미 〔수세미〕
susemi
dish sponge

03 생활필수품 3 saenghwalpilsupum sam | Daily necessities 3

수건
sugeon
towel

비누
binu
soap

치약
chiyak
toothpaste

칫솔
chitsol
toothbrush

샴푸
syampu
shampoo

린스
rinseu
conditioner

04 음식 이름 1 eumsik il | Food 1

떡볶이
tteokbokki
tteokbokki rice cake

김밥
gimbap
gimbap

호떡
hotteok
hotteok

비빔밥
bibimbap
bibimbap

불고기
bulgogi
bulgogi

자장면
jajangmyeon
jajangmyeon

발음규칙 Pronunciation Rules

Liaison (Linking) 연음 법칙
When a syllable ends with a final consonant and is followed by a vowel, then the final phoneme is pronounced as the first phoneme of the following syllable.

$$이것은 \Rightarrow 이거슨$$

이름은 이르믄 **ireumeun** *name is...*
무엇입니까 무어심니까 **mueosimnikka**
　What is...

선생님이에요 선생니미에요 **seonsaengnim ieyo**
　am/is a teacher

Grammar 문법

01 이것 / 그것 / 저것 / 무엇
igeot/geugeot/jeogeot/mueot

This (one) / that (one) / what is —?

이것 igeot	그것 geugeot	저것 jeogeot	무엇 mueot

이것은 교통카드입니다. **igeoseun gyotongkadeuimnida** *This is a transportation card.*

그것은 폰입니다. **geugeoseun ponimnida** *It's a phone.*

저것은 김밥입니다. **jeogeoseun gimbabimnida** *That is gimbap.*

이것은 무엇입니까? **igeoseun mueosimnikka** *What is this?*

02 N은 / 는 N 입니까? N eun/neun N imnikka   Is this / that /it a —?

입니다 is attached to nouns; its equivalent in English is "is," "am," or "are." 입니까? is used to form a question.

이것은 교통카드입니까? **igeoseun gyotongkadeuimnikka** *Is this a transportation card?*

그것은 폰입니까? **geugeoseun ponimnikka** *Is it a phone?*

저것은 김밥입니까? **jeogeoseun gimbabimnikka** *Is that gimbap?*

03 네 , N 입니다 Ne, N imnida
아니요 , N 이 / 가 아닙니다 Aniyo, N i/ga animnida

Yes, it is a —
No, it is not a —

The negative form of 입니다 is 이 / 가 아닙니다. Use N이 아닙니다 when the noun ends in a consonant and use N가 아닙니다 when the noun ends in a vowel.

네, 교통카드입니다. **ne, gyotongkadeuimnida** *Yes, it's a transportation card.*

아니요, 교통카드가 아닙니다. **aniyo, gyotongkadeuga animnida**
  No, it isn't a transportation card.

네, 폰입니다. **ne, ponimnida** *Yes, it's a phone.*

아니요, 폰이 아닙니다. **aniyo, poni animnida** *No, it isn't a phone.*

네, 김밥입니다. **ne, gimbabimnida** *Yes, it's gimbap.*

아니요, 김밥이 아닙니다. **aniyo, gimbabi animnida** *No, it isn't gimbap.*

| **Exercise** | Fill in the blanks. You can find the answers on page 267.

N N *N*	N입니까? **N imnikka** *Is it N?*	N입니다 **N imnida** *It is N*	N이/가 아닙니다 **N i/ga animnida** *It is not N*
교통카드 **gyotongkadeu** *transportation card*	교통카드입니까?	교통카드입니다	교통카드가 아닙니다
시계 **sigye** *watch/clock*		시계입니다	
떡볶이 **tteokbokki** *tteokbokki rice cake*	떡볶이입니까?	떡볶이입니다	
김밥 **gimbap** *gimbap*		김밥입니다	
폰 **pon** *phone*	폰입니까?		

Conversation Practice 회화 연습

01 이것은 무엇입니까 ? **igeoseun mueosimnikka** **What's this?**

Use the example sentences to guide you as you practice. Find model sentences on page 267.

가방
gabang
bag

리리: 이것은 무엇입니까? **igeoseun mueosimnikka**
What's this?

이준기: 그것은 가방입니다. **geugeoseun gabangimnida**
It's a bag.

지갑
jigap
wallet

가: 이것은 무엇입니까?

나: 그것은 _____ 입니다.

안경
angyeong
glasses

가: _____?

나: _____.

구두
gudu
shoe

가: _____?

나: _____.

전화카드
jeonhwa-
kadeu
phone card

가: _____?

나: _____.

02 네, 그것은 김밥입니다. **ne, geugeoseun gimbabimnida** **Yes, it's gimbap.**

Use the example sentences to guide you as you practice. Find model sentences on page 267.

김밥
gimbap
gimbap

리리: 이것은 김밥입니까? igeoseun gimbabimnikka
Is this gimbap?

이준기: 네, 그것은 김밥입니다. **ne, geugeoseun gimbabimnida** *Yes, it's gimbap.*

비빔밥
bibimbap
bibimbap

가: 이것은 비빔밥입니까?

나: 네, 그것은 _____ 입니다.

치약
chiyak
toothpaste

가: _____?

나: _____.

비누
binu
soap

가: _____?

나: _____.

샴푸
syampu
shampoo

가: _____?

나: _____.

03 아니요 , 김밥이 아닙니다 .   aniyo, gimbabi animnida   **No, it isn't gimbap.**

Use the example sentences to guide you as you practice. Find model sentences on page 267.

김밥
gimbap

호떡
hotteok

가: 이것은 김밥입니까? **igeoseun gimbabimnikka**
Is this gimbap?

아니요, 김밥이 아닙니다. **aniyo, gimbabi animnida**
No, it isn't gimbap.

나: 그것은 호떡입니다. **geugeoseun hotteogimnida**
It's hotteok.

비빔밥
bibimbap

삼계탕
samgyetang

가: 이것은 비빔밥입니까?

나: 아니요, _____ 이 / 가 아닙니다.

불고기
bulgogi

자장면
jajang-
myeon

가: _____ ?

나: _____ .

비누
binu
soap

수건
sugeon
towel

가: _____ ?

나: _____ .

숟가락
sutgarak
spoon

젓가락
jeotgarak
chopsticks

가: _____ ?

나: _____ .

ONLINE
AUDIO
02:30

Talking with Lee Joon-gi 이준기와 이야기하기

물건 이름 물어보기 Asking the names of objects

Try having a conversation with Lee Joon-gi as you listen to the audio. You can find a translation of this conversation on page 263.

이준기　이것은 시계입니까? **igeoseun sigyeimnikka**

스테파니　네, 그것은 시계입니다. **ne, geugeoseun sigyeimnida**

이준기　그것은 무엇입니까? **geugeoseun mueosimnikka**

스테파니　이것은 컴퓨터입니다. **igeoseun keompyuteoimnida**

이준기　저것은 전화카드입니까?
jeogeoseun jeonhwakadeuimnikka

스테파니　아니요, 저것은 전화카드가 아닙니다.
aniyo, jeogeoseun jeonhwakadeuga animnida

교통카드입니다. **gyotongkadeuimnida**

Complete the dialogue with this, it, or that.

가 ＿＿＿＿＿ 은/는 ＿＿＿＿＿＿＿＿＿입니까?

나 네, ＿＿＿＿＿ 은/는 ＿＿＿＿＿＿＿＿＿입니다.

가 ＿＿＿＿＿ 은/는 ＿＿＿＿＿＿＿＿＿입니까?

나 ＿＿＿＿＿ 은/는 ＿＿＿＿＿＿＿＿＿입니다.

가 ＿＿＿＿＿ 은/는 ＿＿＿＿＿＿＿＿＿입니까?

나 아니요, ＿＿＿＿＿ 은/는 ＿＿＿＿＿ 이/가 아닙니다.

＿＿＿＿＿＿＿＿＿입니다.

This / That / That / Which
이~ / 그~ / 저~ / 어느~ i/geu/jeo/eoneu

The forms of these words differ depending on whether the following word is a person, an inanimate object, a place, or a direction, as shown in the table below.

	이~ **i** *this*	그~ **geu** *it/that*	저~ **jeo** *that*	어느~ **eoneu** *which*
사람 **saram** *person*	이 사람 **i saram** *this person*	그 사람 **geu saram** *that person*	저 사람 **jeo saram** *that person*	누구 **nugu** *who*
	이분 * **ibun** *this person [honorific]*	그분 **geubun** *that person [honorific]*	저분 **jeobun** *that person [honorific]*	어느 분 **eoneu bun** *who [honorific]*
사물 **samul** *thing*	이것 **igeot** *this*	그것 **geugeot** *it/that*	저것 **jeogeot** *that*	어느 것 **eoneu geot** *which one*
				무엇 **mueot** *what*
장소 **jangso** *place*	여기 **yeogi** *here*	거기 **geogi** *there*	저기 **jeogi** *there*	어디 **eodi** *where*
방향 **banghyang** *direction*	이쪽 **ijjok** *this way*	그쪽 **geujjok** *that way*	저쪽 **jeojjok** *that way*	어느 쪽 **eoneu jjok** *which way*

*분 is the honorific form of 사람 which means "person." 분 is used to show respect to the person the speaker is talking about.

Lee Joon-gi's Guide to Seoul

Insadong

Where Traditional Meets Modern

This area is crowded with traditional-style tea houses wreathed in a refreshing herbal aroma. You'll also find restaurants that serve unique Korean dishes, which may be a little spicier than you are used to, but are still delicious!

You can also enjoy checking out the many galleries that display local art, as well as shops that sell colorful traditional arts and crafts. There are many outdoor stalls that sell sweet pancakes and candies, which you can snack on while strolling around the neighborhood.

How Much Is This Packet of Noodles?

이 라면은 한 개에 얼마예요?

Lesson Goals

Situation
Shopping
Vocabulary
Daily necessities
Food
Counting units
Grammar
This / that / that
It is / it is not
___ and ___
per___
Numbers

ONLINE
AUDIO
00:10

아저씨 ajeossi

어서 오세요.
eoseo oseyo
Welcome.

스테파니 seutepani

이 라면은 한 개에 얼마예요?
i ramyeoneun han gaee eolmayeyo
How much is this packet of noodles?

아저씨 ajeossi

오백 원이에요.
obaek wonieyo
500 won.

스테파니 seutepani

라면 두 개하고 맥주 세 병 주세요.
ramyeon dugaehago maekju se byeong juseyo
I would like two packets of noodles and three bottles of beer, please.

아저씨 ajeossi

모두 오천오백 원입니다. 감사합니다.
안녕히 가세요.
**modu ocheonobaek wonimnida. gamsahamnida.
annyeonghi gaseyo**
That's 5,500 won altogether. Thank you. Goodbye.

스테파니 seutepani

안녕히 계세요.
annyeonghi gyeseyo
Goodbye.

You may often hear people addressing clerks, waiters or waitresses with words such as 아저씨 (ajeossi *Uncle*), 아주머니 (ajumeoni *Ma'am*), 아줌마 (ajumma *Aunt*), or 아가씨 (agassi *Miss*). These expressions are used in informal and friendly settings. Sometimes 어머니 (eomeoni *Mother*) or 이모 (imo *Auntie*) is used instead of 아주머니; and 언니 (eonni *sister*) instead of 아가씨. These are originally terms used to address family members and are even more friendly and casual.

ONLINE
AUDIO
01:18

Vocabulary and Expressions 어휘와 표현

01 생활필수품 4 saenghwalpilsupum sa | Daily necessities 4

건전지 〔건전지〕 **geonjeonji** *battery*

화장지 (티슈) 〔화장지 (티쓔)〕 **hwajangji (tisyu)** *toilet paper (tissue)*

형광등 〔형광등〕 **hyeonggwangdeung** *fluorescent lamp*

휴지 〔휴지〕 **hyuji** *toilet paper*

휴대폰 〔휴대폰〕 **hyudaepon** *phone*

02 식품 sikpum | Food 2

라면 〔라면〕 **ramyeon**
noodles

빵 〔빵〕 **ppang** *bread*

두부 〔두부〕 **dubu** *tofu*

햄 〔햄〕 **haem** *ham*

컵라면 〔컴나면〕 **keomnamyeon**
cup noodles

계란 〔계란/게란〕 **gyeran** *egg*

과자 〔과자〕 **gwaja** *snack*

통조림 〔통조림〕 **tongjorim** *canned food*

03 음료 , 주류 eumnyo, juryu | Drinks

물 〔물〕 **mul** *water*

콜라 〔콜라〕 **kolla** *coke*

우유 〔우유〕 **uyu** *milk*

맥주 〔맥쭈〕 **maekju** *beer*

사이다 〔사이다〕 **saida**
lemon-lime soda

커피 〔커피〕 **keopi** *coffee*

소주 〔소주〕 **soju** *soju*

주스 〔주스〕 **juseu** *juice*

04 과일 gwail   Fruit

사과 〔사과〕 **sagwa** *apple*   배 〔배〕 **bae** *pear*

바나나 〔바나나〕 **banana** *banana*   수박 〔수:박〕 **subak** *watermelon*

딸기 〔딸기〕 **ttalgi** *strawberry*   포도 〔포도〕 **podo** *grapes*

감 〔감:〕 **gam** *persimmon*   귤 〔귤〕 **gyul** *mandarin orange/tangerine*

05 고기 gogi   Meat

소고기 〔소고기〕 **sogogi** *beef*   돼지고기 〔소고기〕 **dwaejigogi** *pork*

닭고기 〔닥꼬기〕 **dakgogi** *chicken (meat)*   생선 〔생선〕 **saengseon** *fish*

06 단위 danwi   Counting units

마리 〔마리〕 **mari** *unit used to count animals*

몇 마리 〔면마리〕 **myeot mari** *how many (for animals)*

킬로그램 〔킬로그램〕 **killogeuraem** *kilogram*

몇 킬로그램 〔면킬로그램〕 **myeot killogeuraem** *how many kilograms*

송이〔송이〕 **songi** *unit used to count flowers by the bunch*

몇 송이 〔면쏭이〕 **myeot songi** *how many bunches*

병 〔병〕 **byeong** *unit used to count bottles*

몇 병 〔면뼝〕 **myeot byeong** *how many bottles*

개 〔개〕 **gae** *unit used to count inanimate objects*

몇 개 〔면깨〕 **myeot gae** *how many objects*

▼

Vocabulary

마리
닭고기, 생선…….

킬로그램 (kg)
포도, 딸기, 돼지고기, 소고기…….

송이
바나나, 포도, 꽃…….

병
맥주, 콜라, 물…….

개
사과, 배, 캔음료, 건전지,
휴지, 라면…….

07 기타 gita   Other useful vocabulary

어서 오세요 〔어서오세요〕 **eoseo oseyo** *Welcome!*

얼마예요? 〔얼마예요〕 **eolmayeyo** *How much is it?*

주세요 〔주세요〕 **juseyo** *I'll take it.*

모두 〔모두〕 **modu** *all, total, altogether*

깎아 주세요 **kkakka juseyo** 〔까까주세요〕 *Please give me a discount.*

뭘 드릴까요? **mwol deurilkkayo** 〔뭘드릴까요〕 *What can I give you?*

값 〔갑〕 **gap** *price*

돈 〔돈:〕 **don** *money*

원 〔원〕 **won** *won (the Korean currency)*

발 음 규 칙 Pronunciation Rules

Tense Consonants 경음화
When the final consonant ㄱ meets with the initial consonants ㄱ, ㄷ, ㅂ, ㅅ or ㅈ on the next syllable, the initial consonants are pronounced as ㄲ, ㄸ, ㅃ, ㅆ or ㅉ respectively.

$$맥주 \Rightarrow 〔맥쭈〕$$

$$
ㄱ +
\begin{matrix} ㄱ \\ ㄷ \\ ㅂ \\ ㅅ \\ ㅈ \end{matrix}
\Rightarrow
\begin{matrix} ㄲ \\ ㄸ \\ ㅃ \\ ㅆ \\ ㅉ \end{matrix}
$$

학교 학꾜 **hakgyo** *school*
닭고기 닥꼬기 **dakgogi** *chicken*

떡볶이 떡뽀끼 **tteokbokki** *tteokbokki rice cake*
읽다 익따 **ikda** *to read*

Grammar 문법

01 이 / 그 / 저 N   i/geu/jeo N

This —?/That —?/
That —?

Use 이 N for a person or object closer to the speaker; use 그 N when the person or object being referred to is closer to the listener. Use 저 N if the person or object is far from both the speaker and the listener.

이 빵은 얼마예요? **i ppangeun eolmayeyo** *How much is this bread?*

그 사과는 얼마예요? **geu sagwaneun eolmayeyo** *How much is that apple?*

저 콜라는 얼마예요? **jeo kollaneun eolmayeyo** *How much is that coke?*

02 N 예요 / 이에요   N yeyo/ieyo
N 이 / 가 아니에요   N i/ga anieyo

It is a —
It is not a —

If the last syllable of the noun does not have a final consonant, use N예요 and N가 아니에요. If the last syllable of the noun has a final consonant, use N이에요 and N이 아니에요. They have the same meanings as N입니다 and N이/가 아닙니다, (see Lesson 2, page 67).

바나나예요. **bananayeyo** *It's a banana.*

바나나가 아니에요. **bananaga anieyo** *It isn't a banana.*

음료수예요. **eumnyosuyeyo** *It's a drink.*

음료수가 아니에요. **eumnyosuga anieyo** *It isn't a drink.*

과일이에요. **gwairieyo** *It's a fruit.*

과일이 아니에요. **gwairi anieyo** *It isn't a fruit.*

03 N 하고 N   N hago N — and —

하고 is a particle that connects two separate nouns. The form N하고 N is used regardless of whether there is a final consonant or not on the last syllable of the noun.

라면하고 두부 **ramyeonhago dubu** *ramen and tofu*

커피하고 우유 **keopihago uyu** *coffee and milk*

사과하고 딸기 **sagwahago ttalgi** *an apple and a strawberry*

맥주하고 소주 **maekjuhago soju** *beer and soju*

휴지하고 건전지 **hyujihago geonjeonji** *a tissue and a battery*

소고기하고 닭고기 **sogogihago dakgogi** *beef and chicken*

| **Exercise** | Fill in the blanks. You can find the answers on page 268.

N N *N*	N하고 N **N hago N** *N and N*
라면, 두부 **ramyeon, dubu** *ramen, tofu*	라면하고두부
커피, 콜라 **keopi, kolla** *coffee, coke*	
햄, 통조림 **haem, tongjorim** *ham, canned food*	
바나나, 수박 **banana, subak** *banana, watermelon*	
건전지, 폰 **geonjeonji, pon** *battery, phone*	
밥, 계란 **bap, gyeran** *rice, egg*	

04 N에 N e   Per —

The form N에 meaning "per" or "for," is used regardless of whether there is a final consonant or not on the last syllable of the noun.

사이다는 한 병에 칠백 원이에요. **saidaneun han byeoge chilbaegwonieyo**
A lemon-lime soda costs 700 won for one bottle.

그 소고기는 일 킬로그램에 얼마예요? **geu sogogineun il killogeuraeme eolmayeyo**
How much does the beef cost for 1 kilogram?

이 화장지는 한 개에 얼마예요? **i hwajangjineun han gaee eolmayeyo**
How much does this tissue box cost for one?

이 생선은 한 마리에 이천 원이에요. **i saengseoneun han marie icheon wonieyo**
This fish costs 2,000 won for one.

| **Exercise** | Fill in the blanks. You can find the answers on page 268.

N N *N*	N예요/이에요 **N yeyo/ieyo** *It is N*	N이/가 아니에요 **N i/ga anieyo** *It is not N*
사과 **sagwa** *apple*	사과예요	사과가 아니에요
포도 **podo** *grape*		포도가 아니에요
바나나 **banana** *banana*		
휴지 **hyuji** *tissue*	휴지예요	휴지가 아니에요
폰 **pon** *phone*		폰이 아니에요
오백 원 **obaek won** *500 won*	오백 원이에요	

05 숫자 sutja

Numbers

Korean uses two number systems. Chinese numbers, below, are used for counting and to refer to the numbers themselves—in math, temperatures, measurements, etc.

1	2	3	4
일 il	이 i	삼 sam	사 sa
5	**6**	**7**	**8**
오 o	육 yuk	칠 chil	팔 pal
9	**10**	**11**	**12**
구 gu	십 sip	십일 sibil	십이 sibi
13	**14**	**15**	**16**
십삼 sipsam	십사 sipsa	십오 sibo	십육 sibyuk
17	**18**	**19**	**20**
십칠 sipchil	십팔 sippal	십구 sipgu	이십 isip
30	**40**	**50**	**60**
삼십 samsip	사십 sasip	오십 osip	육십 yuksip
70	**80**	**90**	**100**
칠십 chilsip	팔십 palsip	구십 gusip	백 baek
1,000	**10,000**	**100,000**	**1,000,000**
천 cheon	만 man	십만 simman	백만 baengman

The native Korean numbers on this page are used for quantities of people or things. Some numbers have shortened forms, shown in brackets, which are used in front of counters.

1	2	3	4
하나 **hana** *(한N **han N**)	둘 **dul** (두N **du N**)	셋 **set** (세N **se N**)	넷 **net** (네N **ne N**)
5	6	7	8
다섯 **daseot**	여섯 **yeoseot**	일곱 **ilgop**	여덟 **yeodeol**
9	10	11	12
아홉 **ahop**	열 **yeol**	열하나 **yeolhana** (열한N **yeolhan N**)	열둘 **yeoldul** (열두N **yeoldu N**)
13	14	15	16
열셋 **yeolset** (열세N **yeolse N**)	열넷 **yeollet** (열네N **yeolne N**)	열다섯 **yeoldaseot**	열여섯 **yeoryeoseot**
17	18	19	20
열일곱 **yeorilgop**	열여덟 **yeoryeodeol**	열아홉 **yeorahop**	스물 **seumul** (스무N **seumu N**)
30	40	50	60
서른 **seoreun**	마흔 **maheun**	쉰 **swin**	예순 **yesun**
70	80	90	100
일흔 **ilheun**	여든 **yeodeun**	아흔 **aheun**	백 **baek**

Conversation Practice 회화 연습

01 이것은 컵라면이에요 ?   **igeoseun keomramyeonieyo**   **Are these cup noodles?**

Use the example sentences to guide you as you practice. Find model sentences on page 268.

| 이것
igeot
this
컵라면
keopramyeon
cup noodles |

스테파니: 이것은 컵라면이에요?
　　　　igeoseun keomramyeonieyo
아저씨: 　*Are these cup noodles?*

네, 그것은 컵라면이에요.
ne geugeoseun keomramyeonieyo
Yes, they are cup noodles.

| 이것 **igeot**
this
통조림 X
tongjorim X
canned food X
햄 **haem**
ham |

가: 　이것은 통조림이에요?

나: 　아니요, 그것은 통조림이 아니에요. 햄이에요.

| 이것
igeot
this
건전지
geonjeonji
battery |

가: 　_____ ?

나: 　_____ .

| 그것 **geugeos**
that
배 **bae**
pear
사과 **sagwa**
apple |

가: 　_____ ?

나: 　_____ .

| 저것 **jeogeot**
that
과자 **gwaja**
snack
빵 **ppang**
bread |

가: 　_____ ?

나: 　_____ .

02 뭘 드릴까요? mwol deurilkkayo What would you like?

Use the example sentences to guide you as you practice. Try reading the key words in the last three sentences without romanization or English! Find model sentences on page 268.

사과 1개 sagwa han gae *1 apple* 딸기 1kg ttalgi il killogeuraem *1 kg strawberries*

아저씨: 뭘 드릴까요? **mwol deurilkkayo**
What would you like?

스테파니: 사과 한 개하고 딸기 일 킬로그램 주세요.
sagwa han gaehago ttalgi il killogeuraem juseyo
One apple and one kilo of strawberries, please.

사이다 3병 saida 3 byeong *3 bottles of soda* 맥주 2병 maekju 2 byeong *2 bottles of beer*

가: 뭘 드릴까요?

나: _____ 하고 _____ 주세요.

돼지고기 1kg 닭고기 1마리

가: _____ ?

나: _____ .

계란 10개 캔 커피 5개 화장지 6개

가: _____ ?

나: _____ .

형광등 1개 휴지 7개 바나나 1송이

가: _____ ?

나: _____ .

03 이 사과는 한 개에 얼마예요 ?
i sagwaneun han gaee eolmayeyo

How much is this apple?

Use the example sentences to guide you as you practice. Find model sentences on page 268.

이 사과 i sagwa
this apple

1 개 han gae
one

오백 원
obaek won
500 won

스테파니:이 사과는 한 개에 얼마예요?
　　　　 i sagwaneun han gaee eolmayeyo
　　　　 How much is this apple?

아저씨: 　그 사과는 한 개에 오백 원이에요.
　　　　 geu sagwaneun han gaee obaek wonieyo
　　　　 It's 500 won.

바나나
bananas
bananas

1송이
han songi
1 bunch

이천 원
icheon won
2,000 won

가: 　이 _____ 은/는 _____ 에 얼마예요?

나: 　이 _____ 은/는 _____ 에 _____ 이에요.

이 콜라

1병

육백 원

가: 　_____ ?

나: 　_____ .

그 소고기

1킬로그램

만 이천 원

가: 　_____ ?

나: 　_____ .

그 생선

1마리

삼천오백 원

가: 　_____ ?

나: 　_____ .

ONLINE
AUDIO
03:51

Talking with Lee Joon-gi 이준기와 이야기하기

물건 사기 **Shopping**

Try having a conversation with Lee Joon-gi as you listen to the audio. You can find a translation of this conversation on page 263.

아주머니   어서 오세요. **eoseo oseyo** 뭘 드릴까요? **mwol deurilkkayo**

이준기   아주머니, 이 사과는 한 개에 얼마예요?
ajumeoni, i sagwaneun han gaee eolmayeyo

아주머니   그 사과는 한 개에 오백 원이에요.
geu sagwaneun han gaee obaeg wonieyo

이준기   그 바나나는 한 송이에 얼마예요?
geu banananeun han songie eolmayeyo

아주머니   이 바나나는 한 송이에 이천 원이에요.
i banananeun han songie icheon wonieyo

이준기   사과 두 개하고 바나나 두 송이 주세요.
sagwa dugaehago banana du songi juseyo

아주머니   여기 있어요. 모두 오천 원이에요.
yeogi isseoyo. modu ocheon wonieyo

이준기   안녕히 계세요. **annyeonghi gyeseyo**

아주머니   감사합니다. 안녕히 가세요.
gamsahamnida. annyeonghi gaseyo

Write a conversation following the model on the previous page.

가 어서 오세요. 뭘 드릴까요?

나 아주머니,＿＿＿＿＿＿＿＿ 은/는 ＿＿＿＿＿＿＿＿ 에 얼마예요?

가 ＿＿＿＿＿＿ 은/는 ＿＿＿＿＿ 에 ＿＿＿＿＿＿ 이에요.

나 ＿＿＿＿＿＿ 은/는 ＿＿＿＿＿ 에 얼마예요?

가 ＿＿＿＿＿＿ 은/는 ＿＿＿＿＿ 에 ＿＿＿＿＿＿ 이에요.

나 ＿＿＿＿＿ 하고 ＿＿＿＿＿＿＿＿＿＿ 주세요.

가 여기 있어요. 모두 ＿＿＿＿＿＿＿＿＿＿＿ 이에요.

나 안녕히 계세요.

가 감사합니다. 안녕히 가세요.

Money 돈 don

십 원
sip won
10 won

오십 원
osip won
50 won

백 원
baek won
100 won

오백 원
obaek won
500 won

천 원
cheon won
1,000 won

오천 원
ocheon won
5,000 won

만 원
man won
10,000 won

오만 원
oman won
50,000 won

Lee Joon-gi's Guide to Seoul

Samcheongdong
Where Korean Design and Architecture Flourish

Palaces built during the Joseon Dynasty surround this Seoul neighborhood; you'll also find many Korean traditional houses, known as *hanok*. You can enjoy walking through labyrinth-like alleyways, where generations-old stores welcome you. Lined with old stone walls, the streets also have stylish and unique cafés on every corner, where you can take a break. Many of the traditional houses have been converted into workshops; some conversions have been carried out by famous architects. There are also many galleries housing unique works of art. It's hard to believe that this ancient neighborhood is in the center of a city with a population of over ten million!

What's the Date Today?

오늘은 며칠이에요?

Lesson Goals

Situation
Talking about dates and days of the week
Vocabulary
Year, months, days
Grammar
What's the date?
When is (special day)?
What kind of N is N?

ONLINE
AUDIO
00:10

이준기 ijungi
비비엔 씨, 오늘은 며칠이에요?
bibien ssi, oneureun myeochirieyo
Vivien, what's the date today?

비비엔 bibien
오늘은 9월 28일이에요.
oneureun guwol isipparirieyo
Today is September 28.

이준기 ijungi
오늘은 무슨 요일이에요?
oneureun museun yoirieyo
What day of the week is it today?

비비엔 bibien
오늘은 목요일이에요.
oneureun mogyoirieyo
It's Thursday.

이준기 ijungi
그럼, 비비엔 씨 생일이 언제예요?
geureom, bibien ssi saengniri eonjeyeyo
Vivien, when is your birthday?

비비엔 bibien
제 생일은 10월 9일이에요.
je saengnireun siwol guirieyo
My birthday is October 9.

Days of the week are ordered starting with Sunday in many cultures, but in Korea the week starts with Monday in the spoken language, although the first column on the Korean calendar is Sundays. Refer to page 103 for more information.

ONLINE
AUDIO
01:10

Vocabulary and Expressions 어휘와 표현

01 해 hae · Year

년 〔건전지〕 **nyeon** *year*
작년〔장년〕 **jangnyeon** *last year*
올해〔올해〕 **olhae** *this year*
내년〔내년〕 **naenyeon** *next year*
몇 년〔면년〕 **myeot nyeon** *how many years/a few years*

02 달 dal · Months

일월〔이뤌〕 **irwol** *January*
삼월〔사뭘〕 **samwol** *March*
오월〔오:뭘〕 **owol** *May*
칠월〔치뤌〕 **chirwol** *July*
구월〔구월〕 **guwol** *September*
십일월〔시비뤌〕 **sibirwol** *November*
몇 월〔며뭘〕 **myeot wol** *what month*
이번 달〔이번딸〕 **ibeon dal** *this month*

이월〔이:월〕 **iwol** *February*
사월〔사:월〕 **sawol** *April*
유월〔유월〕 **yuwol** *June*
팔월〔파뤌〕 **parwol** *August*
시월〔시월〕 **siwol** *October*
십이월〔시비월〕 **sibiwol** *December*
지난달〔지난달〕 **jinandal** *last month*
다음 달〔다음딸〕 **daeum dal** *next month*

03 날 nal · Days

그저께〔그저께〕 **geujeokke** *the day before yesterday*
오늘〔오늘〕 **oneul** *today*
모레〔모레〕 **more** *the day after tomorrow*
며칠〔며칠〕 **myeochil** *how many days/a few days*

어제〔어제〕 **eoje** *yesterday*
내일〔내일〕 **naeil** *tomorrow*
매일〔매일〕 **maeil** *every day*

04 주 ju   Days of the week

월요일〔워료일〕 **woryoil** *Monday*   화요일〔화요일〕 **hwayoil** *Tuesday*

수요일〔수요일〕 **suyoil** *Wednesday*   목요일〔모교일〕 **mogyoil** *Thursday*

금요일〔그묘일〕 **geumyoil** *Friday*   토요일〔토요일〕 **toyoil** *Saturday*

일요일〔이료일〕 **iryoil** *Sunday*   무슨 요일〔무슨뇨일〕 **museun yoil** *what day*

지난주〔지난주〕 **jinanju** *last week*   이번 주〔이번쭈〕 **ibeon ju** *this week*

다음 주 〔다음쭈〕 **daeum ju** *next week*   주말〔주말〕 **jumal** *weekend*

05 기타 gita   Other useful vocabulary

책〔책〕 **chaek** *book*

카푸치노〔카푸치노〕 **kapuchino** *cappuccino*

시험〔시험〕 **siheom** *test/exam/quiz*

수료식〔수료식〕 **suryosik** *graduation ceremony*

방학〔방학〕 **banghak** *vacation*

견학〔견:학〕 **gyeonhak** *field trip*

어!〔어〕 **eo!** *Uh!*

인터뷰〔인터뷰〕 **inteobyu** *interview*

오리엔테이션〔오리엔테이션〕 **orienteisyeon** *orientation*

06 기타 2 gita i　　　　　　　　　　　　　　　Other useful vocabulary 2

언제〔언:제〕 **eonje** *when*

달력〔달력〕 **dallyeok** *calendar*

한글날〔한:글랄〕 **hangeullal** *Hangul Day*

한국어 책〔한:구거책〕 **hangugeo chaek** *Korean book*

영어 책〔영어책〕 **yeongeo chaek** *English book*

생일〔생일〕 **saengnil** *birthday*

생일 축하합니다〔생일추카합니다〕 **saengnil chukahamnida** *Happy birthday*

발음규칙 Pronunciation Rules

Liaison (Linking) 연음 법칙
When a syllable ends with a final consonant and is followed by a vowel, then the final phoneme is pronounced as the first phoneme of the following syllable.

$$오늘은 \Rightarrow [오느른]$$

며칠이에요 머치리에요 **myeochirieyo**
　What's the date?
일월 이뤌 **irwol** *January*

이십팔 일이에요 이:십파리리에요 **isipparirieyo**
　28th (day)
목요일 모교일 **mogyoil** *Thursday*

Grammar 문법

01 N 은 / 는 며칠이에요 ?
N eun/neun myeochirieyo

N 은 / 는 ~ 월 ~ 일이에요
N eun/neun –wol –irieyo

What is the date —?

— is (month) (date)

오늘은 며칠이에요? **oneureun myeochirieyo** *What is the date today?*

오늘은 5월 8일이에요. **oneureun owol paririeyo** *The date today is May 8.*

내일은 며칠이에요? **naeireun myeochirieyo** *What is the date tomorrow?*

내일은 10월 20일이에요. **naeireun siwol isibirieyo** *The date tomorrow is October 20.*

토요일은 며칠이에요? **toyoireun myeochirieyo** *What is the date this Saturday?*

토요일은 12월 25일이에요. **toyoireun sibiwol isiboirieyo**
The date this Saturday is December 25.

02 N 이 / 가 언제예요 ? N i/ga eonjeyeyo
N 은 / 는 ~ 월 ~ 일이에요 N eun/neun –wol –iirieyo

When is —?
— is (month) (date)

생일이 언제예요? **saengniri eonjeyeyo** *When is your birthday?*

제 생일은 1월 5일이에요. **je saengnireun irwol oirieyo** *My birthday is on January 5.*

시험이 언제예요? **siheomi eonjeyeyo** *When is the exam?*

시험은 6월 10일이에요. **siheomeun yuwol sibirieyo** *The exam is on June 10.*

한글날이 언제예요? **hangeullari eonjeyeyo** *When is Hangul Day?*

한글날은 10월 9일이에요. **hangeullareun siwol guirieyo** *Hangul Day is on October 9.*

03 N 은 / 는 무슨 N 예요 / 이에요?
N eun/neun museun N yeyo/ieyo What (kind of) — is —?

N 은 / 는 N 예요 / 이에요
N eun/neun N yeyo/ieyo — is —

오늘은 무슨 요일이에요? **oneureun museun yoirieyo** *What day is today?*

오늘은 수요일이에요. **oneureun suyoirieyo** *Today is Wednesday.*

이것은 무슨 커피예요? **igeoseun museun keopiyeyo** *What kind of coffee is this?*

그것은 카푸치노예요. **geugeoseun kapuchinoyeyo** *It's a cappuccino.*

저것은 무슨 책이에요? **jeogeoseun museun chaegieyo** *What book is that?*

저것은 한국어 책이에요. **jeogeoseun hangugeo chaegieyo** *That's a Korean book.*

| **Exercise** | Fill in the blanks. You can find the answers on page 268.

Date	N월 N일이에요 **N wol N irieyo** *The date is the Nth of N*
May 8	오월 팔일이에요
June 6	
July 7	
August 15	
September 30	
October 5	

Conversation Practice 회화 연습

01 오늘은 며칠이에요 ?   **oneureun myeochirieyo**   **What's the date today?**

Use the example sentences to guide you as you practice. Find model sentences on page 268.

오늘
oneul
today

이준기: 비비엔 씨, 오늘은 며칠이에요?
bibien ssi, oneureun myeochirieyo
Vivien, what's the date today?

비비엔: 오늘은 9월 28일이에요. **oneureun guwol isipparirieyo**
The date today is September 28.

오늘

가: 오늘은 며칠이에요?

나: 오늘은 _____ 이에요.

오늘

가: _____ ?

나: _____ .

내일
naeil
tomorrow

가: _____ ?

나: _____ .

모레
more
day after tomorrow

가: _____ ?

나: _____ .

02 생일이 언제예요 ? saengniri eonjeyeyo　　　　When is your birthday?

Use the example sentences to guide you as you practice. Find model sentences on page 268.

생일
saengnil
birthday

이준기: 비비엔 씨, 생일이 언제예요?
bibien ssi, saengniri eonjeyeyo
Vivien, when is your birthday?

비비엔: 제 생일은 6월 10일이에요.
je saengnireun yuwol sibirieyo
My birthday is on June 10.

시험

가: 시험이 언제예요?

나: 시험은 _____ 이에요.

수료식

가: _____ ?

나: _____ .

방학

가: _____ ?

나: _____ .

오리엔테이션

가: _____ ?

나: _____ .

03 오늘은 무슨 요일이에요 ?   oneureun museun yoirieyo   **What day is it today?**

Use the example sentences to guide you as you practice. Find model sentences on page 268.

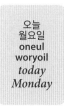

오늘
월요일
oneul
woryoil
today
Monday

이준기: 오늘은 무슨 요일이에요?
oneureun museun yoirieyo
What day is it today?

비비엔: 오늘은 월요일이에요.
oneureun woryoirieyo
Today is Monday.

내일
화요일

가: 내일은 무슨 요일이에요?

나: 내일은 ＿＿＿＿＿＿ 이에요.

모레
수요일

가: ＿＿＿＿＿＿＿＿＿＿ ?

나: ＿＿＿＿＿＿＿＿＿＿ .

7월 3일
일요일

가: ＿＿＿＿＿＿＿＿＿＿ ?

나: ＿＿＿＿＿＿＿＿＿＿ .

오늘
토요일

가: ＿＿＿＿＿＿＿＿＿＿ ?

나: ＿＿＿＿＿＿＿＿＿＿ .

Listening Practice 듣기 연습

01 날짜 받아쓰기 1 **naljja badasseugi il** **Dictating dates 1**

Listen to the question and write the answer, following the example. You can find the answers on page 259.

이준기: 오늘은 며칠이에요? **oneureun myeochirieyo**
What is the date today?

비비엔: 오늘은 5월 5일이에요. **oneureun owol oirieyo**
The date today is May 5.

1. _____ 은/는 _____ 이에요.

2. _____ 은/는 _____ 이에요.

3. _____ 은/는 _____ 이에요.

02 날짜 받아쓰기 2 **naljja badasseugi i** **Dictating dates 2**

Listen to the question and write the answer, following the example. You can find the answers on page 259.

이준기: 비비엔 씨 생일이 언제예요? **bibien ssi saengniri eonjeyeyo**
Vivien, when is your birthday?

비비엔: 제 생일은 5월 8일이에요. **je saengnireun owol paririeyo**
My birthday is May 8.

1. _____ 은/는 _____ 이에요.

2. _____ 은/는 _____ 이에요.

3. _____ 은/는 _____ 이에요.

03 요일 받아쓰기 **yoil badasseugi**   **Dictating days of the week**

Listen to the question and write the answer, following the example. You can find the answers on page 259.

이준기: 내일은 무슨 요일이에요? **naeireun museun yoirieyo**
What day is tomorrow?

비비엔: 내일은 월요일이에요. **naeireun woryoirieyo**
Tomorrow is Monday.

1. _____ 은/는 _____ 이에요.

2. _____ 은/는 _____ 이에요.

3. _____ 은/는 _____ 이에요.

생일 축하합니다 노래 **Happy birthday to you!**

생일 축하합니다.
saengnil chukahamnida
Happy birthday to you.

생일 축하합니다.
saengnil chukahamnida
Happy birthday to you.

사랑하는 _____ 씨

saranghaneun _____ **ssi**

Happy birthday, dear _____

생일 축하합니다.
saengnil chukahamnida
Happy birthday to you.

▼
Koreans traditionally eat 미역국 (miyeokguk *seaweed soup*) on their birthdays. So an alternative birthday greeting to 생일 축하해요 (saengnil chukahaeyo *happy birthday*) is 미역국 드셨어요 (miyeokguk deusyeosseoyo *Did you eat seaweed soup?*).

Talking with Lee Joon-gi 이준기와 이야기하기

날짜 · 요일 · 생일 묻기
Asking about dates, days of the week and birthdays

Try having a conversation with Lee Joon-gi as you listen to the audio. You can find a translation of this conversation on page 263. Then use the gray box below to write your own conversation, following this model.

이준기 비비엔 씨, 오늘은 며칠이에요? **bibien ssi, oneureun myeochirieyo**

비비엔 오늘은 6월 20일이에요. **oneureun yuwol isibirieyo**

이준기 오늘은 월요일이에요? **oneureun woryoirieyo**

비비엔 네, 오늘은 월요일이에요. **ne oneureun woryoirieyo**

이준기 그럼, 비비엔 씨 생일은 언제예요?
geureom, bibien ssi saengnireun eonjeyeyo

비비엔 제 생일은 10월 9일이에요. **je saengnireun siwol guirieyo**

이준기 어? 10월 9일은 한글날이에요. **eo? siwol guireun hangeullarieyo**

비비엔 아, 그렇군요! **a, geureokunyo**

가 _____ 씨, _____?

나 오늘은 _____.

가 오늘은 _____?

나 네, _____.

   (아니요,_____).

가 그럼, _____?

나 제 생일은_____.

가 어? _____.

나 아, 그렇군요!

Reading the Calendar 달력읽기

Read the number first and then read 일 (**il**) when reading the date of the month. For example, the first day of the month is 1일 or 일일 (**iril**), and the tenth day is 10일 or 십일 (**sibil**). Study the calendar below.

달력 읽기   dallyeok ilkki   **Reading the calendar**

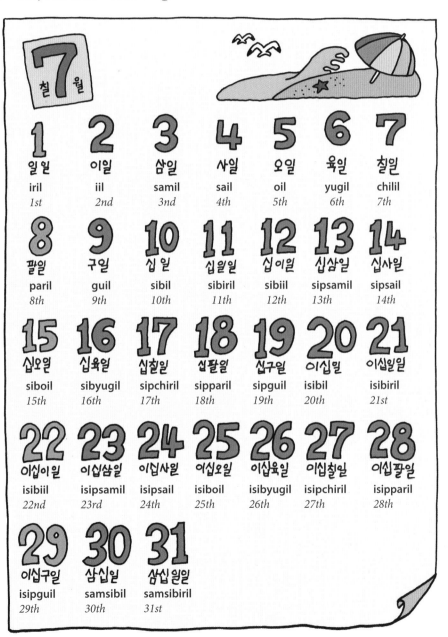

숫자 + 일 sutja + il Number + day

1일 일일 **iril** *1st*	2일 이일 **iil** *2nd*	3일 삼일 **samil** *3rd*
4일 사일 **sail** *4th*	5일 오일 **oil** *5th*	6일 육일 **yugil** *6th*
7일 칠일 **chilil** *7th*	8일 팔일 **paril** *8th*	9일 구일 **guil** *9th*
10일 십일 **sibil** *10th*	11일 십일일 **sibiril** *11th*	12일 십이일 **sibiil** *12th*
13일 십삼일 **sipsamil** *13th*	14일 십사일 **sipsail** *14th*	15일 십오일 **siboil** *15th*
16일 십육일 **sibyugil** *16th*	17일 십칠일 **sipchiril** *17th*	18일 십팔일 **sipparil** *18th*
19일 십구일 **sipguil** *19th*	20일 이십일 **isibil** *20th*	21일 이십일일 **isibiril** *21st*
30일 삼십일 **samsibil** *30th*	31일 삼십일일 **samsibiril** *31st*	

요일 읽기 yoil ilkki Days of the week

Sunday	Monday	Tuesday	Wednesday	Thursday	Friday	Saturday
일요일 **iryoil**	월요일 **woryoil**	화요일 **hwayoil**	수요일 **suyoil**	목요일 **mogyoil**	금요일 **geumyoil**	토요일 **toyoil**

때를 나타내는 말 ttaereul natanaeneun mal Time words

	작년 **jangnyeon** *last year*	올해 **olhae** *this year*	내년 **naenyeon** *next year*	
	지난달 **jinandal** *last month*	이번 달 **ibeon dal** *this month*	다음 달 **daeum dal** *next month*	
	지난주 **jinanju** *last week*	이번 주 **ibeon ju** *this week*	다음 주 **daeum ju** *next week*	
그저께 **geujeokke** *the day before yesterday*	어제 **eoje** *yesterday*	오늘 **oneul** *today*	내일 **naeil** *tomorrow*	모레 **more** *the day after tomorrow*

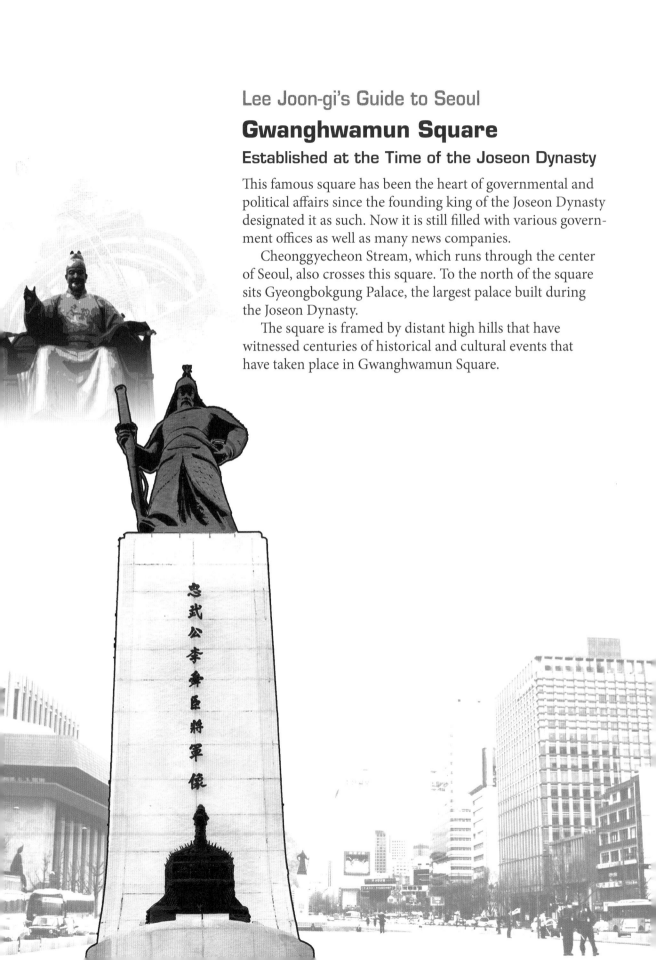

Gwanghwamun Square

Established at the Time of the Joseon Dynasty

This famous square has been the heart of governmental and political affairs since the founding king of the Joseon Dynasty designated it as such. Now it is still filled with various government offices as well as many news companies.

Cheonggyecheon Stream, which runs through the center of Seoul, also crosses this square. To the north of the square sits Gyeongbokgung Palace, the largest palace built during the Joseon Dynasty.

The square is framed by distant high hills that have witnessed centuries of historical and cultural events that have taken place in Gwanghwamun Square.

忠武公李舜臣將軍像

What Time Is It Now?
지금 몇 시예요?

시간 묻고 답하기
Asking and Telling the Time

Lesson Goals

Situation
Asking and telling
the time
Vocabulary
Times of day
Places around town
Grammar
Telling the time

ONLINE
AUDIO
00:10

벤슨 benseun

실례지만, 지금 몇 시예요?
sillyejiman, jigeum myeot siyeyo
Excuse me, but what time is it now?

최지영 choejiyeong

지금 3시 반이에요.
jigeum sesi banieyo
It's 3:30 PM.

벤슨 benseun

한국어 수업은 몇 시부터 몇 시까지예요?
hangugeo sueobeun myeot sibuteo myeot sikkajiyeyo
When is the Korean class?

최지영 choejiyeong

한국어 수업은 9시부터 1시까지예요.
hangugeo sueobeun ahopsibuteo hansikkajiyeyo
The Korean class is from 9 AM to 1 PM.

벤슨 benseun

고맙습니다.
gomapseumnida
Thank you.

▼
When you initiate a talk with a stranger to ask the time or for directions, it is polite to use the phrases 실례지만 (sillyejiman *excuse me*), 고맙습니다 (gomapseumnida) or 감사합니다 (gamsahamnida) which both mean *thank you*.

ONLINE
AUDIO
01:07

Vocabulary and Expressions 어휘와 표현

01 때 ttae   Times

시 [시] **si** *o'clock*   시간 [시간] **sigan** *hour/time*

분 [분] **bun** *minute*   초 [초] **cho** *second*

아침 [아침] **achim** *morning/breakfast*   점심 [점:심] **jeomsim** *lunch time/lunch*

저녁 [저녁] **jeonyeok** *evening/dinner*   낮 [낟] **nat** *daytime*

밤 [밤] **bam** *night*   지금 [지금] **jigeum** *now*

정오 [정:오] **jeongo** *noon*   반 [반:] **ban** *half*

오전 [오전] **ojeon** AM   오후 [오후] **ohu** PM

전 [전] **jeon** *before*   ~쯤(에) [쯔메] **jjeum(e)** *around*

02 공공기관 gonggonggigwan   Places around town

도서관 [도서관] **doseogwan** *library*

은행 [은행] **eunhaeng** *bank*

우체국 [우체국] **ucheguk** *post office*

출입국관리소 [추립꾹꽐리소] **churipgukgwalliso** *Immigration Office*

학교 [학꾜] **hakgyo** *school*

병원 [병:원] **byeongwon** *hospital*

03 장소 jangso   Places

세탁소 [세:탁쏘] **setakso** *laundromat*

학생 식당 [학쌩식땅] **haksaeng sikdang** *student cafeteria*

편의점 [펴니점] **pyeonuijeom** *convenience store*

중국집 [중국찝] **junggukjip** *Chinese restaurant*

동대문 시장 [동대문시장] **dongdaemun sijang** *Dongdaemun Market*

04 기타 **gita**   **Other useful vocabulary**

시계〔시계/시게〕 **sigye** *watch/clock*

한국어 수업〔한:구거수업〕 **hangugeo sueop** *Korean class*

실례지만〔실례지만〕 **sillyejiman** *Excuse me, but …*

고맙습니다〔고:맙씀니다〕 **gomapseumnida** *Thank you*

발 음 규 칙 Pronunciation Rules

Tense Consonants 경음
When the final consonants ㄷ, ㅌ, ㅅ, ㅆ, ㅈ or ㅊ meet with the initial consonants ㄱ, ㄷ, ㅂ, ㅅ or ㅈ on the next syllable, the initial consonants are pronounced as ㄲ, ㄸ, ㅃ, ㅆ or ㅉ respectively.

$$몇 \, 시 \Rightarrow [멷씨]$$

$$ㄷ (ㅌ, ㅅ, ㅆ, ㅈ, ㅊ) + \begin{matrix} ㄱ \\ ㄷ \\ ㅂ \\ ㅅ \\ ㅈ \end{matrix} \Rightarrow \begin{matrix} ㄲ \\ ㄸ \\ ㅃ \\ ㅆ \\ ㅉ \end{matrix}$$

햇빛 핻삗 **haetbit** *sunlight*   같고 갇꼬 **gatgo** *same and*
있다 읻따 **itda** *there is*   맞지만 맏찌만 **majjiman** *although*

Grammar 문법

01 시간 읽기 sigan ilkki — Telling the time

시 si Hour

1	2	3	4	5
한 시 **han si** *1:00*	두 시 **du si** *2:00*	세 시 **se si** *3:00*	네 시 **ne si** *4:00*	다섯 시 **daseot si** *5:00*
6	7	8	9	10
여섯 시 **yeoseot si** *6:00*	일곱 시 **ilgop si** *7:00*	여덟 시 **yeodeol si** *8:00*	아홉 시 **ahop si** *9:00*	열 시 **yeol si** *10:00*
11	12	?		
열한 시 **yeolhan si** *11:00*	열두 시 **yeoldu si** *12:00*	몇 시 **myeot si** *what time*		

분 bun Minute

1	2	3	4	5
일 분 **il bun** *1 minute*	이 분 **i bun** *2 minutes*	삼 분 **sam bun** *3 minutes*	사 분 **sa bun** *4 minutes*	오 분 **o bun** *5 minutes*
6	7	8	9	10
육 분 **yuk bun** *6 minutes*	칠 분 **chil bun** *7 minutes*	팔 분 **pal bun** *8 minutes*	구 분 **gu bun** *9 minutes*	십 분 **sip bun** *10 minutes*
11	12	15	20	25
십일 분 **sibil bun** *11 minutes*	십이 분 **sibi bun** *12 minutes*	십오 분 **sibo bun** *15 minutes*	이십 분 **isip bun** *20 minutes*	이십오 분 **isibo bun** *25 minutes*
30	35	40	45	50
삼십 분/반 **samsip bun/ban** *30 minutes*	삼십오 분 **samsibo bun** *35 minutes*	사십 분 **sasip bun** *40 minutes*	사십오 분 **sasibo bun** *45 minutes*	오십 분 **osip bun** *50 minutes*
55	60	?		
오십오 분 **osibo bun** *55 minutes*	육십 분 **yuksip bun** *60 minutes*	몇 분 **myeot bun** *How many minutes*		

▼

시간 sigan hour
1시간(한 시간)
han sigan
one hour
2시간(두 시간)
du sigan
two hours
10시간(열 시간)
yeol sigan
ten hours
2시간 30분
(두 시간 삼십 분,
두 시간 반)
**du sigan samsip
bun, du sigan ban**
*two hours and
thirty minutes, two
and a half hours*
24시간(이십사 시간)
isipsa sigan
twenty-four hours
몇 시간?
myeot sigan
How many hours?

09 : 00
아홉 시
ahop si
9:00

04 : 30
네 시 삼십 분 / 네 시 반
nesi samsip bun / ne si ban
half past four / four thirty

07 : 55
일곱 시 오십오 분 /
여덟 시 오 분 전
**ilgop si osibo bun /
yeodeol si o bun jeon**
seven fifty-five/ five to eight

10 : 00
오전 열 시
ojeon yeol si
10 AM

22 : 00
밤 열 시
bam yeol si
10 PM

02 N 부터 N 까지 N buteo N kkaji

From — until —

Use ~부터~까지 for a time span. For location, use 에서~까지 instead.

1시~2시 han si – du si
1:00 – 2:00

1시부터 2시까지예요.
han sibuteo du sikkajiyeyo
From 1:00 until 2:00.

아침~저녁 achim – jeonyeok
morning – evening

아침부터 저녁까지예요.
achimbuteo jeonyeokkkajiyeyo
From the morning until the evening.

오늘~ 내일 oneul – naeil
today – tomorrow

오늘부터 내일까지예요.
oneulbuteo naeilkkajiyeyo
From today until tomorrow.

▼

서울 ~부산 seoul – busan
Seoul – Busan

서울~ 서울부터 부산까지 (×)
seoulbuteo busankkaji (×)

서울에서 부산까지 (✓)
seoureseo busankkaji (✓)

from Seoul to Busan

집~학교 jip – hakgyo
home – school

집부터 학교까지 (×)
jipbuteo hakgyokkaji (×)

집에서 학교까지 (✓)
jibeseo hakgyokkaji (✓)

from home to school

Conversation Practice 회화 연습

01 지금 몇 시예요? **jigeum myeot siyeyo**   **What time is it now?**

Use the example sentences to guide you as you practice. Find model sentences on page 269.

벤슨: 실례지만, 지금 몇 시예요?
sillyejiman, jigeum myeot siyeyo
Excuse me, but what time is it now?

최지영: 지금 열한 시예요. **jigeum yeolhan siyeyo**
It's 11:00.

벤슨 : 고맙습니다. **gomapseumnida**
Thank you.

가: 실례지만, 지금 몇 시예요?

나: 지금 _____ 예요.

가: 고맙습니다.

가: _____?
나: _____ .
가: _____ .

가: _____?
나: _____ .
가: _____ .

가: _____?
나: _____ .
가: _____ .

02 수업은 9 시부터 1 시까지예요 .
sueobeun ahop sibuteo han sikkajiyeyo

The class is from 9 AM until 1 PM

Use the example sentences to guide you as you practice. Find model sentences on page 269.

한국어 수업
hangugeo sueop
Korean class

벤슨: 실례지만, 수업은 몇 시부터 몇 시까지예요?
sillyejiman, sueobeun myeot sibuteo myeot sikkajiyeyo
Excuse me, but from what time to what time is the class?

최지영: 수업은 9시부터 1시까지예요. **sueobeun ahop sibuteo han sikkajiyeyo** *The class is from 9AM till 1PM.*

벤슨 : 고맙습니다. **gomapseumnida**
Thank you.

우체국
ucheguk
post office

가: 실례지만, ＿＿＿＿＿＿＿＿ 은/는 몇 시부터 몇 시까지예요?

나: ＿＿＿ 은/는 ＿＿＿＿＿＿＿ 예요.

가: 고맙습니다.

은행

가: ＿＿＿＿＿＿＿＿＿＿＿＿＿＿＿ ?
나: ＿＿＿＿＿＿＿＿＿＿＿＿＿＿＿ .
가: ＿＿＿＿＿＿＿＿＿＿＿＿＿＿＿ .

출입국관리소

가: ＿＿＿＿＿＿＿＿＿＿＿＿＿＿＿ ?
나: ＿＿＿＿＿＿＿＿＿＿＿＿＿＿＿ .
가: ＿＿＿＿＿＿＿＿＿＿＿＿＿＿＿ .

병원

가: ＿＿＿＿＿＿＿＿＿＿＿＿＿＿＿ ?
나: ＿＿＿＿＿＿＿＿＿＿＿＿＿＿＿ .
가: ＿＿＿＿＿＿＿＿＿＿＿＿＿＿＿ .

ONLINE
AUDIO
02:45

Listening Practice 듣기 연습

01 시간 묻고 답하기 **sigan mutgo dapagi**   **Asking for the time**

Listen to the question and write the answer, following the example. You can find the answers on page 259.

벤슨: 실례지만, 지금 몇 시예요? **sillyejiman jigeum myeot siyeyo**
          Excuse me, but what time is it now?

최지영: 지금 11:00예요. **jigeum yeolhan siyeyo** *It's 11:00.*

벤슨: 감사합니다. **gamsahamnida** *Thank you.*

1. 지금 _____ 예요/이에요.

2. 지금 _____ 예요/이에요.

3. 지금 _____ 예요/이에요.

4. 지금 _____ 예요/이에요.

▼
Write down the time first as in the sample text and choose either 예요 or 이에요.

02 영업 시간 묻고 답하기
yeongeop sigan mutgo dapagi   **Asking about business hours**

Listen to the question and write the answer, following the example. You can find the answers on page 259.

벤슨: 실례지만, 한국어 수업은 몇 시부터 몇 시까지예요?
          sillyejiman, hangugeo sueobeun myeot sibuteo myeot sikkajiyeyo?
          Excuse me, but from what time to what time is there a Korean class?

최지영: 한국어 수업은/는 9시부터 1시까지예요.
          hangugeo sueobeun ahop sibuteo han sikkajiyeyo
          There is a Korean class from 9:00 to 1:00.

벤슨: 고맙습니다. **gomapseumnida** *Thank you.*

1. _____ 은/는 _____ 부터 _____ 까지예요.

2. _____ 은/는 _____ 부터 _____ 까지예요.

3. _____ 은/는 _____ 부터 _____ 까지예요.

4. _____ 은/는 _____ 이에요.

ONLINE
AUDIO
07:35

Talking with Lee Joon-gi 이준기와 이야기하기

시간 · 영업 시간 묻고 답하기 Talking about business hours

Try having a conversation with Lee Joon-gi as you listen to the audio. You can find a translation of this conversation on page 263. Then write your own conversation in the gray box below, following this model.

리리   실례지만, 지금 몇 시예요? **sillyejiman jigeum myeot siyeyo**

이준기   지금 2시 45분이에요. **jigeum du si sasibo bunieyo**

리리   은행은 몇 시부터 몇 시까지예요?
          eunhaengeun myeot sibuteo myeot sikkajiyeyo

이준기   은행은 9시부터 4시까지예요.
          eunhaengeun ahop sibuteo ne sikkajiyeyo

리리   동대문 시장은 몇 시부터
          몇 시까지예요?
          dongdaemun sijangeun myeot
          sibuteo myeot sikkajiyeyo

이준기   동대문 시장은 오후 5시부터
          오전 5시까지예요.
          dongdaemun sijangeun ohu daseot
          sibuteo ojeon daseot sikkajiyeyo

리리   감사합니다. **gamsahamnida**

▼

은행 eunhaeng
bank
09:00~16:00

우체국 ucheguk
post office
09:00~18:00

백화점 baekwajeom
department store
10:30~19:30

한국어 수업
hangugeo sueop
Korean class
09:00~13:00

도서관 doseogwan
library
05:00~24:00

중국집 junggukjip
Chinese restaurant
11:00~21:00

동대문 시장
dongdaemun sijang
Dongdaemun Market
17:00~05:00

출입국관리소
churipgukgwalliso
Immigration Office
09:00~17:00

가   실례지만, 지금 몇 시예요?

나   지금 _____이에요.

가   _____ 은/는 _____에요?

나   _____ 은/는 _____에요.

가   _____ 은/는 _____에요?

나   _____ 은/는 _____에요.

가   감사합니다.

I Live in Sinchon
우리 집은 신촌에 있어요

위치 말하기
Describing a Location

Lesson Goals

Situation
Describing a location
Vocabulary
Location
Places
Grammar
Here/there/where
Where is N?
N is (in this location)

ONLINE
AUDIO
00:10

최지영 choejiyeong	로이 씨 집이 어디예요? **roi ssi jibi eodiyeyo** *Roy, where do you live?*	
로이 roi	우리 집은 신촌에 있어요. **uri jibeun sinchone isseoyo** *In Sinchon.*	
최지영 choejiyeong	로이 씨 집은 몇 층에 있어요? **roi ssi jibeun myeot cheunge isseoyo** *What floor is your apartment on?*	
로이 roi	우리 집은 4층이에요. **uri jibeun sacheungieyo** *It's on the 4th floor.*	
최지영 choejiyeong	집에 주차장이 있어요? **jibe juchajangi isseoyo** *Does your building have a parking lot?*	
로이 roi	네, 주차장이 있어요. **ne, juchajangi isseoyo** *Yes, there is one.*	
최지영 choejiyeong	엘리베이터가 있어요? **ellibeiteoga isseoyo** *Does it have an elevator?*	
로이 roi	아니요, 엘리베이터는 없어요. **aniyo, ellibeiteoneun eopseoyo** *No, it doesn't.*	

▼
Koreans prefer the first person plural "we" over the first person singular "I." "Our house," rather than "my house," is predominantly used. Likewise, Koreans are more likely to use expressions like "our family," "our neighborhood," or "our country" rather than "my family," "my neighborhood" or "my country." This aspect of the language reflects the strong sense of communal life and culture among Koreans.

ONLINE
AUDIO
01:28

Vocabulary and Expressions 어휘와 표현

01 위치 wichi   Location

왼쪽
oenjjok
left

오른쪽
oreunjjok
right

위
wi
top

아래 / 밑
area/mit
under/below

앞
ap
front

뒤
dwi
back

안 / 속
an/sok
in

밖
bak
outside

옆
yeop
side

사이
sai
between

근처
geuncheo
around

건너편 / 맞은편
**geonneopyeon/
majeunpyeon**
across/opposite

Koreans do not like the number four as its pronunciation is the same as the Chinese character 死 which means death. You can easily observe this while using an elevator in Korea. Many buildings refer to the fourth floor as the "F floor" rather than using the actual number and some buildings have eliminated the fourth floor altogether. You will never find the fourth floor in a Korean hospital building. What numbers are favored and feared in your culture?

02 ~층 ~cheung   Floors

지하 1층〔지하일층〕 **jihailcheung**
  basement 1/B1

2층〔이:층〕 **icheung** *2nd floor*

4층〔사:층〕 **sacheung** *4th floor*

6층〔육층〕 **yukcheung** *6th floor*

8층〔팔층〕 **palcheung** *8th floor*

10층〔십층〕 **sipcheung** *10th floor*

1층〔일층〕 **ilcheung** *1st floor*

3층〔삼층〕 **samcheung** *3rd floor*

5층〔오:층〕 **ocheung** *5th floor*

7층〔칠층〕 **chilcheung** *7th floor*

9층〔구층〕 **gucheung** *9th floor*

몇 층〔면층〕 **myeot cheung** *which
  floor*

03 동네에서 dongneeseo In town

꽃 가게 〔꼳까게〕 **kkot gage** *flower shop*

공원 〔공원〕 **gongwon** *park*

주유소 〔주유소〕 **juyuso** *gas station*

미용실 〔미용실〕 **miyongsil** *hairdresser's*

커피숍 〔커피숍〕 **keopisyop** *coffee shop*

슈퍼마켓 / 슈퍼 〔슈퍼마켇 / 슈퍼〕
syupeomaket/syupeo *supermarket*

04 집 / 아파트에서 jip/apateueseo In a house/apartment

집 〔집〕 **jip** *house*

방 〔방〕 **bang** *room*

거실 〔거:실〕 **geosil** *living room*

현관 〔현관〕 **hyeongwan** *front door*

엘리베이터 〔엘리베이터〕 **ellibeiteo**
elevator

계단 〔계단 / 게단〕 **gyedan** *staircase*

아파트 〔아파트〕 **apateu** *apartment*

화장실 〔화장실〕 **hwajangsil** *bathroom/toilet/restroom*

부엌 〔부억〕 **bueok** *kitchen*

주차장 〔주차장〕 **juchajang** *parking lot*

에스컬레이터 〔에스컬레이터〕 **eseukeolleiteo**
escalator

창문 〔창문〕 **changmun** *window*

05 기타 gita Other useful vocabulary

실례합니다 〔실례함니다〕 **sillyehamnida** *Excuse me*

텔레비전 〔텔레비전〕 **tellebijeon** *television*

책상 〔책쌍〕 **chaeksang** *desk*

아무것 / 아무것도 〔아무걷 / 아무걷또〕
amugeot/amugeotdo *anything/nothing*

신촌 〔신촌〕 **sinchon** *Sinchon*

우리 〔우리〕 **uri** *we/our/us*

컴퓨터 〔컴퓨터〕 **keompyuteo** *computer*

의자 〔의자〕 **uija** *chair*

한남동 〔한남동〕 **hannamdong**
Hannam-dong

Grammar 문법

01 여기 / 거기 / 저기 / 어디
yeogi/geogi/jeogi/eodi

Here / there / (over)there / where

여기 yeogi	거기 geogi	저기 jeogi	어디 eodi

▼

여기 and 거기 can be used interchangeably because they refer to broad areas. But 여기 is where the speaker is and 거기 is where the listener is when the speakers are far away from each other, as in telephone conversations.

화장실은 여기에 있어요. **hwajangsireun yeogie isseoyo**
There is a toilet here.

편의점은 거기에 있어요. **pyeonuijeomeun geogie isseoyo**
There is a convenience store there.

병원은 저기에 있어요. **byeongwoneun jeogie isseoyo**
There is a hospital over there.

계단은 어디에 있어요? **gyedaneun eodie isseoyo**
Where are the stairs?

02 N 이 / 가 어디에 있어요 ?
N i/ga eodie isseoyo

Where is —?

N이 어디에 있어요? is used when the last syllable of a noun has a final consonant, and N가 어디에 있어요? otherwise.

슈퍼마켓이 어디에 있어요? **syupeomakesi eodie isseoyo**
Where is the supermarket?

꽃 가게가 어디에 있어요? **kkot gagega eodie isseoyo**
Where is the flower shop?

컴퓨터가 어디에 있어요? **keompyuteoga eodie isseoyo**
Where is the desktop computer?

03 N 은 / 는 N 에 있어요 N   N 은 / 는 N 에 없어요 N   — is on/in/at
N eun/neun N e isseoyo   N eun/neun N e eopseoyo   — isn't on/in/ at

슈퍼마켓은 공원 건너편에 있어요. **syupeomakeseun gongwon geonneopyeone isseoyo**
There is a supermarket on the opposite side of the park.

슈퍼마켓은 공원 건너편에 없어요. **syupeomakeseun gongwon geonneopyeone eopseoyo**
There isn't a supermarket on the opposite side of the park.

꽃 가게는 오른쪽에 있어요. **kkot gageneun oreunjjoge isseoyo**
There is a flower shop on the right.

꽃 가게는 오른쪽에 없어요. **kkot gageneun oreunjjoge eopseoyo**
There isn't a flower shop on the right.

컴퓨터는 책상 위에 있어요. **keompyuteoneun chaeksang wie isseoyo**
There is a desktop computer on the desk.

컴퓨터는 책상 위에 없어요. **keompyuteoneun chaeksang wie eopseoyo**
There isn't a desktop computer on the desk.

| **Exercise** | Fill in the blanks. You can find the answers on page 269.

Conversation Practice 회화 연습

01 엘리베이터가 어디에 있어요? **ellibeiteoga eodie isseoyo** **Where is the elevator?**

Use the example sentences to guide you as you practice. You can find the answers on page 269.

엘리베이터
ellibeiteo
elevator

로이: 실례합니다. 엘리베이터가 어디에 있어요?
sillyehamnida. ellibeiteoga eodie isseoyo
Excuse me. Where is the elevator?

최지영: 엘리베이터는 화장실 옆에 있어요.
ellibeiteoneun hwajangsil yeope isseoyo
The elevator is next to the toilet.

로이: 감사합니다. **gamsahamnida** *Thank you.*

화장실

가: 실례합니다. _____ 이/가 어디에 있어요?
나: _____ 은/는 _____ 에 있어요.
가: 감사합니다.

계단

가: _____ ?
나: _____ .
가: _____ .

휴지통

가: _____ ?
나: _____ .
가: _____ .

구두

가: _____ ?
나: _____ .
가: _____ .

02 커피숍은 공원 옆에 있어요.
keopisyobeun gongwon yeope isseoyo

The coffee shop is next to the park.

Use the example sentences to guide you as you practice. You can find the answers on page 269.

로이: 실례합니다. 커피숍이 어디에 있어요?
sillyehamnida. keopisyobi eodie isseoyo
Excuse me. Where is the coffee shop?

> 커피숍
> keopisyop
> *coffee shop*

최지영: 커피숍은 공원 옆에 있어요.
keopisyobeun gongwon yeope isseoyo
The coffee shop is next to the park.

로이: 감사합니다. **gamsahamnida** *Thank you.*

가: 실례합니다. _____
이 / 가 어디에있어요?

나: _____ 은 / 는 _____ 에
있어요.

> 세탁소

가: 감사합니다.

가: _____ ?
나: _____ .
가: _____ .

> 은행

가: _____ ?
나: _____ .
가: _____ .

> 꽃 가게

가: _____ ?
나: _____ .
가: _____ .

> 주유소

03 엘리베이터 옆에 계단이 있어요.
ellibeiteo yeope gyedani isseoyo

There are stairs next to the elevator.

Use the example sentences to guide you as you practice. You can find the answers on page 269.

엘리베이터 옆 계단

로이: 엘리베이터 옆에 계단이 있어요?
ellibeiteo yeope gyedani isseoyo
Are there stairs next to the elevator?

최지영: 네, 엘리베이터 옆에 계단이 있어요.
ne, ellibeiteo yeope gyedani isseoyo
Yes, there are stairs next to the elevator.

로이 책상 위 책

가: 로이 씨 책상 위에 책이 있어요?
나: 아니요, 로이 씨 책상 위에 책이 없어요.

비비엔 뒤 퍼디

가: _____?
나: _____.

책상 위 컴퓨터

가: _____?
나: _____.

가방 안 옷

가: _____?
나: _____.

04 커피숍이 몇 층에 있어요 ?
keopisyobi myeot cheunge isseoyo

What floor is the coffee shop on?

Use the example sentences to guide you as you practice. You can find answers on page 270.

로이: 실례합니다. 커피숍이 몇 층에 있어요?
sillyehamnida. keopisyobi myeot cheunge isseoyo
Excuse me. What floor is the coffee shop on?

최지영: 커피숍은 5층에 있어요.
keopisyobeun ocheunge isseoyo
It's on the 5th floor.

로이: 감사합니다. **gamsahamnida** *Thank you.*

커피숍
keopisyop
coffee shop

가: 실례합니다. _____ 이/가 어디에있어요?
나: _____ 은/는 _____ 에 있어요.
가: 감사합니다.

냉장고

가: _____ ?
나: _____ .
가: _____ .

화장실

가: _____ ?
나: _____ .
가: _____ .

지갑

가: _____ ?
나: _____ .
가: _____ .

주차장

ONLINE
AUDIO
04:15

Listening Practice 듣기 연습

01 장소 찾기 **jangso chatgi** **Finding places**

Listen to the dialogues and write the missing words, following the example.
You can find the answers on page 259.

로이: 실례합니다.영화관이 어디에 있어요?
sillyehamnida. yeonghwagwani eodie isseoyo
Excuse me. Where is the cinema?

최지영: 영화관은 공원 앞에 있어요.
yeonghwagwaneun gongwon ape isseoyo
It's in front of the park.

로이: 고맙습니다. **gomapseumnida** *Thank you.*

1. 은행 **bank**

가: 실례합니다. _____ 이 어디에 있어요?

나: 은행은 _____ 하고 _____ 사이에 있어요,

가: 고맙습니다.

2. 과일 가게 fruit shop

가: 실례합니다. _____ 가 어디에 있어요?

나: 과일 가게는 _____ 앞에 있어요.

가: 고맙습니다.

3. 식당 restaurant

가: 실례합니다. _____ 이 어디에 있어요?

나: 식당은 _____ 옆에 있어요.

가: 고맙습니다.

4. 슈퍼마켓 supermarket

가: 실례합니다. _____ 이 어디에 있어요?

나: 수퍼마켓은 _____ 하고 _____ 사이에 있어요.

가: 고맙습니다.

5. 병원 hospital

가: 실례합니다. _____ 이 어디에 있어요?

나: 병원은 _____ 옆에 있어요.

가: 고맙습니다.

6. 주유소 gas station

가: 실례합니다. _____ 가 어디에 있어요?

나: 주유소는 _____ 옆에 있어요.

가: 고맙습니다.

Talking with Lee Joon-gi 이준기와 이야기하기

세계의 유명한 곳 물어보기 **Asking questions about famous places**

Try having a conversation with Lee Joon-gi as you listen to the audio. You can find a translation of this conversation on page 263.

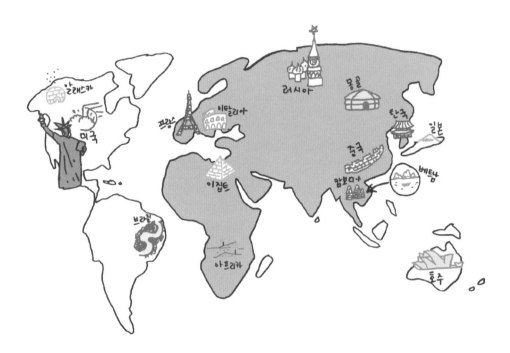

이준기	스테파니 씨, 오페라 하우스가 어디에 있어요? **seutepani ssi, opera hauseuga eodie isseoyo**
스테파니	오페라 하우스는 시드니에 있어요. **opera hauseuneun sideunie isseoyo**
이준기	피라미드가 어디에 있어요? **piramideuga eodie isseoyo**
스테파니	피라미드는 이집트에 있어요. **piramideuneun ijipteue isseoyo**
이준기	에펠 탑이 독일에 있어요? **epel tabi dogire isseoyo**
스테파니	아니요, 에펠 탑은 프랑스에 있어요. **aniyo, epel tabeun peurangseue isseoyo.**
이준기	감사합니다. **gamsahamnida.**

Make a dialogue using the model below, using place names and country names from the chart.

	한국 **hanguk** **Korea**	숭례문 **sungnyemun** *Sungnyemun Gate*		일본 **ilbon** **Japan**	후지 산 **huji san** *Mt. Fuji*
	중국 **jungguk** **China**	만리장성 **mallijangseong** *The Great Wall*		캄보디아 **kambodia** **Cambodia**	앙코르 와트 **angkoreu wateu** *Angkor Wat*
	베트남 **beteunam** **Vietnam**	하롱베이 **harongbei** *Ha Long Bay*		호주 **hoju** **Australia**	오페라 하우스 **opera hauseu** *Sydney Opera House*
	이집트 **ijipteu** **Egypt**	피라미드 **piramideu** *the pyramids*		러시아 **reosia** **Russia**	크렘린 궁 **keuremnin gung** *the Kremlin*
	몽골 **monggol** **Mongolia**	게르 **gereu** *yurt*		이탈리아 **itallia** **Italy**	피사의 사탑 **pisaui satap** *Leaning Tower of Pisa*
	프랑스 **peurangseu** **France**	에펠 탑 **epel tap** *Eiffel Tower*		알래스카 **allaeseuka** **Alaska**	이글루 **igeullu** *igloo*
	미국 **miguk** **USA**	자유의 여신상 **jayuui yeosinsang** *Statue of Liberty*		캐나다 **kaenada** **Canada**	나이아가라 폭포 **naiagara pokpo** *Niagara Falls*
	브라질 **beurajil** **Brazil**	아마존 강 **amajon gang** *Amazon River*		아프리카 **apeurika** **Africa**	사하라 사막 **sahara samak** *Sahara Desert*

가 _____ 씨, _____ 이/가 어디에 있어요?

나 _____ 은/는 _____ 에 있어요.

가 _____ 이/가 어디에 있어요?

나 _____ 은/는 _____ 에 있어요.

가 _____ 이/가 _____ 에 있어요?

나 아니요, _____ 은/는 _____ 에 있어요.

가 감사합니다.

Sinchon

The College District

Korea's top-notch colleges—Yonsei University, Ewha Womans University, and Sogang University—are within a few kilometers distance from each other in the Sinchon neighborhood. The cafés that can be found on every street in this district are packed with college students working at their laptops or chatting to their friends. A lot of the students proudly wear their college shirts, although most Korean colleges do not have uniforms. These students will be the leaders of Korea tomorrow, so it wouldn't be a bad experience to spend some time socializing with them!

I'm Watching a Movie Today

저는 오늘 영화를 봅니다

07

일정 묻고 답하기
Talking about Schedules

Lesson Goals

Situation
Asking and answering questions about schedules
Vocabulary
Basic verbs
Grammar
Asking questions
Answering questions
Time particles
Also/as well

▼
Multiplex buildings that contain movie theaters, shopping malls and food courts are popular with young people in Korea because of their convenience—you can watch a movie, go shopping and eat dinner in the same building without having to move to different places.

ONLINE
AUDIO
00:10

다이애나 daiaena
이준기 씨, 오늘 무엇을 합니까 ?
ijungi ssi, oneul mueoseul hamnikka
Joon-gi, what are you doing today?

이준기 ijungi
저는 오늘 영화를 봅니다.
jeoneun oneul yeonghwareul bomnida
I'm watching a movie today.
다이애나 씨는 오늘 무엇을 합니까 ?
daiaena ssineun oneul mueoseul hamnikka
What are you doing today, Diana?

다이애나 daiaena
저는 오늘 한국어를 공부합니다.
jeoneun oneul hangugeoreul gongbuhamnida
I'm studying Korean.

이준기 ijungi
내일도 한국어를 공부합니까 ?
naeildo hangugeoreul gongbuhamnikka
Are you studying Korean tomorrow, too?

다이애나 daiaena
아니요, 주말에는 한국어를 공부하지 않습니다.
aniyo, jumareneun hangugeoreul gongbuhaji ansseumnida
No, I don't study Korean at the weekends.
친구를 만납니다.
chingureul mannamnida
I hang out with my friends.

Vocabulary and Expressions 어휘와 표현

01	동사 1 어간에 받침이 있는 동사 dongsa il eogane batchimi inneun dongsa	**Verbs 1** **Stem ends with a** **consonant**

먹다〔먹따〕 **meokda** *to eat*

읽다〔익따〕 **ikda** *to read*

듣다〔듣따〕 **deutda** *to listen/to hear*

02	동사 2 어간에 받침이 없는 동사 dongsa i eogane batchimi eomneun dongsa	**Verbs 2** **Stem ends with a** **vowel**

보다〔보다〕 **boda** *to watch*

(그림을) 그리다〔(그ː리믈)그리다〕 **(geurimeul) geurida** *to draw (a picture)*

마시다〔마시다〕 **masida** *to drink*

요리하다〔요리하다〕 **yorihada** *to cook*

숙제하다〔숙쩨하다〕 **sukjehada** *to do one's homework*

배우다〔배우다〕 **baeuda** *to learn*

청소하다〔청소하다〕 **cheongsohada** *to clean*

가르치다〔가르치다〕 **gareuchida** *to teach*

노래하다〔노래하다〕 **noraehada** *to sing (a song)*

잠을 자다〔자믈자다〕 **jameul jada** *to sleep*

운동하다〔운ː동하다〕 **undonghada** *to work out*

03 동사 3 어간에 'ㄹ' 받침이 있는 동사
dongsa sam eogane 'r' batchimi inneun dongsa

Verbs 3
Stem ends with ㄹ

만들다〔만들다〕 **mandeulda** *to make something*
살다〔살:다〕 **salda** *to live*

04 기타 **gita**

Other useful vocabulary

일정〔일쩡〕 **iljeong** *schedule*
밥〔밥〕 **bap** *rice/a meal*
영화 촬영〔영화촤령〕 **yeonghwa charyeong** *shooting a movie*

〔발〕〔음〕〔규〕〔칙〕 **Pronunciation Rules**

Nasalization of Consonants 비음화
The sounds ㅂ, ㄷ and ㄱ become ㅁ, ㄴ and ㅇ respectively before the nasal vowels ㄴ, ㅁ and ㅇ.

안녕하십니다까 ⇒ 안녕하심니까〕
ㅂ + ㄷ ⇒ ㅁ + ㄴ

봅니다 봄니다 **bomnida** *see*   만납니다 만남니다 **mannamnida** *meet*
않습니다 안씀니다 **ansseumnida** *not*   배웁니다 배움니다 **baeumnida** *learn*

Grammar 문법

01 N 을 / 를 V – ㅂ / 습니까?   Do/does subject + V + object?
N eul/reul V-b/seumnikka

To indicate that a noun is the object of a verb, attach the particle 을 or 를 after the noun. Use 을 for nouns with a final consonant on the last syllable and 를 for nouns that do not have a final consonant on the last syllable.

리리 씨는 한국어를 공부합니까? **riri ssineun hangugeoreul gongbuhamnikka**
   Lili, do you study Korean?

비비엔 씨는 일요일에 친구를 만납니까?
   bibien ssineun iryoire chingureul mannamnikka
   Vivien, do you meet your friend on Sundays?

로이 씨는 커피를 마십니까? **roi ssineun keopireul masimnikka**
   Roy, do you drink coffee?

02 N 을 / 를 V – ㅂ / 습니다   N eul/reul V-b/seumnida   Subject + V + object
N 을 / 를 V- 지 않습니다   N eul/reul V-ji ansseumnida   Present simple

In order to negate a verb, replace –다 with –지 않습니다 whether there is a final consonant on the last syllable or not.

네, 한국어를 공부합니다. **ne, hangugeoreul gongbuhamnida.** *Yes, I study Korean.*

아니요, 한국어를 공부하지 않습니다. **aniyo, hangugeoreul gongbuhaji ansseumnida**
   No, I do not study Korean.

네, 일요일에 친구를 만납니다. **ne, iryoire chingureul mannamnida**
   Yes, I meet my friend on Sundays.

아니요, 일요일에 친구를 만나지 않습니다.
   aniyo, iryoire chingureul mannaji ansseumnida
   No, I do not meet my friend on Sundays.

explanation | Converting to the V-ㅂ/습니다 form |

The form V ㅂ/습니다 is added to a verb stem; the verb stem can be found by simply removing the final syllable 다 of the base form of the verb. ㅂ니다 is added to verb stems ending in a vowel and 습니다 is added to verb stems ending in a consonant. One exception is when the verb stem has the final consonant ㄹ. In this case, replace the ㄹ with ㅂ니다.

When the last syllable of the stem does NOT have a final consonant:
가다 + ㅂ니다 ⇒ 갑니다

When the last syllable of the stem has a final consonant:
먹다 + 습니다 ⇒ 먹습니다

When the last syllable of the stem has the final consonant ㄹ:
살다 + ㅂ니다 ⇒ 삽니다

03 N 에 (시간의 '에') N e (siganui 'e')   Particle indicating the time

In general, – 에 is used for nouns that indicate time but not for 오늘, 어제, 그저께, 내일 or 모레. For example, both 내일에 and 매일에 are grammatically incorrect.

언제 – 을/를 – ㅂ/습니까? **eonje -eul/reul -b/seumnikka** *When . . . ?*

~에 – 을/를 – ㅂ/습니다. **-e -eul/reul b/seumnida** *at . . .*

언제 밥을 먹습니까? **eonje babeul meokseumnikka** *When do you eat a meal?*

7시에 밥을 먹습니다. **ilgopsie babeul meokseumnida** *I eat a meal at 7:00.*

언제 친구를 만납니까? **eonje chingureul mannamnikka** *When do you meet your friend?*

주말에 친구를 만납니다. **jumare chingureul mannamnida** *I meet my friend at the weekend.*

언제 한국어를 공부합니까? **eonje hangugeoreul gongbuhamnikka**
  When do you study Korean?

내일 한국어를 공부합니다. **naeil hangugeoreul gongbuhamnida**
  I will study Korean tomorrow.

04 N도 N do
— as well/too/also

스테파니 씨는 한국어를 공부합니다. **seutepani ssineun hangugeoreul gongbuhamnida**
Stephanie studies Korean.

로베르토 씨도 한국어를 공부합니다. **robereuto ssido hangugeoreul gongbuhamnida**
Roberto also studies Korean.

다이애나 씨는 라면을 먹습니다. **daiaena ssineun ramyeoneul meokseumnida**
Diana eats ramen.

퍼디 씨도 라면을 먹습니다. **peodi ssido ramyeoneul meokseumnida**
Ferdy eats ramen too.

저는 목요일에 학교에 갑니다. **jeoneun mogyoire hakgyoe gamnida**
I go to school on Thursday.

저는 금요일에도 학교에 갑니다. **jeoneun geumyoiredo hakgyoe gamnida**
I go to school on Friday as well.

| **Exercise** | Fill in the blanks. You can find the answers on page 270.

Base Form	V-ㅂ/습니까 V–b/seumnikka *question form*	V-ㅂ/습니다 V –b/seumnida *present tense*	V-지 않습니다 V–ji ansseumnida *negative*
가르치다 gareuchida *to teach*	가르칩니까?	가르칩니다	가르치지 않습니다
배우다 baeuda *to learn*	배웁니까?	배웁니다	
마시다 masida *to drink*		마십니다	마시지 않습니다
쓰다 sseuda *to write*	씁니까?		
만나다 mannada *to meet*		만납니다	
먹다 meokda *to eat*	먹습니까?		먹지 않습니나

Conversation Practice 회화 연습

01 지금 무엇을 합니까 ? **jigeum mueoseul hamnikka** **What are you doing now?**

Use the example sentences to guide you as you practice. Find model sentences on page 270.

다이애나
daiaena
Diana

이준기: 다이애나 씨, 지금 무엇을 합니까?
daiaena ssi, jigeum mueoseul hamnikka
Diana, what are you doing now?

다이애나: 저는 지금 한국어를 공부합니다.
jeoneun jigeum hangugeoreul gongbuhamnida
I am studying Korean now.

로이

가: _____, 지금 무엇을 합니까?

나: 저는 _____ .

비비엔

가: _____ ?

나: _____ .

왕샤워

가: _____ ?

나: _____ .

퍼디

가: _____ ?

나: _____ .

---

02 언제 한국어를 공부합니까?
eonje hangugeoreul gongbuhamnikka

When do you study Korean?

Use the example sentences to guide you as you practice. Find model sentences on page 270.

수요일
suyoil
Wednesday

이준기: 다이애나 씨, 언제 한국어를 공부합니까?
daiaena ssi, eonje hangugeoreul gongbuhamnikka
Diana, when do you study Korean?

다이애나: 저는 수요일에 한국어를 공부합니다.
jeoneun suyoire hangugeoreul gongbuhamnida
I study Korean on Wednesdays.

주말

가: 언제 친구를 만납니까?

나: 저는 _____ .

아침

가: _____ ?

나: _____ .

잠자기 전

가: _____ ?

나: _____ .

토요일
일요일

가: _____ ?

나: _____ .

03 오늘 책을 읽습니까? oneul chaegeul ikseumnikka Are you reading a book today?

Use the example sentences to guide you as you practice. Find model sentences on page 270.

오늘 책을 읽다 ✓
oneul
chaegeul ikda
*to read
a book today*

이준기: 다이애나 씨, 오늘 책을 읽습니까?
daiaena ssi, oneul chaegeul ikseumnikka
Diana, are you reading a book today?

다이애나: 네, 책을 읽습니다.
ne, chaegeul ikseumnida
Yes, I am reading a book.

오늘 영화를 보다 X
oneul
yeonghwareul
boda
*to watch
a movie today*

친구를 만나다 ✓
chingureul
mannada
*to meet
a friend*

이준기: 다이애나 씨, 오늘 영화를 봅니까?
daiaena ssi, oneul yeonghwareul bomnikka
Diana, are you watching a movie today?

다이애나: 아니요, 영화를 보지 않습니다.
aniyo, yeonghwareul boji ansseumnida
No, I am not watching a movie.
친구를 만납니다.
chingureul mannamnida
I am meeting my friend.

이준기
피자를 먹다 ✓

가: _____ ?
나: _____ .

벤슨 책을 읽다 X
텔레비전을 보다 ✓

가: _____ ?
나: _____ .
_____ .

왕샤워 영화를
보다 X
음악을 듣다 ✓

가: _____ ?
나: _____ .
_____ .

ONLINE
AUDIO
02:48

Talking with Lee Joon-gi 1 이준기와 이야기하기1

일정 묻고 답하기   **Asking about someone's schedule**

Try having a conversation with Lee Joon-gi as you listen to the audio. You can find a translation of this conversation on page 264. Then write your own conversation in the gray box below, following this model.

이준기	다이애나 씨, 지금 무엇을 합니까?
	daiaena ssi, jigeum mueoseul hamnikka
다이애나	저는 지금 책을 읽습니다.
	jeoneun jigeum chaegeul ikseumnida
이준기	다이애나 씨, 내일은 무엇을 합니까?
	daiaena ssi, naeireun mueoseul hamnikka
다이애나	저는 내일 영화를 봅니다.
	jeoneun naeil yeonghwareul bomnida
이준기	그럼, 주말에는 무엇을 합니까?
	geureom, jumareneun mueoseul hamnikka
다이애나	주말에는 친구를 만납니다.
	jumareneun chingureul mannamnida

가 _____ 씨, 지금 무엇을 합니까?

나 저는 지금 _____.

가 _____ 씨, 내일은 무엇을 합니까?

나 저는 내일 _____.

가 그럼, 주말에는 무엇을 합니까?

나 _____

ONLINE
AUDIO
03:44

Talking with Lee Joon-gi 2   이준기와 이야기하기2

이준기의 일주일 일정   Lee Joon-gi's weekly schedule

Write your weekly schedule, using Lee Joon-gi's plan as a model. You can find translations of the text on this page on page 264.

저는 월요일하고 화요일에 중국어를 공부합니다.
jeoneun woryoilhago hwayoire junggugeoreul gongbuhamnida

금요일에도 중국어를 공부합니다.
geumyoiredo junggugeoreul gongbuhamnida

수요일에는 중국어를 공부하지 않습니다.
suyoireneun junggugeoreul gongbuhaji ansseumnida

영화 촬영을 합니다.
yeonghwa chwaryeongeul hamnida

목요일에는 책을 읽습니다.
mogyoireneun chaegeul ikseumnida

그리고 주말에는 친구를 만납니다.
geurigo jumareneun chingureul mannamnida

Hongdae

Seoul's Mecca of Underground Culture

Korea's underground culture has found its home in the area surrounding Hongik University, which has Korea's best fine arts department. Flashy graffiti artists have decorated most of the street walls, and there are literally dozens and dozens of clubs and cafés along these streets. Each of them has a unique atmosphere that attracts young men and women seeking rebellion. There are always performances big and small. At the weekends, if it's not raining, you'll find a flea market and "Hope Market," which will give you a glimpse of the unique artistic culture of this area. The last Friday of each month is called "Live Club Day." With a ticket, you can hop from club to club and enjoy various genres of dance and music.

I'm Going to Myeongdong This Weekend

주말에 명동에 갑니다

Lesson Goals

Situation
Talking about plans
Vocabulary
Verbs for leaving
and arriving
Verbs for shopping
Places
Grammar
Particles to indicate
destination
Particles to indicate
place
Joining two verbs
together

▼

Since the beginning of the
digital age, Korea has had
easy and ubiquitous access
to the Internet—it is available
at libraries, public offices and
subway stations and in every
neighborhood café.

ONLINE
AUDIO
00:10

최지영 choejiyeong	퍼디 씨, 주말에 어디에 갑니까? **peodi ssi, jumare eodie gamnikka** *Ferdy, where are you going this weekend?*
퍼디 peodi	저는 주말에 명동에 갑니다. **jeoneun jumare myeongdonge gamnida** *I'm going to Myeongdong this weekend.*
최지영 choejiyeong	명동에서 무엇을 합니까? **myeongdongeseo mueoseul hamnikka** *What are you going to do in Myeongdong?*
퍼디 peodi	명동에서 영화를 봅니다. **myeongdongeseo yeonghwareul bomnida** *I'm going to see a movie.* 최지영 씨는 주말에 무엇을 합니까? **choejiyeong ssineun jumare mueoseul hamnikka** *What are you doing this weekend, Jiyoung?*
최지영 choejiyeong	저는 도서관에 갑니다. **jeoneun doseogwane gamnida** *I'm going to the library.*
퍼디 peodi	도서관에서 무엇을 합니까? **doseogwaneseo mueoseul hamnikka** *What are you going to do at the library?*
최지영 choejiyeong	도서관에서 책을 읽고 인터넷을 합니다. **doseogwaneseo chaegeul ilkko inteoneseul hamnida** *I'm going to read a book and surf the Internet.*

Vocabulary and Expressions 어휘와 표현

| **01** 동사 4 dongsa sa | **Verbs 4** |

N에 가다〔에네가다〕 **N e gada** *to go to (a place)*

내리다〔내리다〕 **naerida** *to get off (a vehicle)*

N에 오다〔에네오다〕 **N e oda** *to come to (a place)*

갈아타다〔가라타다〕 **garatada** *to transit*

걷다〔걷:따〕 **geotda** *to walk*

건너다〔건너다〕 **geonneoda** *to cross*

달리다〔달리다〕 **dallida** *to run*

운전하다〔운:전하다〕 **unjeonhada** *to drive (a vehicle)*

타다〔타다〕 **tada** *to get on (a vehicle)*

| **02** 동사 5 dongsa o | **Verbs 5** |

사다〔사다〕 **sada** *to buy*

고르다〔고르다〕 **goreuda** *to choose*

팔다〔팔다〕 **palda** *to sell*

쇼핑하다〔쇼핑하다〕 **syopinghada** *to shop*

바꾸다〔바꾸다〕 **bakkuda** *to change*

인터넷하다〔인터네타다〕 **inteonetada** *to surf the Internet*

03 기타 gita — Other useful vocabulary

나〔나〕 **na** *I (informal)*

명동〔명동〕 **myeongdong** *Myeongdong*

저〔저〕 **jeo** *I (polite)*

교실〔교:실〕 **gyosil** *classroom*

교회〔교:훼〕 **gyohoe** *church*

식당〔식땅〕 **sikdang** *restaurant*

광화문〔광화문〕 **gwanghwamun** *Gwanghwamun (gate of Gyeongbokgung Palace)*

신문〔신문〕 **sinmun** *newspaper*

전시회〔전:시훼〕 **jeonsihoe** *exhibition*

발 음 규 칙 Pronunciation Rules

Liaison (Linking) 연음 법칙
When a syllable ends with a final consonant and is followed by a vowel, then the final phoneme is pronounced as the first phoneme of the following syllable.

주말에 ⇒ 〔주마레〕

도서관에 도서과네 **doseogwane** *to the library*   책을 채글 **chaegeul** *book*

인터넷을 인터네슬 **inteoneseul** *internet*   신문을 신무늘 **sinmuneul** *newspaper*

Grammar 문법

01 N 은 / 는 N 에 가다 / 오다
N eun/neun N e gada/oda
— go(goes)/come(comes) to —

The particle 에 attached to a noun shows that the noun is the destination indicated by the verbs 가다 and 오다.

선생님은 학교에 갑니다. **seonsaengnimeun hakgyoe gamnida** *The teacher goes to school.*

로이 씨는 명동에 갑니다. **roi ssineun myeongdonge gamnida**
Roy goes to Myeongdong.

스테파니 씨는 내일 한국에 옵니다. **seutepani ssineun naeil hanguge omnida**
Stephanie is coming to Korea tomorrow.

02 N 은 / 는 N 에서 N 을 / 를 V- ㅂ / 습니다
N eun/neun N eseo N eul/reul V –b/seumnida
N is V+N in/at N

Nouns that indicate a place take the particle 에서 if the verb used is neither 가다 or 오다.

선생님은 한국대학교에서 한국어를 가르칩니다.
seonsaengnimeun hangukdaehakgyoeseo hangugeoreul gareuchimnida
The teacher teaches Korean at Hanguk University.

마스미 씨는 백화점에서 쇼핑을 합니다.
maseumi ssineun baekwajeomeseo syopingeul hamnida
Masumi does the shopping at the department store.

벤슨 씨는 도서관에서 책을 읽습니다.
benseun ssineun doseogwaneseo chaegeul ikseumnida
Benson reads a book in the library.

03 V-고 V–go V **V and V**

If there are two consecutive verbs in a sentence, attach the suffix – 고 to the stem of the first verb and then follow with the second verb. Regardless of whether there is a final consonant on the last syllable of the verb stem, use 고. For example, 읽다 → 읽고 or 보다→보고.

저는 주말에 한국어를 공부하고 친구를 만납니다.
jeoneun jumare hangugeoreul gongbuhago chingureul mannamnida
I study Korean and meet my friend at the weekend.

비비엔 씨는 주말에 영화를 보고 커피를 마십니다.
bibien ssineun jumare yeonghwareul bogo keopireul masimnida
Vivien watches a movie and drinks coffee at the weekend.

스테파니 씨는 텔레비전을 보고 영화를 봅니다.
seutepani ssineun tellebijeoneul bogo yeonghwareul bomnida
Stephanie watches television and sees a movie.

| **Exercise** | Fill in the blanks. You can find the answers on page 270.

한국어를 공부하다/친구를 만나다 **hangugeoreul gongbuhada/ chingureul mannada** *study Korean/ meet a friend*	한국어를 공부하고 친구를 만납니다 **hangugeoreul gongbuhago chingureul mannamnida** *I study Korean and meet my friend.*
책을 읽다/편지를 쓰다 **chaegeul ikda/pyeonjireul sseuda** *read a book/write a letter*	
텔레비전을 보다/잠을 자다 **tellebijeoneul boda/jameul jada** *watch television/sleep*	
밥을 먹다/영화를 보다 **babeul meokda/yeonghwareul boda** *eat a meal/watch a movie*	
친구를 만나다/도서관에 가다 **chingureul mannada/doseogwane gada** *meet a friend/go to the library*	
커피를 마시다/음악을 듣다 **keopireul masida/eumageul deutda** *drink coffee/listen to music*	
백화점에 가다/쇼핑하다 **baekwajeome gada/syopinghada** *go to the department store/ do the shopping*	

Conversation Practice 회화 연습

01 어디에 갑니까 ? eodie gamnikka   **Where are you going?**

Use the example sentences to guide you as you practice. Find model sentences on page 270.

	퍼디 광화문 **peodi gwanghwamun** *Ferdy Gwanghwamun*	최지영: 퍼디 씨, 어디에 갑니까? **peodi ssi, eodie gamnikka** *Ferdy, where are you going?* 퍼디: 저는 광화문에 갑니다. **jeoneun gwanghwamune gamnida** *I am going to Gwanghwamun.*

- -

	최지영 명동	가: ＿＿＿＿＿＿＿＿＿＿＿＿＿＿ 씨, 어디에 갑니까? 나: 저는 ＿＿＿＿＿＿＿＿＿＿＿ 에 갑니다.

- -

	리리 교회	가: ＿＿＿＿＿＿＿＿＿＿＿＿＿＿＿＿＿？ 나: ＿＿＿＿＿＿＿＿＿＿＿＿＿＿＿＿＿．

- -

	마스미 백화점	가: ＿＿＿＿＿＿＿＿＿＿＿＿＿＿＿＿＿？ 나: ＿＿＿＿＿＿＿＿＿＿＿＿＿＿＿＿＿．

- -

	왕사위 식당	가: ＿＿＿＿＿＿＿＿＿＿＿＿＿＿＿＿＿？ 나: ＿＿＿＿＿＿＿＿＿＿＿＿＿＿＿＿＿．

- -

02 어디에서 커피를 마십니까 ? eodieseo keopireul masimnikka	**Where do you drink coffee?**

Use the example sentences to guide you as you practice. Find model sentences on page 270.

커피를
마시다
커피숍

최지영: 로베르토 씨, 어디에서 커피를 마십니까?
robereuto ssi, eodieseo keopireul masimnikka
Roberto, where do you drink coffee?

로베르토: 저는 커피숍에서 커피를 마십니다.
jeoneun keopisyobeseo keopireul masimnida
I drink coffee at a coffee shop.

한국어를
가르치다
학교

가: 어디에서 한국어를 가르칩니까?

나: 저는 _____ 에서 _____ .

친구를
만나다
명동

가: _____?

나: _____.

비빔밥을
먹다
식당

가: _____?

나: _____.

책을 읽다
도서관

가: _____?

나: _____.

03 요리하고 청소합니다   yorihago cheongsohamnida   **I cook and clean.**

Use the example sentences to guide you as you practice. Find model sentences on page 271.

주말
jumal
weekend
요리하다
yorihada
to cook
청소하다
cheongsohada
to clean

최지영: 퍼디 씨, 주말에 무엇을 합니까?
peodi ssi, jumare mueoseul hamnikka
Ferdy, what do you do at the weekend?

퍼디: 저는 주말에 요리하고 청소합니다.
jeoneun jumare yorihago cheongsohamnida
I cook and clean at the weekend.

오늘 오후
텔레비전을
보다
편지를 쓰다

가: 오늘 오후에 무엇을 합니까?
나: 저는 _____ 에 _____ 고
_____ .

오늘 오후
명동에서
영화를 보다
친구를 만나다

가: _____ ?
나: _____
_____ .

일요일
공원에서
운동하다
그림을 그리다

가: _____ ?
나: _____
_____ .

내일
신문을 읽다
커피를 마시다

가: _____ ?
나: _____
_____ .

ONLINE
AUDIO
02:57

Listening Practice 듣기 연습

01 주말 활동 묻기 jumal hwaldong mutgi   **Weekend activities**

Listen carefully to the audio, write the number of each activity mentioned, then make sentences, following the example below. Find the answers on page 260.

왕샤위: 스테파니 씨, 주말에 무엇을 합니까?
seutepani ssi, jumare mueoseul hamnikka
Stephanie, what do you do at the weekend?

스테파니: 저는 주말에 공원에서 운동하고 친구 집에 갑니다.
jeoneun jumare gongwoneseo undonghago chingu jibe gamnida
I exercise at a park and visit my friend's house at the weekend.

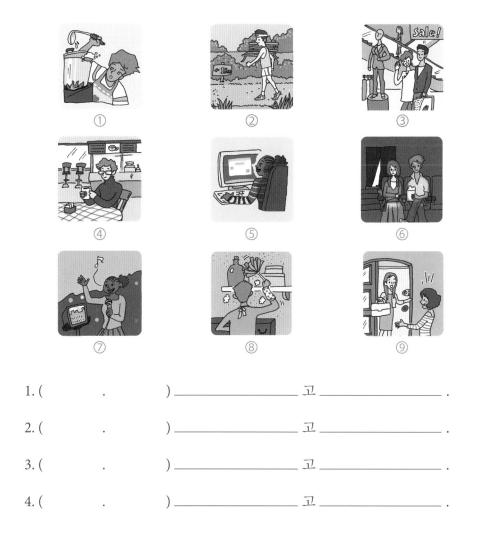

1. (.   ) ———————— 고 ———————— .

2. (.   ) ———————— 고 ———————— .

3. (.   ) ———————— 고 ———————— .

4. (.   ) ———————— 고 ———————— .

ONLINE
AUDIO
05:16

Talking with Lee Joon-gi 이준기와 이야기하기

주말 계획 묻고 답하기 Asking and answering questions about the weekend.

Try having a conversation with Lee Joon-gi as you listen to the audio. You can find a translation of this conversation on page 264.

이준기	최지영 씨, 주말에 어디에 갑니까? **choejiyeong ssi, jumare eodie gamnikka**
최지영	저는 주말에 광화문에 갑니다. **jeoneun jumare gwanghwamune gamnida**
이준기	광화문에서 무엇을 합니까? **gwanghwamuneseo mueoseul hamnikka**
최지영	광화문에서 전시회를 보고 커피를 마십니다. **gwanghwamuneseo jeonsihoereul bogo keopireul masimnida** 이준기 씨는 주말에 어디에 갑니까? **ijungi ssineun jumare eodie gamnikka**
이준기	저는 주말에 신촌에 갑니다. **jeoneun jumare sinchone gamnida**
최지영	신촌에서 무엇을 합니까? **sinchoneseo mueoseul hamnikka**
이준기	신촌에서 가방을 사고 밥을 먹습니다. **sinchoneseo gabangeul sago babeul meokseumnida**

Use the pictures to help you write a dialogue.

가 _____ 씨, 주말에 어디에 갑니까?

나 저는 _____.

가 _____ 에서 무엇을 합니까?

나 _____ 고 _____.

_____ 씨는 주말에 어디에 갑니까?

가 저는 _____.

나 _____ 에서 무엇을 합니까?

가 _____ 고 _____.

Verbs 동사

가다
gada
to go

오다
oda
to come

보다
boda
to watch

만나다
mannada
to meet

먹다
meokda
to eat

마시다
masida
to drink

듣다
deutda
to listen to

읽다
ikda
to read

편지를 쓰다
pyeonjireul sseuda
to write a letter

이야기하다
iyagihada
to talk to

춤을 추다
chumeul chuda
to dance

그림을 그리다
geurimeul geurida
to draw a picture

가르치다
gareuchida
to teach

배우다
baeuda
to learn

자다
jada
to sleep

일어나다
ireonada
to get up

만들다
mandeulda
to make

사다
sada
to buy

팔다
palda
to sell

바꾸다
bakkuda
to change

타다
tada
to get on, ride

(차에서) 내리다
chaeseo naerida
to get off/out of (a vehicle)

갈아타다
garatada
to transit

청소하다
cheongsohada
to clean

노래하다
noraehada
to sing (a song)

운동하다
undonghada
to work out

요리하다
yorihada
to cook

세수하다
sesuhada
to wash the face

샤워하다
syawohada
to take a shower

수영하다
suyeonghada
to swim

인터넷하다
inteonetada
to surf the Internet

공부하다
gongbuhada
to study

Lee Joon-gi's Guide to Seoul

Yeouido

The Epicenter of The Korean Wave

If you have been wondering where to find the epicenter of the
Korean wave, or Hallyu, you should visit Yeouido. This small
island in the middle of the Han River, just like Manhattan
Island in New York, is home to all the Korean broadcasting
companies, and of course, all the TV and radio stars naturally
commute to this district. As well as star-spotting, you might
catch teams of filmmakers at work! You're extremely lucky
if you happen to be visiting in early spring, because Yeouido
has streets filled with cherry trees that blossom like magic.
Imagine bumping into one of your favorite celebrities while
taking a walk beneath the blooms!

How Is the Weather Today?

오늘은 날씨가 어떻습니까?

Lesson Goals

Situation
Talking about the weather
Vocabulary
Verbs: weather
Adjectives: weather
Basic adjectives
Grammar
How is —?
Questions with adjectives
Joining two adjectives together

▼

The expression 삼한사온 (sam-hansaon *three cold [days] and four warm [days]*) is used to describe the typical spring weather pattern in Korea. Spring generally begins in March when warmer days are briefly followed by colder days. This cold weather is referred as 꽃샘추위 (kkoch-saemchuwi), meaning the cold weather is jealous of the emerging flower blossom.

ONLINE
AUDIO
00:10

왕샤위 wangsyawi	스테파니 씨, 오늘은 날씨가 어떻습니까? **seutepani ssi, oneureun nalssiga eotteoseumnikka** *Stephanie, how is the weather today?*
스테파니 seutepani	오늘은 날씨가 좋습니다. **oneureun nalssiga joseumnida** *The weather is nice today.*
왕샤위 wangsyawi	호주는 요즘 날씨가 어떻습니까? **hojuneun yojeum nalssiga eotteoseumnikka** *What's the weather like in Australia at the moment?*
스테파니 seutepani	호주는 요즘 날씨가 덥고 비가 옵니다. **hojuneun yojeum nalssiga deopgo biga omnida** *It's hot and rainy at the moment.*
	중국은 요즘 날씨가 어떻습니까? **junggugeun yojeum nalssiga eotteoseumnikka** *What's the weather like in China at the moment?*
왕샤위 wangsyawi	중국은 요즘 날씨가 좋지만 춥습니다. **junggugeun yojeum nalssiga jochiman chupseumnida** *The weather is nice but cold at the moment.*

Vocabulary and Expressions 어휘와 표현

01 동사 6 날씨 **dongsa yuk nalssi** **Verbs 6 Weather**

(비가) 오다 〔(비가)오다〕 (**biga) oda** *(rain) comes*

(비가) 내리다 〔(비가)내리다〕 **(biga) naerida** *(rain) falls*

(눈이) 오다 〔(누:니)오다〕 **(nuni) oda** *(snow) comes*

(눈이) 내리다 〔(누:니)내리다〕 **(nuni) naerida** *(snow) falls*

(바람이) 불다 〔(바라미)불:다〕 **(barami) bulda** *(wind) blows*

(천둥이) 치다 〔(천둥이)치다〕 **(cheondungi) chida** *(thunder) rolls*

(번개가) 치다 〔(번개가)치다〕 **(beongaega) chida** *(lightning) flashes*

(안개가) 끼다 〔(안:개가)끼:다〕 **(angaega) kkida** *(fog) rolls*

(구름이) 끼다 〔(구르미)끼:다〕 **(gureumi) kkida** *(cloud) rolls*

02 형용사 1 날씨 **hyeongyongsa il nalssi** **Adjectives 1 Weather**

덥다 〔덥:따〕 **deopda** *hot*	춥다 〔춥따〕 **chupda** *cold*
따뜻하다 〔따뜨타다〕 **ttatteutada** *warm*	시원하다 〔시원하다〕 **siwonhada** *nice and cool*
쌀쌀하다 〔s쌀쌀하다〕 **ssalssalhada** *chilly*	맑다 〔막따〕 **makda** *sunny*
흐리다 〔흐리다〕 **heurida** *cloudy*	

03 형용사 2 맛 **hyeongyongsa i mat** **Adjectives 2 Taste**

맛있다 〔마싣따〕 **masitda** *delicious*	맛없다 〔마덥따〕 **madeopda** *not tasty*
맵다 〔맵따〕 **maepda** *spicy*	짜다 〔짜다〕 **jjada** *salty*
달다 〔달다〕 **dalda** *sweet*	싱겁다 〔싱겁따〕 **singgeopda** *bland*
쓰다 〔쓰다〕 **sseuda** *bitter*	시다 〔시다〕 **sida** *sour*

04 형용사 3 hyeongyongsa sam **Adjectives 3**

빠르다 〔빠르다〕 **ppareuda** *fast*

쉽다 〔쉽ː따〕 **swipda** *easy*

재미있다 〔재미읻따〕 **jaemiitda** *fun*

어떻다 〔어떠타〕 **eotteota** *how*

복잡하다 〔복짜파다〕 **bokjapada** *complicated*

친절하다 〔친절하다〕 **chinjeolhada** *kind*

기쁘다 〔기쁘다〕 **gippeuda** *happy*

나쁘다 〔나쁘다〕 **nappeuda** *bad*

크다 〔크다〕 **keuda** *big*

많다 〔만ː타〕 **manta** *many*

넓다 〔널따〕 **neolda** *wide*

싸다 〔싸다〕 **ssada** *inexpensive*

편리하다 〔펄리하다〕 **pyeollihada** *convenient*

느리다 〔느리다〕 **neurida** *slow*

어렵다 〔어렵따〕 **eoryeopda** *difficult*

재미없다 〔재미업따〕 **jaemieopda** *boring*

멋있다 〔머싣따〕 **meositda** *gorgeous*

예쁘다 〔예ː쁘다〕 **yeppeuda** *pretty*

불친절하다 〔불친절하다〕 **bulchinjeolhada** *unkind*

슬프다 〔슬프다〕 **seulpeuda** *sad*

좋다 〔조ː타〕 **jota** *good*

작다 〔작ː다〕 **jakda** *small*

적다 〔적ː따〕 **jeokda** *few*

좁다 〔좁따〕 **jopda** *narrow*

비싸다 〔비싸다〕 **bissada** *expensive*

불편하다 〔불편하다〕 **bulpyeonhada** *inconvenient*

05 기타 gita **Other useful vocabulary**

요즘 〔요즘〕 **yojeum** *these days*

한국 음식 〔한ː구금식〕 **hanguk eumsik** *Korean food*

물건 〔물건〕 **mulgeon** *object*

김치 〔김치〕 **gimchi** *kimchi*

발음규칙 Pronunciation Rules

Aspiration (Pronouncing consonants with a burst of air) 격음화

Before or after ㅎ, the consonants ㄱ, ㄷ, ㅂ and ㅈ combine with the ㅎ to become the aspirated consonants ㅋ, ㅌ, ㅍ and ㅊ.

$$좋지만 \Rightarrow [조ː치만]$$
$$ㅎ + ㅈ \Rightarrow ㅊ$$

많지 만ː치 **manchi** *a lot*

그렇지 그러치 **geureochi** *yes*

빨갛지 빨가치 **ppalgachi** *red*

노랗지 노ː라치 **norachi** *yellow*

Grammar 문법

01 N 이 / 가 어떻습니까? N i/ga eotteoseumnikka
N 이 / 가 A- ㅂ / 습니다   N i/ga A–b/seumnida   **How is N? N is A**

For adjective stems whose last syllable has a final consonant, attach －습니다 to the stem. When the last syllable of the adjective stem does not have a final consonant, use － ㅂ니다 instead. This is similar to the case of the suffix V － ㅂ / 습니까. When the last syllable ends with the final consonant ㄹ, then remove the ㄹ and attach － ㅂ니다 in its place.

날씨가 어떻습니까? **nalssiga eotteoseumnikka** *How is the weather?*

날씨가 좋습니다. **nalssiga joseumnida** *The weather is good.*

교실이 어떻습니까? **gyosiri eotteoseumnikka** *How is the classroom?*

교실이 덥습니다. **gyosiri deopseumnida** *The classroom is hot.*

한국 음식이 어떻습니까? **hanguk eumsigi eotteoseumnikka** *How is Korean food?*

한국 음식이 맛있습니다. **hanguk eumsigi masitseumnida** *Korean food is tasty.*

02 N 이 / 가 A- ㅂ / 습니까? N i/ga A–b/seumnikka
N 이 / 가 A- 지 않습니다 N i/ga A–ji ansseumnida   **Is N A? N is not A**

A － 지 않습니다 is the negative form of A － ㅂ / 습니다, regardless of whether the last syllable of the adjective stem has a final consonant or not.

날씨가 좋습니까? **nalssiga joseumnikka** *Is the weather good?*

날씨가 좋지 않습니다. 비가 옵니다. **nalssiga jochi ansseumnida. biga omnida**
The weather isn't good. It's rainy.

불고기가 맵습니까? **bulgogiga maepseumnikka** *Is bulgogi spicy?*

불고기가 맵지 않습니다. **bulgogiga maepji ansseumnida** *Bulgogi isn't spicy.*

한국어 공부가 어렵습니까? **hangugeo gongbuga eoryeopseumnikka**
Is studying Korean hard?

한국어 공부가 어렵지 않습니다. **hangugeo gongbuga eoryeopji ansseumnida**
Studying Korean isn't hard.

03 A– 고 A A–go A

A and A

To indicate that another adjective is coming in the sentence, attach the suffix – 고 to the first adjective stem and then follow with the next adjective. Use – 고 regardless of whether there is a final consonant in the last syllable of the adjective stem.

오늘은 날씨가 덥고 비가 옵니다. **oneureun nalssiga deopgo biga omnida**
  It's hot and rainy today.

지하철은 빠르고 편리합니다. **jihacheoreun ppareugo pyeollihamnida**
  The subway is fast and convenient.

한국어 선생님은 친절하고 예쁩니다.
  hangugeo seonsaengnimeun chinjeolhago yeppeumnida
  The Korean language teacher is kind and pretty.

04 A–지만 A A–jiman A

A but A

To follow an adjective with an adjective that contrasts in meaning, attach the suffix –지만 to the stem of the first adjective. This serves the same function as the word "but" in English. This suffix is the same whether there is a final consonant or not at the end of the first adjective stem.

서울은 복잡하지만 깨끗합니다. **seoureun bokjapajiman kkaekkeutamnida**
Seoul is crowded but clean.

김치는 맵지만 맛있습니다. **gimchineun maepjiman masitseumnida**
Kimchi is spicy but tasty.

이 음악은 좋지만 슬픕니다. **i eumageun jochiman seulpeumnida**
This music is good but sad.

| **Exercise** | Fill in the blanks. You can find the answers on page 271.

Base Form	When the last syllable has no final consonant: V–ㅂ니다 / A–지 않습니다 **A–bnida/A–ji ansseumnida** When the last syllable has a final consonant: : A–습니다 / A–지 않습니다 **A–seumnida/A–ji ansseumnida**	
덥다 **deopda** *to be hot*	덥습니다	
춥다 **chupda** *to be cold*		춥지 않습니다
따뜻하다 **ttatteutada** *to be warm*	따뜻합니다	따뜻하지 않습니다
시원하다 **siwonhada** *to be cool*	시원합니다	
비가 오다 **biga oda** *to rain*	비가 옵니다	
눈이 내리다 **nuni naerida** *to snow*		눈이 내리지 않습니다

Conversation Practice 회화 연습

01 날씨가 어떻습니까?   nalssiga eotteoseumnikka   **How is the weather?**

Use the example sentences to guide you as you practice. Find model sentences on page 271.

오늘
날씨
좋다

왕샤위: 스테파니 씨, 오늘은 날씨가 어떻습니까?
seutepani ssi, oneureun nalssiga eotteoseumnikka
Stephanie, how is the weather today?

스테파니: 오늘은 날씨가 좋습니다.
oneureun nalssiga joseumnida
It's good today.

호주
날씨
덥다

가: 호주는 날씨가 어떻습니까?

나: _____ .

일본
날씨
덥고 비가 오다

가: _____ ?

나: _____ .

홍콩
날씨
시원하다

가: _____ ?

나: _____ .

제주도
날씨
따뜻하다

가: _____ ?

나: _____ .

02 날씨가 좋지만 춥습니다
nalssiga jochiman chupseumnida

The weather's nice but cold.

Use the example sentences to guide you as you practice. Find model sentences on page 271.

오늘 날씨
oneul nalssi
today weather
좋다 / 춥다
jota / chupda
good / cold

왕샤위: 스테파니 씨, 오늘은 날씨가 어떻습니까?
seutepani ssi, oneureun nalssiga eotteoseumnikka
Stephanie, how is the weather today?

스테파니: 오늘은 날씨가 좋지만 춥습니다.
oneureun nalssiga jochiman chupseumnida
It's good but cold.

김치
맵다 / 맛있다

가: 김치는 어떻습니까?

나: _____ .

한국 음식
맛있다 /
비싸다

가: _____ ?

나: _____ .

지하철
빠르다 /
복잡하다

가: _____ ?

나: _____ .

한국어 공부
어렵다 /
재미있다

가: _____ ?

나: _____ .

03 아니요, 춥지 않습니다 aniyo, chupji ansseumnida   No, it's not cold.

Use the example sentences to guide you as you practice. Find model sentences on page 271.

오늘 날씨
oneul nalssi
today weather
춥다 X
chupda
to be cold
따뜻하다 ✓
ttatteutada
to be warm

왕샤위: 스테파니 씨, 오늘은 날씨가 춥습니까?
seutepani ssi, oneureun nalssiga chupseumnikka
Stephanie, is it cold weather today?

스테파니: 아니요, 오늘은 날씨가 춥지 않습니다. 따뜻합니다.
aniyo, oneureun nalssiga chupji ansseumnida
ttatteutamnida
No, it's not cold today. It's warm.

김치
맵다 X
맛있다 ✓

가: 김치는 맵습니까?

나: 아니요, 김치는 _____ .

만들기
어렵다 X
쉽다 ✓

가: _____ ?
나: _____ .
_____ .

버스
사람이 적나 X
사람이 많다 ✓

가: _____ ?
나: _____ .
_____ .

백화점
싸다 X
비싸다 ✓

가: _____ ?
나: _____ .
_____ .

ONLINE
AUDIO
04:30

Talking with Lee Joon-gi 이준기와 이야기하기

날씨와 한국에 대한 인상 묻기
Asking about the weather and impressions of Korea

Try having a conversation with Lee Joon-gi as you listen to the audio. You can find a translation of this conversation on page 264.

이준기 왕샤위 씨는 어느 나라 사람입니까?
wangsyawi ssineun eoneu nara saramimnikka

왕샤위 저는 중국 사람입니다. **jeoneun jungguk saramimnida**

이준기 중국은 요즘 날씨가 어떻습니까?
junggugeun yojeum nalssiga eotteoseumnikka

왕샤위 중국은 요즘 날씨가 시원합니다.
junggugeun yojeum nalssiga siwonhamnida

이준기 한국은 날씨가 어떻습니까?
hangugeun nalssiga eotteoseumnikka

왕샤위 한국은 날씨가 따뜻하고 좋습니다.
hangugeun nalssiga ttatteutago joseumnida

이준기 한국어 공부와 한국어 선생님은 어떻습니까?
hangugeo gongbuwa hangugeo seonsaengnimeun eotteoseumnikka

왕샤위 한국어 공부는 어렵지만 재미있고, 한국어 선생님은 재미있고 친절합니다.
hangugeo gongbuneun eoryeopjiman jaemiitgo, hangugeo seonsaengnimeun jaemiitgo chinjeolhamnida

Look at the pictures, and complete the dialogue.

가 _____ 씨는 어느 나라 사람입니까?

나 저는 _____.

가 _____ 은/는 요즘 날씨가 _____?

나 _____ 은/는 요즘 날씨가 _____.

나 _____ 은/는 날씨가 _____.

나 _____ 은/는 날씨가 _____.

가 _____ 은/과 _____ 은/는 _____?

나 _____ 은/는 _____.

_____ 은/는 _____.

Adjectives 형용사

크다
keuda
big

작다
jakda
small

많다
manta
many

적다
jeokda
few

길다
gilda
long

짧다
jjalda
short

무겁다
mugeopda
heavy

가볍다
gabyeopda
light

높다
nopda
high

낮다
natda
low

빠르다
ppareuda
fast

느리다
neurida
slow

재미있다
jaemiitda
fun

재미없다
jaemieopda
boring

맛있다
masitda
delicious

맛없다
madeopda
not tasty

Special Feature

어렵다
eoryeopda
difficult

쉽다
swipda
easy

뜨겁다
tteugeopda
hot

차갑다
chagapda
cold

밝다
bakda
bright

어둡다
eodupda
dark

넓다
neolda
wide

좁다
jopda
narrow

멀다
meolda
far

가깝다
gakkapda
near

편리하다
pyeollihada
convenient

불편하다
bulpyeonhada
inconvenient

복잡하다
bokjapada
complicated

바쁘다
bappeuda
busy

예쁘다
yeppeuda
pretty

맵다
maepda
spicy

친절하다
chinjeolhada
kind

불친절하다
bulchinjeolhada
unkind

깨끗하다
kkaekkeutada
clean

더럽다
deoreopda
dirty

기쁘다
gippeuda
happy

슬프다
seulpeuda
sad

좋다
jota
good/nice

나쁘다
nappeuda
bad

덥다
deopda
hot

춥다
chupda
cold

따뜻하다
ttatteutada
warm

시원하다
siwonhada
cool

맑다
makda
sunny

흐리다
heurida
cloudy

싸다
ssada
inexpensive

비싸다
bissada
expensive

اللّٰه أكبر

Lee Joon-gi's Guide to Seoul

Itaewon

A Global Village in Seoul

People from all over the world have settled in Seoul's Itaewon district in one way or another. In this neighborhood you can see various cultural elements from Asia, the Americas, Europe, the Middle East and Africa. Renowned in the world as a shopping avenue, Itaewon is generally recognized among Koreans as the most culturally diverse district in Seoul. The jewel in this diversity is Korea's largest mosque, which sits at the top of a hill overlooking the Itaewon area.

What Are You Going to Do Today?
오늘 뭐 해요?

Lesson Goals

Situation
Asking about
destinations
Vocabulary
Famous places in
Seoul
Hanging out
Grammar
Present simple
tense

▼

Korea's government and
colleges have built many
libraries that you can visit
free of charge. Notable
libraries include the National
Assembly Library, which
has the largest collection of
books in Korea, and Namsan
Public Library, which has a
gorgeous path for walking.
Seeing many books in those
libraries might motivate you
to study the Korean language
more diligently!

ONLINE
AUDIO
00:10

이준기 ijungi	리리 씨, 어디에 가요? **riri ssi, eodie gayo** *Lili, where are you going?*	
리리 riri	저는 지금 도서관에 가요. **jeoneun jigeum doseogwane gayo** *I am going to the library.*	
	이준기 씨도 도서관에 가요? **ijungi ssido doseogwane gayo** *Are you also going to the library, Joon-gi?*	
이준기 ijungi	아니요, 저는 도서관에 안 가요. **aniyo, jeoneun doseogwane an gayo** *No, I am not.*	
	명동에 가요. **myeongdonge gayo** *I am going to Myeongdong.*	
리리 riri	벤슨 씨도 같이 명동에 가요? **benseun ssido gachi myeongdonge gayo** *Benson, are you going to Myeongdong with Joon-gi?*	
벤슨 benseun	네, 저도 명동에 가요. **ne, jeodo myeongdonge gayo** *Yes, I am also going to Myeongdong.*	
리리 riri	명동에서 뭐 해요? **myeongdongeseo mwo haeyo** *What are you going to do in Myeongdong?*	
벤슨 benseun	우리는 같이 명동에서 쇼핑하고 밥을 먹어요. **urineun gachi myeongdongeseo syopinghago** **babeul meogeoyo** *We are going to do some shopping and eat some food.*	

Vocabulary and Expressions 어휘와 표현

01 장소 1 서울 근교의 유명한 장소 jangso il
seoul geungyoui yumyeonghan jangso **Famous places in
Seoul**

민속촌 〔민속촌〕 **minsokchon** *folk village*

신촌 〔신촌〕 **sinchon** *Sinchon*

롯데월드 〔롣떼월드〕 **rotdewoldeu** *Lotte World*

강남 〔강남〕 **gangnam** *Gangnam*

서울랜드 〔서울랜드〕 **seoullaendeu** *Seoul Land*

대학로 〔대항노〕 **daehakgyo** *Daehangno*

에버랜드 〔에버랜드〕 **ebeoraendeu** *Everland*

이태원 〔이태원〕 **itaewon** *Itaewon*

명동 〔명동〕 **myeongdong** *Myeongdong*

동대문 시장 〔동대문시장〕 **dongdaemun sijang** *Dongdaemun Market*

인사동 〔인사동〕 **insadong** *Insadong*

남대문 시장 〔남대문시장〕 **namdaemun sijang** *Namdaemun Market*

02 동사 7 놀이 **dongsa chil nori** **Verbs 7 Hanging out**

바이킹을 타다 〔바이킹을타다〕 **baikingeul tada** *to ride a pirate ship*

전통차를 마시다 〔전통차를마시다〕 **jeontongchareul masida**
to drink traditional tea

놀이 기구를 타다 〔노리기구를타다〕 **nori gigureul tada**
to go on a ride in an amusement park

롤러코스터를 타다 〔롤러코스터를타다〕 **rolleokoseuteoreul tada**
to ride a rollercoaster

선물을 사다 〔선:무를사다〕 **seonmureul sada** *to buy a gift*

노래방에 가다 〔노래방에가다〕 **noraebange gada** *to go to karaoke*

연극을 보다 〔연:그글보다〕 **yeongeugeul boda** *to watch a play*

춤을 추다 〔추믈추다〕 **chumeul chuda** *to dance*

03 기타 gita   **Other useful vocabulary**

무엇/뭐 〔무얼/뭐〕 **mueot/mwo** *what*

혼자 〔혼자〕 **honja** *alone/by oneself*

촬영 〔촤령〕 **chwaryeong** *shooting/filming*

같이 〔가치〕 **gachi** *together*

방송국 〔방:송국〕 **bangsongguk** *TV/radio station*

여의도 〔여이도〕 **yeouido** *Yeouido*

발 음 규 칙 **Pronunciation Rules**

Palatalization 구개음화
If the consonant ㅌ or ㄷ is placed at the bottom of the syllable and followed by 이, it is pronounced ㅈ [j] or ㅊ [ch] .

$$같이 \Rightarrow 〔가치〕$$

ㅌ+이→치	같이 가치 **gachi** *together*	붙이다 부치다 **buchida** *attach*
ㄷ+이→지	굳이 구지 **guji** *unnecessarily*	맏이 마지 **maji** *firstborn*
ㄷ+히→치	닫히다 다치다 **dachida** *shut*	굳히다 구치다 **guchida** *harden*

발 음 규 칙 **Pronunciation Rules**

Tense Consonants 경음화
When the final consonants ㅂ(ㅍ) meet with the initial consonants ㄱ, ㄷ, ㅂ, ㅅ or ㅈ on the next syllable, these initial consonants are pronounced as ㄲ, ㄸ, ㅃ, ㅆ and ㅉ respectively.

$$춥습니다 \Rightarrow 〔춥씀니다〕$$

$$ㅂ(ㅍ) + \begin{matrix} ㄱ \\ ㄷ \\ ㅂ \\ ㅅ \\ ㅈ \end{matrix} \Rightarrow \begin{matrix} ㄲ \\ ㄸ \\ ㅃ \\ ㅆ \\ ㅉ \end{matrix}$$

맵다 맵따 **maepda** *spicy*
높다 놉따 **nopda** *high*

덥고 덥:꼬 **deobgo** *hot*
좁다 좁따 **jopda** *narrow*

Grammar 문법

01 A/V- 아 / 어요 A/V–a/eoyo   A / V Present simple tense

The meaning and the degree of politeness of A/V – 아/어요 is the same as – ㅂ니다(습니다) but is used in informal settings.

가다 ⇒ (가아요) ⇒ 가요 **gada** ⇒ **(gaayo)** ⇒ **gayo** *to go* ⇒ *go(es)*

좋다 ⇒ 좋아요 **jota** ⇒ **joayo** *to be good* ⇒ *am/is/are good*

서다 ⇒ (서어요) ⇒ 서요 **seoda** ⇒ **(seoeoyo)** ⇒ **seoyo** *to stand* ⇒ *stand(s)*

먹다 ⇒ 먹어요 **meokda** ⇒ **meogeoyo** *to eat* ⇒ *eat(s)*

마시다 ⇒ 마셔요 **masida** ⇒ **masyeoyo** *to drink* ⇒ *drink(s)*

가르치다 ⇒ 가르쳐요 **gareuchida** ⇒ **gareuchyeoyo** *to teach* ⇒ *teach(es)*

explanation | Converting to the A/V-아/어요 form |

When converting an adjective or a verb to the –아/어요 form, the following rules apply. If the last syllable of the adjective/verb stem is 하, replace it with 해요. Use –아요 when it is not 하 but contains either ㅏ or ㅗ. Use –어요 when it is not 하 AND does not contain ㅏ or ㅗ.

Verbs with the vowels ㅏ or ㅗ in the last syllable of the stem:
좋다 → 좋다 + 아요 → 좋아요

Verbs with the other vowels in the last syllable of the stem:
먹다 → 먹다 + 어요 → 먹어요

Verbs that end with the suffix -하다:
공부하다 → 공부하다 + 해요 → 공부해요

02 안 A/V− 아 / 어요 an A/V–a/eoyo

A / V Present simple negative form

To make the negative present tense form, simply attach 안 before the stem, so that the base form becomes 안 A/V − 아/어요. Note that when a verb ends with − 하다 as in the case of 공부하다, the negative form is 공부 안 해요, not 안 공부해요.

가다 ⇒ 안 가요 **gada** ⇒ **an gayo** *to go* ⇒ *do(es)n't go*

보다 ⇒ 안 봐요 **boda** ⇒ **an bwayo** *to see* ⇒ *do(es)n't see*

서다 ⇒ 안 서요 **seoda** ⇒ **an seoyo** *to stand* ⇒ *do(es)n't stand*

배우다 ⇒ 안 배워요 **baeuda** ⇒ **an baewoyo** *to learn* ⇒ *do(es)n't learn*

공부하다 ⇒ 공부 안 해요 **gongbuhada** ⇒ **gongbu an haeyo** *to study* ⇒ *do(es)n't study*

03 A/V− 지 않아요 A/V –ji anayo

A / V Present simple negative form

A/V − 지 않아요 is a more formal negative form than 안 A/V − 아/어요.

가다 ⇒ 가지 않아요 **gada** ⇒ **gaji anayo** *to go* ⇒ *do(es) not go*

바쁘다 ⇒ 바쁘지 않아요 **bappeuda** ⇒ **bappeuji anayo** *to be busy* ⇒ *am/is/are not busy*

먹다 ⇒ 먹지 않아요 **meokda** ⇒ **meokji anayo** *to eat* ⇒ *do(es) not eat*

덥다 ⇒ 덥지 않아요 **deopda** ⇒ **deopji anayo** *to be hot* ⇒ *am/is/are not hot*

따뜻하다 ⇒ 따뜻하지 않아요 **ttatteutada** ⇒ **ttatteutaji anayo**
  to be warm ⇒ *am/is/are not warm*

| **Exercise** | Fill in the blanks. You can find the answers on page 271.

Base Form	A/V-아/어요 A/V-a/eoyo *A/V present tense*	안 A/V-아/어요 an A/V-a/eoyo *do(es)n't V isn't/aren't A*	A/V-지 않아요 A/V -ji anayo *do(es)n't V isn't/am not/aren't A*
가다 gada *to go*	가요	안 가요	가지 않아요
만나다 mannada *to meet*			
오다 oda *to come*			
보다 boda *to see*			
앉다 anda *to sit*			
서다 seoda *to stand*			
배우다 baeuda *to learn*			
먹다 meokda *to eat*			
그리다 geurida *to draw*			
가르치다 gareuchida *to teach*			
마시다 masida *to drink*			
요리하다 yorihada *to cook*			
청소하다 cheongsohada *to clean*			
춥다 chupda *to be cold*			
덥다 deopda *to be hot*			

Conversation Practice 회화 연습

01 어디에 가요 ? **eodie gayo**   **Where are you going?**

Use the example sentences to guide you as you practice. Find model sentences on page 271.

공원
gongwon
park

이준기: 퍼디 씨, 어디에 가요? **peodi ssi, eodie gayo**
Ferdy, where are you going?

퍼디: 저는 공원에 가요. **jeoneun gongwone gayo**
I'm going to the park.

도서관 X
doseogwan
library

은행 ✓
eunhaeng
bank

이준기: 퍼디 씨, 도서관에 가요?
peodi ssi, doseogwane gayo
Ferdy, are you going to the library?

퍼디: 아니요, 도서관에 안 가요. 은행에 가요.
aniyo, doseogwane an gayo? eunhaenge gayo
No, I'm not going to the library. I'm going to the bank.

민속촌

가: _____ ?
나: _____ .

민속촌 X
롯데월드 ✓

가: _____ ?
나: _____ .
   _____ .

강남 X
신촌 ✓

가: _____ ?
나: _____ .
   _____ .

02 오늘 뭐 해요?　oneul mwo haeyo　**What are you doing today?**

Use the example sentences to guide you as you practice. Find model sentences on page 272.

대학로
daehangno
Daehangno
연극을 보다
yeongeugeul
boda
to see a play

이준기: 리리 씨, 오늘 뭐 해요? **riri ssi, oneul mwo haeyo**
Lili, what are you doing today?

리리: 저는 대학로에서 연극을 봐요.
jeoneun daehangnoeseo yeongeugeul bwayo
I'm going to see a play in Daehangno.

롯데월드
바이킹을 타다

가: 오늘 뭐 해요?

나: 저는 _____.

인사동
전통차를
마시다

가: _____?

나: _____.

공원
그림을
그리다

가: _____?

나: _____.

강남
떡볶이를
먹고
쇼핑을 하다

가: _____?

나: _____.

03 아니요, 책을 안 읽어요. **aniyo, chaegeul an ilgeoyo**　　　**No, I don't read books.**

Use the example sentences to guide you as you practice. Find model sentences on page 272.

도서관
doseogwan
library
책을 읽다
chaegeul ikda
to read a book
인터넷하다
inteonetada
to go on the Internet

이준기: 퍼디 씨, 도서관에서 책을 읽어요?
peodi ssi, doseogwaneseo chaegeul ilgeoyo
Ferdy, do you read books in the library?

퍼디: 아니요, 저는 책을 안 읽어요. 인터넷해요.
aniyo, jeoneun chaegeul an ilgeoyo. Inteonetaeyo
No, I don't read books. I go on the Internet.

명동
영화를 보다 X

친구를
만나다 ✓

가: 명동에서 영화를 봐요?

나: 아니요, 저는 _____ .
_____ .

학교 한국어를
공부하다 X

영어를 가르치다 ✓

가: _____ ?

나: _____ .
_____ .

집 텔레비전을
보다 X

청소하다 ✓

가: _____ ?

나: _____ .
_____ .

롯데월드
바이킹을
타다 X

롤러코스터를
타다 ✓

가: _____ ?

나: _____ .
_____ .

ONLINE
AUDIO
03:18

Listening Practice 듣기 연습

01 주말에 뭐 해요?
jumare mwo haeyo?

What do you do at the weekend?

Listen carefully to the audio, write the number of each activity mentioned, then make sentences, following the example below. You can find the answers on page 260.

왕샤위: 리리 씨, 주말에 뭐 해요? **riri ssi, jumare mwo haeyo**
Lili, what do you do at the weekend?

리리 :   명동에서 쇼핑하고 맥주를 마셔요.
myeongdongeseo syopinghago maekjureul masyeoyo
I do the shopping and have a beer in Myeongdong.

1. (.   ) ——————————— 고 ——————————— .

2. (.   ) ——————————— 고 ——————————— .

3. (.   ) ——————————— 고 ——————————— .

4. (.   ) ——————————— 고 ——————————— .

Talking with Lee Joon-gi 이준기와 이야기하기

친구의 오늘 일정 묻기 Asking about your friend's daily routine

Try having a conversation with Lee Joon-gi as you listen to the audio. You can find a translation of this conversation on page 264. Then write your own conversation in the gray box below, following this model.

이준기　리리 씨, 오늘 뭐 해요? **riri ssi, oneul mwo haeyo**

리리　저는 오늘 한국어를 공부해요.
jeoneun oneul hangugeoreul gongbuhaeyo

이준기　어디에서 한국어를 공부해요?
eodieseo hangugeoreul gongbuhaeyo

리리　도서관에서 한국어를 공부해요.
doseogwaneseo hangugeoreul gongbuhaeyo

이준기 씨는 오늘 뭐 해요?
ijungi ssineun oneul mwo haeyo

이준기　저는 오늘 여의도에 가요.
jeoneun oneul yeouidoe gayo

리리　여의도에서 뭐 해요?
yeouidoeseo mwo haeyo

이준기　여의도 방송국에서 촬영이 있어요.
yeouido bangsonggugeseo chwaryeongi isseoyo

가　_____ 씨, 오늘 뭐 해요?

나　저는 _____.

가　어디에서 _____?

나　_____ 에서 _____.

　　_____ 씨는 _____?

가　저는 _____.

나　_____ 에서 _____?

가　_____ 에서 _____.

Verb and Adjective Conjugation Table
동사 · 형용사 활용표

The following is a conjugation table of the various forms of verbs and adjectives that have been covered so far. Use the table for your review.

Base Form	A/V-ㅂ/습니다 A/V–b/seumnida *A/V present tense*	A/V-지 않습니다 A/V–ji ansseumnida *do(es) not V, am/is/are not A*	A/V-아/어요 A/V–a/eoyo *A/V present tense*	안 A/V-아/어요 an A/V–a/eoyo *do(es)n't V, am/is/are not A*
가다 gada *to go*	갑니다	가지 않습니다	가요	안 가요
만나다 **mannada** *to meet*	만납니다	만나지 않습니다	만나요	안 만나요
보다 **boda** *to watch*	봅니다	보지 않습니다	봐요	안 봐요
오다 **oda** *to come*	옵니다	오지 않습니다	와요	안 와요
먹다 **meokda** *to eat*	먹습니다	먹지 않습니다	먹어요	안 먹어요
마시다 **masida** *to drink*	마십니다	마시지 않습니다	마셔요	안 마셔요
만들다 **mandeulda** *to make*	만듭니다	만들지 않습니다	만들어요	안 만들어요
팔다 **palda** *to sell*	팝니다	팔지 않습니다	팔아요	안 팔아요
듣다 **deutda** *to listen to*	듣습니다	듣지 않습니다	들어요	안 들어요

Base Form	A/V-ㅂ/습니다 A/V-b/seumnida *A/V present tense*	A/V-지 않습니다 A/V-ji ansseumnida *do(es) not V, am/is/are not A*	A/V-아/어요 A/V-a/eoyo *A/V present tense*	안 A/V-아/어요 an A/V-a/eoyo *do(es)n't V, am/is/are not A*
요리하다 yorihada *to cook*	요리합니다	요리하지 않습니다	요리해요	요리 안 해요
청소하다 cheongsohada *to clean*	청소합니다	청소하지 않습니다	청소해요	청소 안 해요
춥다 chupda *to be cold*	춥습니다	춥지 않습니다	추워요	안 추워요
덥다 deopda *to be hot*	덥습니다	덥지 않습니다	더워요	안 더워요
맛있다 masitda *to be tasty*	맛있습니다	맛있지 않습니다	맛있어요	안 맛있어요
좋다 jota *to be good*	좋습니다	좋지 않습니다	좋아요	안 좋아요
많다 manta *to be a lot*	많습니다	많지 않습니다	많아요	안 많아요
비싸다 bissada *to be expensive*	비쌉니다	비싸지 않습니다	비싸요	안 비싸요
친절하다 chinjeolhada *to be kind*	친절합니다	친절하지 않습니다	친절해요	안 친절해요

I Go Shopping at a Department Store

백화점에 가서 쇼핑해요

하루 일과 말하기
Talking about Daily Activities

Lesson Goals

Situation
Daily activities
Vocabulary
Verbs for daily activities
Grammar
Connecting verbs

▼
Instant coffee is popular among Koreans. Many expatriates who have lived in Korea for more than a few years discover that not only are they getting used to spicy food, they're developing a liking for instant coffee too!

ONLINE AUDIO 00:10

최지영 choejiyeong
벤슨 씨, 주말에 보통 뭐 해요?
benseun ssi, jumare botong mwo haeyo
Benson, what do you usually do at the weekend?

벤슨 benseun
저는 주말에 보통 아침에 일어나서 커피를 마셔요.
jeoneun jumare botong achime ireonaseo keopireul masyeoyo
At the weekend I usually have some coffee in the morning.

그리고 백화점에 가서 쇼핑해요.
geurigo baekwajeome gaseo syopinghaeyo
Then, I go shopping at a department store.

오후에 친구를 만나서 영화를 봐요.
ohue chingureul mannaseo yeonghwareul bwayo
In the afternoon, I watch a movie with a friend.

저녁에 요리해서 친구와 같이 먹어요.
jeonyeoge yorihaeseo chinguwa gachi meogeoyo
In the evening, I cook dinner and eat it with a friend.

ONLINE
AUDIO
01:15

Vocabulary and Expressions 어휘와 표현

01 동사 8 일상생활   Verbs 8 Daily activities
dongsa pal ilsangsaenghwal

주다 〔주다〕 **juda** *to give (something/to someone)*

보내다 〔보내다〕 **bonaeda** *to send (something)*

일어나다 〔이러나다〕 **ireonada** *to wake up/get up/stand up*

샤워하다 〔샤워하다〕 **saewohada** *to take a shower*

선물하다 〔선:물하다〕 **seonmulhada** *to give a present*

편지를 쓰다 〔편:지를쓰다〕 **pyeonjireul sseuda** *to write a letter*

테니스를 치다 〔테니쓰를치다〕 **teniseureul chida** *to play tennis*

농구를 하다 〔농구를하다〕 **nonggureul hada** *to play basketball*

자전거를 타다 〔자전거를타다〕 **jajeongeoreul tada** *to cycle/to go by bicycle*

정리하다 〔정:니하다〕 **jeongnihada** *to go over/arrange/sort out*

02 기타 gita   Other useful vocabulary

신문〔신문〕 **sinmun** *newspaper*

대학교 〔대학꾜〕 **daehakgyo** *university*

일과 〔일과〕 **ilgwa** *daily routine*

보통 〔보:통〕 **botong** *usually*

발음규칙 Pronunciation Rules

Aspiration (Pronouncing consonants with a burst of air) 격음화
Before or after ㅎ, the consonants ㄱ, ㄷ, ㅂ and ㅈ combine with the ㅎ
and become the aspirated consonants ㅋ, ㅌ, ㅍ and ㅊ respectively.

$$백화점 \Rightarrow 〔배콰점〕$$
$$ㄱ + ㅎ \Rightarrow ㅋ$$

축하해요 추카해요 **chukahaeyo** *congratulations*

박하사탕 바카사탕 **bakasatang** *peppermint candy*

각하 가카 **gaka** *dismissal*

낙하산 나카산 **nakasan** *parachute*

Grammar 문법

01 V– 아 / 어서 V V–a/eoseo V   V and V

아침에 일어나서 커피를 마셔요. **achime ireonaseo keopireul masyeoyo**
I get up in the morning and drink coffee.

아침에 일어나서 샤워를 해요. **achime ireonaseo syaworeul haeyo**
I get up in the morning and take a shower.

학교에 와서 공부해요. **hakgyoe waseo gongbuhaeyo** *I come to school and study.*

도서관에 가서 책을 읽어요. **doseogwane gaseo chaegeul ilgeoyo**
I go to the library and read a book.

친구를 만나서 영화를 봐요. **chingureul mannaseo yeonghwareul bwayo**
I meet my friend and watch a movie.

로이 씨를 만나서 쇼핑해요. **roi ssireul mannaseo syopinghaeyo**
I meet Roy and do the shopping.

explanation The form ∨고 ∨ from Lesson 8 simply connects verbs. The above ∨ 아/어/서 ∨ form on the other hand implies that there is a time order of the verbs, and has three meanings as follows: 1. in that place, 2. together with that person, 3. for that.

아침에 일어나요 → (아침에) → 커피를 마셔요 ⇒ 아침에 일어나서 커피를 마셔요.
친구를 만나요 → (그 친구와 같이) → 영화를 봐요 ⇒ 친구를 만나서 영화를 봐요.
빵을 사요 → (그 빵을) → 먹어요 ⇒ 빵을 사서 먹어요.
학교에 가요 → (학교에서) → 공부해요 ⇒ 학교에서 공부해요.

explanation | Making the V1-아/어서 V2 form is the same as in V-아/어요. |

If the last syllable of the adjective/verb stem is 하, replace it with 해서. Use –아서 when it is not 하 but contains either ㅏ or ㅗ. Use – 어서 when it is not 하 and does not contain ㅏ or ㅗ.

Verbs with the vowels ㅏ or ㅗ in the last syllable of the stem:
일어나다 → 일어나다 + 아서 → 일어나서

Verbs with the other vowels in the last syllable of the stem:
만들다 → 만들다 + 어서 → 만들어서

Verbs that end with the suffix -하다 :
요리하다 → 요리하다 + 해서 → 요리해서

Conversation Practice 회화 연습

01 아침에 일어나서 커피를 마셔요.
achime ireonaseo keopireul masyeoyo

I get up in the morning and have some coffee.

Use the example sentences to guide you as you practice. Find model sentences on page 272.

아침에
일어나다
커피를
마시다

최지영: 벤슨 씨, 아침에 일어나서 보통 뭐 해요?
benseun ssi, achime ireonaseo botong mwo haeyo
Benson, what do you usually do when you get up in the morning?

벤슨: 저는 아침에 일어나서 커피를 마셔요.
jeoneun achime ireonaseo keopireul masyeoyo
I get up in the morning and have some coffee.

아침에
일어나다
신문을 읽다

가: _____ 뭐 해요?

나: 저는 _____ .

아침에
일어나다
청소하다

가: _____ ?

나: _____ .

아침에
일어나다
샤워하다

가: _____ ?

나: _____ .

아침에
일어나다
밥을 먹다

가: _____ ?

나: _____ .

02 학교에 가서 공부해요. hakgyoe gaseo gongbuhaeyo **I go to school and study.**

Use the example sentences to guide you as you practice. Find model sentences on page 272.

학교에 가다
공부하다

최지영: 비비엔 씨, 학교에 가서 보통 뭐 해요?
bibien ssi, hakgyoe gaseo botong mwo haeyo
Vivien, what do you usually do when you go to school?

비비엔: 저는 학교에 가서 공부해요.
jeoneun hakgyoe gaseo gongbuhaeyo
I go to school and study.

학교에 가다
친구를
만나다

가: _____ 뭐 해요?

나: 저는 _____ .

동대문시장에
가다
옷을 사다

가: _____ ?

나: _____ .

이태원에
가다
맥주를
마시다

가: _____ ?

나: _____ .

인사동에
가다
선물을 사다

가: _____ ?

나: _____ .

03 친구를 만나서 테니스를 쳐요.
chingureul mannaseo teniseureul chyeoyo

I meet my friend and play tennis.

Use the example sentences to guide you as you practice. Find model sentences on page 272.

친구를
만나다
테니스를
치다

최지영: 친구를 만나서 보통 뭐 해요?
chingureul mannaseo botong mwo haeyo
What do you usually do when you meet your friend?

벤슨: 저는 친구를 만나서 테니스를 쳐요.
jeoneun chingureul mannaseo teniseureul chyeoyo
I meet my friend and play tennis with them.

친구를 만나다
커피를
마시다

가: _____ 뭐 해요?

나: 저는 _____ .

친구를
만나다
영화를 보다

가: _____ ?

나: _____ .

이준기 씨를
만나다
피자를 먹다

가: _____ ?

나: _____ .

로이 씨를
만나다
놀이 기구를
타다

가: _____ ?

나: _____ .

04 꽃을 사서 친구에게 줘요 .   **I buy flowers and**
kkocheul saseo chinguege jwoyo   **give them to my friend.**

Use the example sentences to guide you as you practice. Find model sentences on page 272.

꽃을 사다
친구에게
주다

최지영: 꽃을 사서 뭐 해요? **kkocheul saseo mwo haeyo**
What do you do when you buy flowers?

벤슨: 꽃을 사서 친구에게 줘요.
kkocheul saseo chinguege jwoyo
When I buy flowers I give them to my friend.

요리하다
친구와
같이 먹다

가: _____ 뭐 해요?

나: 저는 _____ .

김치를
만들다
친구에게
주다

가: _____ ?

나: _____ .

스파게티를
만들다
친구와
같이 먹나

가: _____ ?

나: _____ .

편지를 쓰다
친구에게
보내다

가: _____ ?

나: _____ .

ONLINE
AUDIO
02:13

Listening Practice 듣기 연습

01 하루 일과 묻기 haru ilgwa mutgi **Asking about daily routine**

Listen carefully to the audio, write the number of each activity mentioned, then make sentences, following the example below. You can find the answers on page 260.

최지영: 벤슨 씨, 보통 아침에 일어나서 뭐 해요?
benseun ssi, botong achime ireonaseo mwo haeyo
Benson, what do you usually do after getting up in the morning?

벤슨: 저는 아침에 일어나서 샤워하고 커피를 마셔요.
jeoneun achime ireonaseo syawohago keopireul masyeoyo
I get up in the morning, take a shower and drink coffee.

1. (.   ) ——————— 고 ——————— .

2. (.   ) ——————— 고 ——————— .

3. (.   ) ——————— 고 ——————— .

4. (.   ) ——————— 고 ——————— .

ONLINE
AUDIO
04:45

Talking with Lee Joon-gi 이준기와 이야기하기

친구의 생활에 대해 묻기 Asking about your friend's everyday schedule

Have a conversation with Lee Joon-gi as you listen to the audio. A translation of this conversation is on page 264. Write your own dialogue in the gray box.

벤슨　이준기 씨, 보통 아침에 일어나서 뭐 해요?
　　　ijungi ssi, botong achime ireonaseo mwo haeyo

이준기　저는 보통 아침에 일어나서 공원에서 운동해요.
　　　jeoneun botong achime ireonaseo gongwoneseo undonghaeyo

　　　그리고 집에 와서 샤워하고,
　　　요리해서 밥을 먹어요.
　　　geurigo jibe waseo syawohago
　　　yorihaeseo babeul meogeoyo

벤슨　주말에는 보통 뭐 해요?
　　　jumareneun botong mwo haeyo

이준기　태국 친구를 만나서 태국어 공부를 해요.
　　　taeguk chingureul mannaseo taegugeo
　　　gongbureul haeyo

　　　그리고 집에 와서 일주일 일과를 정리하고 자요.
　　　geurigo jibe waseo iljuil ilgwareul jeongnihago jayo

　　　벤슨 씨는 주말에 보통 뭐 해요?
　　　benseun ssineun jumare botong mwo haeyo

벤슨　저는 주말에 보통 영화를 보고 친구를 만나요.
　　　jeoneun jumare botong yeonghwareul bogo chingureul mannayo

가　_____ 씨, 보통 아침에 일어나서 뭐 해요?

나　저는 _____.

　　그리고 _____?

가　주말에는 보통 뭐 해요?

나　_____.

　　_____저는 _____?

가　저는 _____.

The ㅡ Irregular Rule

For the verb or adjective stems that end in ㅡ, ㅡ is dropped when followed by a vowel and their forms change as shown below. Following the pattern in the chart, write the correct verb forms for numbers 1 to 8. You can find the answers on page 272.

When the vowel before ㅡ is ㅏ or ㅗ, drop ㅡ and add ㅏ.
바쁘다 ⇒ 바쁘 + ㅏ요 ⇒ 바빠요   고프다 ⇒ 고프 + ㅏ요 ⇒ 고파요

When the vowel before ㅡ is other than ㅏ or ㅗ, or the stem is just one syllable, drop ㅡ and add ㅓ.
기쁘다 ⇒ 기쁘+ ㅓ요 ⇒ 기뻐요   쓰다 ⇒ 쓰 + ㅓ요 ⇒ 써요

Base Form	A/V-ㅂ/습니다 **A/V–b/seumnida** *A/V present tense* A/V-아/어요 **A/V–a/eoyo** *A/V present tense*	A/V-지 않습니다 **A/V–ji ansseumnida** *do(es) not V, am/is/are not A* 안 A/V-아/어요 **an A/V–a/eoyo** *do(es)n't V, isn't/aren't A*	A/V-고 **A/V–go** *A/V and* A/V-지 않아요 **A/V –ji anayo** *do(es) not V, am/is/are not A*	A/V-지만 **A/V–jiman** *A/V but* V-아/어서 **V–a/eoseo V** *V and then V*
바쁘다 **bappeuda** *to be busy*	바쁩니다 바빠요	바쁘지 않습니다 안 바빠요	바쁘고 바쁘지 않아요	바쁘지만 바빠서
아프다 **apeuda** *to be ill*	①	아프지 않습니다 안 아파요	아프고 아프지 않아요	아프지만 아파서
예쁘다 **yeppeuda** *to be pretty*	예쁩니다 예뻐요	②	예쁘고 예쁘지 않아요	③
기쁘다 **gippeuda** *to be happy*	④	기쁘지 않습니다 안 기뻐요	⑤	⑥
쓰다 **sseuda** *to write*	씁니다 써요	⑦	쓰고 쓰지 않아요	쓰지만 써서

The ㄷ Irregular Rule

When the final consonant ㄷ in the verb stem is followed by a vowel, ㄷ changes to ㄹ.

Examples of how to apply the ㄷ irregular rule to an adjective/verb

듣다 ⇒ (들어요) ⇒ 들어요   듣다 ⇒ (들어서) ⇒ 들어서

Some verbs with stem ending in ㄷ are conjugated regularly.

받다 to receive ⇒ 받아요   닫다 to open ⇒ 닫아요

Base Form	A/V-ㅂ/습니다 **A/V-b/seumnida** *A/V present tense* A/V-아/어요 **A/V-a/eoyo** *A/V present tense*	A/V-고 **A/V-go** *A/V and* V-(으)ㄹ까요? **V-(eu)rkkayo?** *Shall we/I V?*	A/V-지만 **A/V-jiman** *A/V but* V-(으)ㅂ시다 **V-(eu)bsida** *Let's V*	A/V-(으)면 **A/V-(eu) myeon** *when A/V*	V-(으)ㄹ세요 **V-(eu)seyo** *V, please*
듣다 **deutda** *to listen to*	듣습니다 들어요	듣고 들을까요?	듣지만 들읍시다	들으면	들으세요
걷다 **geotda** *to walk*	걷습니다 걸어요	걷고 걸을까요?	걷지만 걸읍시다	걸으면	걸으세요
묻다 **mutda** *to ask*	묻습니다 물어요	묻고 물을까요?	묻지만 물읍시다?	물으면	물으세요

Apgujeong

The Place Where Luxurious Lifestyle and Celebrities Mix

You will probably bump into celebrities in Seoul's Apgujeong district, where luxury shops and fancy restaurants thrive. Koreans who love to follow the latest fashions enjoy strolling around the neighborhood. Celebrities can often be seen in the luxurious restaurants and bars that line the streets here.

Apgujeong is also a center for the arts and entertainment: many high-end wedding shops, talent agencies, movie and music production offices are located here. There also are many aesthetics clinics that attract those who wish to improve their looks. Aren't you already tempted to take a leisurely walk around this star-studded area?

I Saw a Movie Yesterday
어제 영화를 봤어요

12

Lesson Goals

Situation
Talking about the past
Vocabulary
Food
Tourist destinations
Hobbies
Grammar
The past tense
The possessive particle

▼

The King and the Clown, a 2005 historical drama film, starring Lee Joon-gi sold more than 10 million tickets in Korea, which has a population of about 50 million. Lee Joon-gi became a Korean wave celebrity as a result of this success. The movie beautifully portrays the art and culture of the common people during the Joseon Dynasty.

ONLINE
AUDIO
00:10

이준기 ijungi	마스미 씨, 어제 무엇을 했어요? **maseumi ssi, eoje mueoseul haesseoyo** *Masumi, what did you do yesterday?*
마스미 maseumi	명동에서 커피를 마시고 영화를 봤어요. **myeongdongeseo keopireul masigo yeonghwareul bwasseoyo** *I had a coffee and saw a movie in Myeongdong.*
이준기 ijungi	무슨 영화를 봤어요? **museun yeonghwareul bwasseoyo** *What movie did you see?*
마스미 maseumi	<왕의 남자>를 봤어요. **<wangui namja>reul bwasseoyo** *I saw The King and the Clown.* 이준기 씨는 어제 뭘 했어요? **ijungi ssineun eoje mwol haesseoyo** *What did you do yesterday, Joon-gi?*
이준기 ijungi	친구와 같이 동대문 시장에 갔어요. **chinguwa gachi dongdaemun sijange gasseoyo** *I went to Dongdaemun Market with a friend.*
마스미 maseumi	동대문 시장에서 뭘 했어요? **dongdaemun sijangeseo mwol haesseoyo** *What did you do at Dongdaemun Market?*
이준기 ijungi	동대문 시장에서 옷을 사고 비빔국수를 먹었어요. **dongdaemun sijangeseo oseul sago bibimguksureul meogeosseoyo** *I bought some clothes and had bibimguksu spicy noodles.*

ONLINE
AUDIO
01:27

Vocabulary and Expressions 어휘와 표현

01 음식 eumsik   Food 3

비빔국수 〔비빔국 쑤〕 **bibimguksu**
bibimguksu spicy noodles

비빔밥 〔비빔빱〕 **bibimbap**
bibimbap

김치찌개 〔김치찌개〕 **gimchijjigae**
kimchi stew

된장찌개 〔된장찌개〕 **doenjangjjigae**
doenjang stew

피자 〔피자〕 **pija** *pizza*

만두 〔만두〕 **mandu** *dumplings*

갈비탕 〔갈비탕〕 **galbitang**
galbitang short rib soup

냉면 〔냉면〕 **naengmyeon**
naengmyeon noodles

칼국수 〔칼국쑤〕 **kalguksu**
kalguksu (noodle dish)

02 여행지 yeohaengji   Tourist destinations

산 〔산〕 **san** *mountain*

설악산 〔서락산〕 **seoraksan**
Mt. Seorak

바다 〔바다〕 **bada** *the sea*

온천 〔온천〕 **oncheon** *spa*

북한산 〔부칸산〕 **bukansan** *Mt. Bukhan*

도봉산 〔도봉산〕 **dobongsan**
Mt. Dobong

놀이동산 〔노리동산〕 **noridongsan**
amusement park

호수 〔호수〕 **hosu** *lake*

03 동사 9 취미 dongsa gu chwimi   Verbs 9 Hobbies

등산을 하다 〔등사늘하다〕 **deungsaneul hada** *to go hiking*

피아노〔기타〕를 치다 〔피아노를치다/기타를치다〕 **piano(gita)reul chida**
to play the piano/guitar

골프〔테니스/볼링〕을/를 치다 〔골프를치다/테니쓰를치다/볼링을치다〕
golpeu(teniseu/bolling)eul/reul chida *to play golf/tennis/bowling*

스키〔스케이트〕를 타다 〔스키를타다/스케이트를타다〕
seuki(seukeiteu)reul tada *to ski/skate*

태권도를 하다 〔태꿘도를하다〕 **taegwondoreul hada** *to do taekwondo*

수영〔축구〕을/를 하다 〔수영을하다/축꾸를하다〕
suyeong(chukgu)eul/reul hada *to swim/play soccer*

04 기타 gita **Other useful vocabulary**

무엇을 = 뭘 〔무어슬 = 뭘〕 **mueoseul = mwol** *what*

왕의 남자 〔왕에남자〕 **wangui namja** *The King and the Clown*

테니스장 〔테니쓰장〕 **teniseujang** *tennis court*

태권도장 〔태꿘도장〕 **taegwondojang** *taekwondo studio/gym*

우리 동네 〔우리동네〕 **uri dongne** *my neighborhood/my town*

바 〔바〕 **ba** *bar*

발음규칙 Pronunciation Rules

Pronunciation of the syllable 의
The sound of the vowel ㅢ varies depending on the circumstances.

▶ When the vowel ㅢ is placed in the first syllable of word and ○ appears at the
▶ beginning of the syllable, ㅢ is pronounced [ui]: 의사 uisa *doctor*
▶ When the syllable with the vowel ㅢ begins with a consonant, ㅢ is pronounced [i]:
　 희망 himang *hope*
▶ When the vowel ㅢ is not in the first syllable of word and ○ appears at the beginning
　 of the syllable, ㅢ is pronounced [ui] or [i]: 민주주의 minjujuui / minjujui *democracy*
▶ When the vowel ㅢ is used as a possessive particle, ㅢ is pronounced [ui] or [e].
　 왕의 남자 wangui / wangue namja *The King and the Clown* (lit. the king's clown)

Grammar 문법

01 A/V- 았 / 었어요 A/V–at/eosseoyo   A/V Past tense

가다 ⇒ 갔어요 **gada** ⇒ **gasseoyo** *to go* ⇒ *went*

좋다 ⇒ 좋았어요 **jota** ⇒ **joasseoyo** *to be good* ⇒ *was/were good*

배우다 ⇒ 배웠어요 **baeuda** ⇒ **baewosseoyo** *to learn* ⇒ *learned*

먹다 ⇒ 먹었어요 **meokda** ⇒ **meogeosseoyo** *to eat* ⇒ *ate*

읽다 ⇒ 읽었어요 **ikda** ⇒ **ilgeosseoyo** *to read* ⇒ *read*

explanation | Converting to the A/V-았/었어요 form |

This is a past tense form of adjectives and verbs. Remove 다 from the base form. When the last syllable of the stem has ㅏ or ㅗ as its vowel, attach 았어요. For other vowels, use 었어요 instead.

When the syllable of the stem contains the medial vowels ㅏ or ㅗ:
좋다 → 좋다 + 았어요 → 좋았어요

When the syllable of the stem does NOT contain the medial vowels ㅏ or ㅗ:
먹다 → 먹다 + 었어요 → 먹었어요

Verbs that take the 하다 suffix: 공부하다 → 공부하다 + 했어요 → 공부했어요

explanation | A simple way to make the A/V-았/었어요 form |

Simply add 써어요 to the verb stem.
가요 → 가요 + 써어요 → 갔어요
먹어요 → 먹어요 + 써어요 → 먹었어요
공부해요 → 공부해요 + 써어요 → 공부했어요

02 안 A/V– 았 / 었어요 an A/V–at/eosseoyo

Did not V/ was not (were not) A

가다 ⟹ 안 갔어요 **gada** ⟹ **an gasseoyo** *to go* ⟹ *didn't go*

좋다 ⟹ 안 좋았어요 **jota** ⟹ **an joasseoyo** *to be good* ⟹ *wasn't/weren't good*

먹다 ⟹ 안 먹었어요 **meokda** ⟹ **an meogeosseoyo** *to eat* ⟹ *didn't eat*

공부하다 ⟹ 공부 안 했어요 **gongbuhada** ⟹ **gongbu an haesseoyo**
 to study ⟹ *didn't study*

03 A/V– 지 않았어요 A/V–ji anasseoyo

Did not V/ was not (were not) A

가다 ⟹ 가지 않았어요 **gada** ⟹ **gaji anasseoyo** *to go* ⟹ *did not go*

마시다 ⟹ 마시지 않았어요 **masida** ⟹ **masiji anasseoyo** *to drink* ⟹ *did not drink*

읽다 ⟹ 읽지 않았어요 **ikda** ⟹ **ikji anasseoyo** *to read* ⟹ *did not read*

공부하다 ⟹ 공부하지 않았어요 **gongbuhada** ⟹ **gongbuhaji anasseoyo**
 to study ⟹ *did not study*

04 N의 N Nui N

N's N

왕의 남자 **wangui namja** *The King and the Clown (Korean movie; Lit. king's man)*

스테파니 씨의 친구 **seutepani ssiui chingu** *Stephanie's friend*

유 선생님의 학생 **yu seonsaengnimui haksaeng** *Teacher Yu's student*

최지영 씨의 폰 **choejiyeong ssiui pon** *Jiyoung Choi's phone*

한국의 산 **hangugui san** *mountains in Korea*

오늘의 뉴스 **oneurui nyuseu** *today's news*

| **Exercise** | Fill in the blanks. You can find the answers on page 272.

Base Form	A/V-았/었어요 **A/V–at/eosseoyo** *A/V past tense*	안 A/V-았/었어요 **an A/V–at/eosseoyo** *not V/A*	A/V-지 않았어요 **A/V–ji anasseoyo** *not V/A*
가다 **gada** *to go*	갔어요	안 갔어요	가지 않았어요
만나다 **mannada** *to meet*	만났어요		만나지 않았어요
오다 **oda** *to come*	왔어요		
보다 **boda** *to watch*	봤어요	안 봤어요	
앉다 **anda** *to sit*		안 앉았어요	앉지 않았어요
배우다 **baeuda** *to learn*			배우지 않았어요
읽다 **ikda** *to read*			읽지 않았어요
그리다 **geurida** *to draw*		안 그렸어요	

Conversation Practice 회화 연습

01 지난 주말에 어디에 갔어요 ?
jinan jumare eodie gasseoyo

Where did you go last weekend?

Use the example sentences to guide you as you practice. Find model sentences on page 273.

지난 주말
바다

이준기: 마스미 씨, 지난 주말에 어디에 갔어요?
maseumi ssi, jinan jumare eodie gasseoyo
Masumi, where did you go last weekend?

마스미: 저는 지난 주말에 바다에 갔어요.
jeoneun jinan jumare badae gasseoyo
I went to the seaside last weekend.

지난 주말
도서관

가: 지난 주말에 어디에 갔어요?

나: 저는 _____ .

지난 주말
설악산

가: _____ ?

나: _____ .

지난 주말
온천

가: _____ ?

나: _____ .

지난 주말
놀이동산

가: _____ ?

나: _____ .

02 지난 주말에 민속촌에 갔어요 ?
jinan jumare minsokchone gasseoyo
Did you go to the folk village last weekend?

Use the example sentences to guide you as you practice. Find model sentences on page 273.

민속촌 X
롯데월드 ✓

이준기: 마스미 씨, 지난 주말에 민속촌에 갔어요?
maseumi ssi, jinan jumare minsokchone gasseoyo
Masumi, did you go to the folk village last weekend?

마스미: 아니요, 저는 민속촌에 안 갔어요.
aniyo, jeoneun minsokchone an gasseoyo
No, I didn't go to the folk village.

롯데월드에 갔어요. **rotdewoldeue gasseoyo**
I went to Lotte World.

도서관 X
백화점 ✓

가: 지난 주말에 도서관에 갔어요?

나: 아니요, 저는 _____ 에 안 갔어요.

_____ .

설악산 X
온천 ✓

가: _____ ?

나: _____ .

_____ .

바다 X
산 ✓

가: _____ ?

나: _____ .

_____ .

부산 X
제주도 ✓

가: _____ ?

나: _____ .

_____ .

03 어제 무엇을 했어요?
eoje mueoseul haesseoyo

What did you do yesterday?

Use the example sentences to guide you as you practice. Find model sentences on page 273.

어제, 집
텔레비전을
보다
책을 읽다

이준기: 마스미 씨, 어제 무엇을 했어요?
maseumi ssi, eoje mueoseul haesseoyo
Masumi, what did you do yesterday?

마스미: 저는 어제 집에서 텔레비전을 보고 책을 읽었어요.
jeoneun eoje jibeseo tellebijeoneul bogo chaegeul ilgeosseoyo
I watched television and read a book at home.

어제, 영화관
영화를 보다
술을 마시다

가: 어제 무엇을 했어요?

나: _____

_____ .

어제, 집
텔레비전을
보다
청소하다

가: _____ ?

나: _____

_____ .

지난 주말
명동
피자를 먹다
쇼핑을 하다

가: _____ ?

나: _____

_____ .

지난 주말
이태원
술을 마시다
춤을 추다

가: _____ ?

나: _____

_____ .

---

04 아니요 , 태권도를 안 했어요 . No, I didn't do taekwondo.
aniyo, taegwondoreul an haesseoyo

Use the example sentences to guide you as you practice. Find model sentences on page 273.

| 어제, 학교 |
| 태권도를 하다 X |
| 테니스를 치다 ✓ |

이준기: 마스미 씨, 어제 학교에서 태권도를 했어요?
maseumi ssi, eoje hakgyoeseo taegwondoreul haesseoyo *Did you do taekwondo at school yesterday?*

마스미: 아니요, 저는 태권도를 안 했어요.
aniyo, jeoneun taegwondoreul an haesseoyo
No, I didn't do taekwondo.

테니스를 쳤어요. **teniseureul chyeosseoyo**
I played tennis.

| 어제, 명동 |
| 영화를 보다 X |
| 친구를 만나다 ✓ |

가: 어제 명동에서 영화를 봤어요?

나: 아니요, 저는 ＿＿＿＿＿＿ 를 안 봤어요.

＿＿＿＿＿＿＿＿＿＿＿＿ .

| 어제, 도서관 |
| 책을 읽다 X |
| 인터넷을 하다 ✓ |

가: ＿＿＿＿＿＿＿＿＿＿ ?
나: ＿＿＿＿＿＿＿＿＿＿ .

＿＿＿＿＿＿＿＿＿＿ .

| 어제, 집 |
| 피아노를 치다 X |
| 기타를 치다 ✓ |

가: ＿＿＿＿＿＿＿＿＿＿ ?
나: ＿＿＿＿＿＿＿＿＿＿ .

＿＿＿＿＿＿＿＿＿＿ .

| 지난 주말 |
| 등산을 하다 X |
| 골프를 치다 ✓ |

가: ＿＿＿＿＿＿＿＿＿＿ ?
나: ＿＿＿＿＿＿＿＿＿＿ .

＿＿＿＿＿＿＿＿＿＿ .

Listening Practice 듣기 연습

01 지난 일 묻기 **jinan il mutgi** **Asking about past activities**

Listen carefully to the audio, write the number of each activity mentioned, then make sentences, following the example below. You can find the answers on page 260.

퍼디: 마스미 씨, 지난 주말에 무엇을 했어요?
maseumi ssi, jinan jumare mueoseul haesseoyo
Masumi, what did you do last weekend?

마스미 : 저는 지난 주말에 스키를 타고 수영을 했어요.
jeoneun jinan jumare seukireul tago suyeongeul haesseoyo
I skied and swam last weekend.

1. (.   ) _____ 고 _____ .

2. (.   ) _____ 고 _____ .

3. (.   ) _____ 고 _____ .

4. (.   ) _____ 고 _____ .

ONLINE
AUDIO
05:48

Talking with Lee Joon-gi 1 이준기와 이야기하기 1

지난 주말 활동 이야기하기 Talking about what you did at the weekend

Have a conversation with Lee Joon-gi as you listen to the audio. A translation of this conversation is on page 265. Write your own dialogue in the gray box.

이준기   비비엔 씨, 주말에 뭐 했어요?
          bibien ssi, jumare mwo haesseoyo

비비엔   저는 주말에 친구와 같이 쇼핑했어요.
          jeoneun jumare chinguwa gachi syopinghaesseoyo

이준기   어디에서 쇼핑했어요?
          eodieseo syopinghaesseoyo

비비엔   명동에서 쇼핑했어요.
          myeongdongeseo syopinghaesseoyo

          이준기 씨는 주말에 뭐 했어요?
          ijungi ssineun jumare mwo haesseoyo

이준기   저는 주말에 운동했어요.
          jeoneun jumare undonghaesseoyo

비비엔   무슨 운동을 했어요?
          museun undongeul haesseoyo

이준기   태권도를 했어요.   taegwondoreul haesseoyo

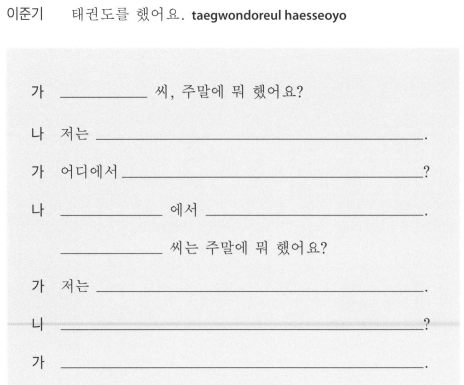

가   _____ 씨, 주말에 뭐 했어요?

나   저는 _____.

가   어디에서 _____?

나   _____ 에서 _____.

     _____ 씨는 주말에 뭐 했어요?

가   저는 _____.

나   _____?

가   _____.

ONLINE
AUDIO
06:53

Talking with Lee Joon-gi 2   이준기와 이야기하기 2

일기 쓰기   Writing a diary

Read Lee Joon-gi's diary and then write your own diary entry.

5월 5일 맑다 **owol oil makda**

어제는 날씨가 아주 좋았어요. **eojeneun nalssiga aju joasseoyo**

선생님과 친구들이 우리 집에 왔어요.
　　seonsaengnimgwa chingudeuri uri jibe wasseoyo

비비엔 씨는 남자 친구하고 같이 왔어요.
　　bibien ssineun namja chinguhago gachi wasseoyo

우리는 같이 스페인 음식과 중국 음식을 먹고 일본 차를 마셨어요.
　　urineun gachi seupein eumsikgwa jungguk eumsigeul meokgo ilbon cha-
　　reul masyeosseoyo

비비엔 씨와 로베르토 씨는 노래를 했어요.
　　bibien ssiwa robereuto ssineun noraereul haesseoyo

로이 씨도 홍콩 노래를 했어요. **roi ssido hongkong noraereul haesseoyo**

아주 좋았어요. **aju joasseoyo**

· ·

년　　월　　일

Hobbies

독서
dokseo
reading

음악 감상
eumak gamsang
listening to music

인터넷을 하다
inteoneseul hada
to surf the Internet

그림을 그리다
geurimeul geurida
to draw a picture

노래하다
noraehada
to sing (a song)

요리하다
yorihada
to cook

춤을 추다
chumeul chuda
to dance

텔레비전을 보다
tellebijeoneul boda
to watch TV

테니스를 치다
teniseureul chida
to play tennis

기타를 치다
gitareul chida
to play the guitar

수영하다
suyeonghada
to swim

골프를 치다
golpeureul chida
to play golf

스키를 타다
seukireul tada
to ski

태권도를 하다
taegwondoreul hada
to do taekwondo

농구를 하다
nonggureul hada
to play basketball

쇼핑하다
syopinghada
to go shopping

등산을 하다
deungsaneul hada
to go hiking

스케이트를 타다
seukeiteureul tada
to skate

피아노를 치다
pianoreul chida
to play the piano

영화를 보다
yeonghwareul boda
to watch a movie

걷기
geotgi
walking

공연을 보다
gongyeoneul boda
to watch a play

놀이공원에 가다
norigongwone gada
*to go to an
amusement park*

산책을 하다
sanchaegeul hada
to take a walk

신문을 보다
sinmuneul boda
to read the newspaper

야구를 하다
yagureul hada
to play baseball

여행을 가다
yeohaengeul gada
to travel go on a trip

연을 날리다
yeoneul nallida
to fly a kite

운동을 하다
undongeul hada
to work out

차를 마시다
chareul masida
to have some tea

클럽에 가다
keulleobe gada
to go to a club

편지를 쓰다
pyeonjireul sseuda
to write a letter

Lee Joon-gi's Guide to Seoul

Daehangno
Seoul's Theater District

It would not be an exaggeration to state that Korea's modern theater culture was born in Daehangno. It's a place that inspires every young actor with dreams of success, and it's safe to assume that many of the people you rub shoulders with in Daehangno are aspiring thespians. You can enjoy watching their performances in the many small theaters here, or you may be lucky enough to come across an outdoor performance in the neighborhood's Marronnier Park.

How About a Drink Tonight?
오늘 한잔 어때요?

13

약속하기
Making Plans

Lesson Goals

Situation
Making plans
Vocabulary
Verbs
Grammar
Intentions
Suggestions
The conditional with "when"

▼

Bars that sell beer are called 호프 (hopeu) in Korea. You can find many of them near colleges or business districts. Quite a few of them sell a wide variety of beer from all over the world. Koreans love to order side dishes such as chicken and pork cutlet along with their beer.

ONLINE
AUDIO
00:10

최지영
choejiyeong

퍼디 씨, 오늘 시간이 있으면 한잔 어때요?
peodi ssi, oneul sigani isseumyeon hanjan eottaeyo
Ferdy, how about a drink tonight if you are free?

퍼디
peodi

좋아요. 어디로 갈까요?
joayo. eodiro galkkayo
Sounds good. Where shall we go?

최지영
choejiyeong

광화문 호프로 갑시다.
gwanghwamun hopeuro gapsida
Let's go to a beer bar in Gwanghwamun.

퍼디
peodi

네, 좋아요.
ne, joayo
Ok, then.

그럼 어디에서 만날까요?
geureom eodieseo mannalkkayo
Where shall we meet?

최지영
choejiyeong

오늘 저녁 6시에 한국대학교 앞에서 만납시다.
oneul jeonyeok yeoseotsie hangukdaehakgyo apeseo mannapsida
Let's meet in front of Hankuk University at 6 PM.

퍼디
peodi

네, 좋아요.
ne, joayo
Sure. That sounds good.

Vocabulary and Expressions 어휘와 표현

01 동사 10 약속 dongsa sip yaksok   Verbs 10 Appointments

끝나다 〔끈나다〕 kkeunnada *to be done/to be finished*

방학하다(= 방학을 하다) 〔방학카다(= 방하클하다)〕
  banghakada(= banghageul hada) *school holiday starts*

파티를 하다 〔파티를하다〕 patireul hada *to have a party*

여행하다(= 여행을 가다) 〔여행하다(= 여행을가다)〕
  yeohaenghada(= yeohaengeul gada) *to go on a trip*

한잔하다 〔한잔하다〕 hanjanhada *to have an (alcoholic) drink*

시간이 있다 〔시가니읻따〕 sigani itda *to have some free time*

시간이 없다 〔시가니업:따〕 sigani eopda *to have no free time*

02 기타 gita   Other useful vocabulary

경복궁 〔경:보꿍〕 gyeongbokgung
  Gyeongbokgung

고향 〔고향〕 gohyang *hometown*

호프 〔호프〕 hopeu *pub*

007 〔공공칠〕 gonggongchil *007*

타이타닉 〔타이타닉〕 taitanik
  the Titanic

유럽 〔유럽〕 yureop *Europe*

약 〔약〕 yak *medicine*

발음규칙 Pronunciation Rules

Omission of ㅎ
The final consonant ㅎ is omitted before a syllable that starts with a vowel.

$$좋아요 \Rightarrow 〔조:아요〕$$

$$ㅎ + ㅇ \Rightarrow \emptyset + ㅇ$$

많아요 마:나요 manayo *a lot*   않아요 아나요 anayo *not*

Grammar 문법

01 V-(으)ㄹ까요? 의향 묻기
V–(eu)rkkayo? uihyang mutgi

가다 ⇒ 오늘 오후에 명동에 갈까요? gada ⇒ oneul ohue myeongdonge galkkayo
to go ⇒ Shall we go to Myeongdong this afternoon?

먹다 ⇒ 오늘 저녁에 생선을 먹을까요?
meokda ⇒ **oneul jeonyeoge saengseoneul meogeulkkayo**
to eat ⇒ Shall we eat fish for dinner?

만들다 ⇒ 주말에 같이 김치를 만들까요?
mandeulda ⇒ **jumare gachi gimchireul mandeulkkayo**
to make ⇒ Shall we make kimchi together at the weekend?

explanation | Converting to the V- (으)ㄹ까요? form |

Remove the –다 suffix from the base verb form. When the last syllable of the verb stem does not have a final consonant, ㄹ까요 is used, but if there is a final consonant, 을까요 is used instead. One exception to the rule is when the final consonant is ㄹ, then ㄹ까요 is used.

When the last syllable of the stem does NOT have a final consonant:
가다 → 가다 + ㄹ까요→갈까요?

When the last syllable of the stem has a final consonant:
먹다 → 먹다 + 을까요→먹을까요?

When the last syllable of the stem has the final consonant ㄹ:
만들다 → 만들다 + ㄹ까요→만들까요?

| **Exercise** | Fill in the blanks. You can find the answers on page 273.

Base Form	-(으)ㄹ까요? –(eu)rkkayo *Shall we V?*		
가다 gada *to go*	갈까요?	만나다 **mannada** *to meet*	
보다 boda *to watch*		마시다 **masida** *to drink*	

02 V-(으)ㅂ시다 V-(eu)bsida

Let's V

가다 ⇒ 일요일에 민속촌에 갑시다. **gada** ⇒ **iryoire minsokchone gapsida**
to go ⇒ *Let's go to the folk village on Sunday.*

읽다 ⇒ 도서관에서 한국어 책을 읽읍시다.
ikda ⇒ **doseogwaneseo hangugeo chaegeul ilgeupsida**
to read ⇒ *Let's read a Korean book in the library.*

만들다 ⇒ 주말에 같이 김치를 만듭시다.
mandeulda ⇒ **jumare gachi gimchireul mandeupsida**
to make ⇒ *Let's make kimchi together at the weekend.*

explanation | Converting to the V- (으)ㅂ시다 form |

Remove 다 from the base form first, then attach – ㅂ시다 when the last syllable of the stem does not have a final consonant. When there is a final consonant, use -읍시다 instead. When it is ㄹ, remove ㄹ and attach – ㅂ시다.

When the last syllable of the stem does NOT have a final consonant:
가다 → 가다 + ㅂ시다 → 갑시다

When the last syllable of the stem has a final consonant:
먹다 → 먹다 + 읍시다 → 먹읍시다

When the last syllable of the stem has the final consonant ㄹ:
만들다 → 만들다 + ㅂ시다 → 만듭시다

| **Exercise** | Fill in the blanks. You can find the answers on page 273.

Base Form	-(으)ㅂ시다 (eu)bsida *Let's V*		
가다 gada *to go*	갑시다	만나다 **mannada** *to meet*	
보다 boda *to watch*		마시다 **masida** *to drink*	

03 A/V-(으)면 A/V–(eu)myeon
The conditional with "when"

방학을 하다 ⇒ 방학을 하면 뭐 해요?
banghageul hada ⇒ **banghageul hamyeon mwo haeyo**
school holiday starts ⇒ *what do you do when your school holiday starts?*

수업이 끝나다 ⇒ 수업이 끝나면 친구를 만나서 영화를 봐요.
sueobi kkeunnada ⇒ **sueobi kkeunnamyeon chingureul mannaseo yeonghwareul bwayo**
a class finishes ⇒ *I meet my friend and watch a movie when the class finishes.*

빵을 먹다 ⇒ 빵을 먹으면 기분이 좋아요.
ppangeul meokda ⇒ **ppangeul meogeumyeon gibuni joayo**
to eat bread ⇒ *I feel good when I eat bread.*

explanation | Converting to the V- (으)ㄹ까요? form |

Remove –다 from the base form of the adjective/verb, and attach the suffix –면 if the final consonant on the last syllable of the stem is either ㄹ or null. For any other consonant, attach –으면 instead.

When the last syllable of the stem does NOT have a final consonant:
하다 → 하다 + 면 → 하면

When the last syllable of the stem has a final consonant:
먹다 → 먹다 + 으면 → 먹으면

When the last syllable of the stem has the final consonant ㄹ:
만들다 → 만들다 + 면 → 만들면

| **Exercise** | Fill in the blanks. You can find the answers on page 273.

Base Form	A/V-(으)면 A/V–(eu)myeon *if/when A/V*		
방학을 하다 **banghageul hada** *school holiday starts*	방학을 하면	시간이 있다 **sigani itda** *to have some free time*	
수업이 끝나다 **sueobi kkeunnada** *class finishes*		시간이 없다 **sigani eopda** *to have no free time*	

Conversation Practice 회화 연습

01 영화를 볼까요? **yeonghwareul bolkkayo** **Shall we watch a movie?**

Use the example sentences to guide you as you practice. Find model sentences on page 273.

오늘
영화를 보다

최지영: 퍼디 씨, 오늘 영화를 볼까요?
peodi ssi, oneul yeonghwareul bolkkayo
Ferdy, shall we watch a movie today?

퍼디: 네, 좋아요. 영화를 봅시다.
ne, joayo. yeonghwareul bopsida
Yes, that sounds good. Let's watch a movie.

내일
점심을 먹다

가: 내일 점심을 먹을까요?

나: 네, 좋아요. _____ .

소주 삼겹살

오늘 저녁
술을 마시다

가: _____ ?

나: _____ .

이번 주말
온천에 가다

가: _____ ?

나: _____ .

내일
농구를 하다

가: _____ ?

나: _____ .

02 경복궁에 갑시다.   gyeongbokgunge gapsida   Let's go to Gyeongbokgung.

Use the example sentences to guide you as you practice. Find model sentences on page 273.

주말
버스 X
지하철 ✓

최지영: 퍼디 씨, 주말에 경복궁에 갑시다. 버스를 탈까요?
지하철을 탈까요?
peodi ssi, jumare gyeongbokgunge gapsida. beoseureul talkkayo. jihacheoreul talkkayo
Ferdy, let's go to Gyeongbokgung at the weekend. Shall we take a bus? Or shall we take the subway?

퍼디:　지하철을 탑시다.
jihacheoreul tapsida
Let's take the subway.

주말
수영 X
골프 ✓

가: 주말에 운동을 합시다.
　　_____ ? _____ ?

나: 골프를 합시다.

오늘
비빔밥 X
비빔국수 ✓

가: _____ ?
나: _____ ? _____ ?
　　_____ .

금요일
007 X
타이타닉 ✓

가: _____ ?
나: _____ ? _____ ?
　　_____ .

주말
스케이트 X
스키 ✓

가: _____ ?
나: _____ ? _____ ?
　　_____ .

03 방학을 하면 뭐 해요 ?
banghageul hamyeon mwo haeyo

What do you do in school holidays?

Use the example sentences to guide you as you practice. Find model sentences on page 274.

방학을 하다
고향에 가다

최지영: 퍼디 씨, 방학을 하면 뭐 해요?
peodi ssi, banghageul hamyeon mwo haeyo
Ferdy, what do you do in the school holidays?

퍼디: 저는 방학을 하면 고향에 가요.
jeoneun banghageul hamyeon gohyange gayo
I go to my hometown in the school holidays.

수업이
끝나다
친구를
만나다

가: 마스미 씨, 수업이 끝나면 뭐 해요?

나: _____ .

친구를
만나다
농구를 하다

가: _____ ?

나: _____ .

집에 가다
텔레비전을
보다

가: _____ ?

나: _____ .

인사동에
가다
전통차를
마시다

가: _____ ?

나: _____ .

---

04 방학을 하면 고향에 가요?
banghageul hamyeon gohyange gayo

Do you go to your hometown during school holidays?

Use the example sentences to guide you as you practice. Find model sentences on page 274.

방학을 하다
고향에 가다 X
유럽에 가다 ✓

최지영: 퍼디 씨, 방학을 하면 고향에 가요?
peodi ssi, banghageul hamyeon gohyange gayo
Ferdy, do you go to your hometown in the school holidays?

퍼디: 아니요, 저는 고향에 안 가요. 유럽에 가요.
aniyo, jeoneun gohyange an gayo. yureobe gayo
No, I don't go to my hometown. I go to Europe.

- -

수업이 끝나다
집에 가다 X
도서관에 가다 ✓

가: 수업이 끝나면 집에 가요?

나: 아니요, _____ .
_____ .

- -

아침에 일어나다
신문을 읽다 X
커피를 마시다 ✓

가: _____ ?
_____ .

나: _____ .

- -

시간이 있다
영화를 보다 X
경복궁에 가다 ✓

가: _____ ?
_____ .

나: _____ .

- -

수업이 끝나다
숙제하다 X
명동에 가다 ✓

가: _____ ?

나: _____ .
_____ .

- -

ONLINE
AUDIO
02:16

Listening Practice 듣기 연습

01 방학 계획 묻기
banghak gyehoek mutgi

Asking about school holidays

Listen carefully to the audio, write the number of each activity mentioned, then make sentences, following the example below. You can find the answers on page 261.

왕샤위: 스테파니 씨, 방학을 하면 뭐 해요?
seutepani ssi, banghageul hamyeon mwo haeyo
Stephanie, what do you do in the school holidays?

스테파니: 저는 방학을 하면 친구와 같이 스키를 타고 사진을 찍어요.
**jeoneun banghageul hamyeon chinguwa gachi seukireul tago
sajineul jjigeoyo**
I ski with my friends and take photos in the school holidays.

1. (.   ) _____ 고 _____ .

2. (.   ) _____ 고 _____ .

3. (.   ) _____ 고 _____ .

4. (.   ) _____ 고 _____ .

ONLINE
AUDIO
04:38

Talking with Lee Joon-gi 이준기와 이야기하기

의향 묻고 대답하기 Talking about plans

Try having a conversation with Lee Joon-gi as you listen to the audio. You can find a translation of this conversation on page 265. Write your own conversation in the gray box below, following this model.

이준기	마스미 씨, 이번 주말에 경복궁에 갈까요? **maseumi ssi, ibeon jumare gyeongbokgunge galkkayo**
마스미	네, 좋아요. **ne, joayo**
이준기	버스를 탈까요? 지하철을 탈까요? **beoseureul talkkayo. jihacheoreul talkkayo**
마스미	지하철을 탑시다. 이준기 씨, 오늘 점심에 뭘 먹을까요? **jihacheoreul tapsida.** **ijungi ssi, oneul jeomsime** **mwol meogeulkkayo**
이준기	비빔밥을 먹읍시다. **bibimbabeul meogeupsida**
마스미	네, 좋아요. **ne, joayo**

가 _____ 씨, 이번 주말에 _____?

나 네, 좋아요.

가 _____? _____?

나 _____ 을/를 _____.

_____ 씨, 오늘 _____.

가 _____ 을/를 _____.

나 네, 좋아요.

Particles 조사

Let's review particles.

Particle	When to use		Meaning
N은/는 N eun/neun	When the last syllable has a final consonant	은	Marks the subject of the sentence.
	When the last syllable has no final consonant	는	
N이/가 N i/ga	When the last syllable has a final consonant	이	Mainly used in questions and descriptions using adjectives, and marks the subject of the sentence.
	When the last syllable has no final consonant	가	
N을/를 N eul/reul	When the last syllable has a final consonant	을	Marks the object of the sentence.
	When the last syllable has no final consonant	를	
N와/과 N wa/gwa	When the last syllable has a final consonant	과	Used to join two nouns, like "and" in English
	When the last syllable has no final consonant	와	
N하고 N hago	When the last syllable has a final consonant	하고	Used to join more than two nouns and is more informal than 와 or 과.
	When the last syllable has no final consonant		
N도 N do	When the last syllable has a final consonant	도	Signifies that the following sentence has the same content as the previous one.
	When the last syllable has no final consonant		

Particle	When to use		Meaning
N에 **N e**	*When the last syllable has a final consonant*	에	1) Place/Destination as in N에 가다 or N에 오다. To mark the place that the subject of the verb moves to use N에.
	When the last syllable has no final consonant		2) Per/For as in N□ 얼마예요? The particle 에 is used to mean "per" or "for" with numbers and counting units. 3) Time as in 1시에 만나요. N에 marks the time of the action.
N부터 **N buteo**	*When the last syllable has a final consonant*	부터	Indicates the beginning and ending of a time much like from __ until __ in English.
	When the last syllable has no final consonant		
N까지 **N kkaji**	*When the last syllable has a final consonant*	까지	N부터 N까지 marks the time span from A to B. N에서 N까지 marks the space between A and B.
	When the last syllable has no final consonant		
N에서 **N eseo**	*When the last syllable has a final consonant*	에서	1) N에서 V-아/어요 indicates the physical range of locations. 2) N에서 N까지 expresses the distance from something to something.
	When the last syllable has no final consonant		

Namdaemun Market

Korea's Largest Traditional Market

Namdaemun Market is Korea's largest and most comprehensive traditional market place. All sorts of clothes, food, electronics and local produce are displayed under colorful awnings. There are over 5,400 shops in here. Make sure you try a tteokbokki rice cake dipped in spicy sauce. The fiery taste is surprisingly addictive.

I'm Drinking a Glass of Wine Now

지금 와인을 마시고 있어요

14
현재 진행과
습관 말하기
**Present
Continuous and
Present Simple
Tenses**

Lesson Goals

Situation
Talking about the
present
Vocabulary
Verbs: daily habits
Grammar
Polite verb forms
—ing form

▼

Wine has been catching on
in Korea in recent years. A
wide variety of wines are
imported from Europe and
South America. An increasing
number of cultural centers
have been offering courses
on wine, reflecting its
growning popularity.

ONLINE
AUDIO
00:10

이준기
ijungi
안녕하세요? 다이애나 씨.
annyeonghaseyo daiaena ssi
Hello, Diana.

다이애나
daiaena
안녕하세요? 이준기 씨 오랜만이에요.
annyeonghaseyo ijungi ssi oraenmanieyo
Hello, Joon-gi. Long time no see.

이준기
ijungi
다이애나 씨, 지금 뭘 마시고 있어요?
daiaena ssi, jigeum mwol masigo isseoyo
Diana, what are you drinking now?

다이애나
daiaena
저는 지금 와인을 마시고 있어요.
jeoneun jigeum waineul masigo isseoyo
I'm drinking a glass of wine.

이준기
ijungi
다이애나 씨는 요즘 뭐 하세요?
daiaena ssineun yojeum mwo haseyo
Diana, what are you doing these days?

다이애나
daiaena
저는 요즘 기타를 배우고 있어요.
jeoneun yojeum gitareul baeugo isseoyo
I'm learning to play the guitar.

이준기
ijungi
다이애나 씨, 와인 다 마셨어요?
daiaena ssi, wain da masyeosseoyo
Diana, is your glass empty?

다이애나
daiaena
아니요, 아직 마시고 있어요.
aniyo, ajik masigo isseoyo
No, it's still full.

Vocabulary and Expressions 어휘와 표현

01 동사 11, 습관
dongsa sibil, seupgwan   **Verbs 11 Daily habits**

드시다 〔드시다〕 **deusida** *to eat (polite)*

주무시다 〔주무시다〕 **jumusida** *to sleep (polite)*

(사진을) 찍다 〔(사지늘)찍다〕 **(sajineul) jjikda** *to take (a picture)*

(전화를) 하다 〔(전:화를)하다〕 **(jeonhwareul) hada** *to make (a phone call)*

(담배를) 피우다 〔(담:배를)피우다〕 **(dambaereul) piuda** *to smoke*

걷다 〔걷:따〕 **geotda** *to walk*

묻다 〔묻:따〕 **mutda** *to ask*

계시다/있다 〔계:시다, 게:시다/읻따〕 **gyesida/itda** *to be/exist (polite)*

기다리다 〔기다리다〕 **gidarida** *to wait*

02 기타 gita   **Other useful vocabulary**

아직 〔아직〕 **ajik** *yet*

오랜만이에요 〔오랜마니에요〕 **oraenmanieyo**
  it's been a long time/long time no see

와인 〔와인〕 **wain** *wine*

기타 〔기타〕 **gita** *guitar*

드라마 〔드라마〕 **deurama** *drama*

거문고 〔거문고〕 **geomungo** *geomungo (stringed instrument)*

발음규칙 Pronunciation Rules

Liaison (Linking) 연음 법칙
When a syllable ends with a final consonant and is followed by a vowel,
then the final unit of sound is pronounced as the first unit of sound of
the following syllable.

$$있어요 \Rightarrow 〔이써요〕$$

오랜만이에요 오랜마니에요 **oraenmanieyo**
  long time no see
마셨어요 마셔써요 **masyeosseoyo** *drank*

와인을 와이늘 **waineul** *wine*
했어요 해써요 **haesseoyo** *did*

Grammar 문법

01 V–(으)세요 V–(eu)seyo **Honorific form of V아/어요**

어머니는 주말에 백화점에 가세요. **eomeonineun jumare baekwajeome gaseyo**
My mother goes to the department store at the weekend.

아버지는 지금 텔레비전을 보세요. **abeojineun jigeum tellebijeoneul boseyo**
My father is watching television now.

어머니는 아버지에게 운전을 배우세요. **eomeonineun abeojiege unjeoneul baeuseyo**
My mother learns how to drive from my father.

아버지는 신문을 읽으세요. **abeojineun sinmuneul ilgeuseyo**
My father reads a newspaper.

어머니는 김치를 만드세요. **eomeonineun gimchireul mandeuseyo**
My mother makes kimchi.

explanation | Converting to the V–(으)세요 form |

This suffix is used to describe an action by another person who is usually senior to the speaker. Remove –다 from the base form and add –세요 when the last syllable of the stem does not have a final consonant, or –으세요 otherwise.

When the last syllable of the stem does NOT have a final consonant:
요리하다 → 요리하다 → 요리하+세요 → 요리하세요

When the last syllable of the stem has a final consonant:
읽다 → 읽다 → 읽 + 으세요 → 읽으세요

When the last syllable of the stem has the final consonant ㄹ:
만들다 → 만들다 → 만드 + 세요 → 만드세요

Most verbs follow this pattern, but here are a few examples of irregular verbs.

먹다, 마시다 → 드시다 → 드세요
자다 → 주무시다 → 주무세요
있다 → 계시다 → 계세요

02 V- 고 있다 V-go itda

Be V-ing

커피를 마시다 ⇒ 커피를 마시고 있다. **keopireul masida** ⇒ **keopireul masigo itda**
to drink coffee ⇒ am/is/are drinking coffee.

빵을 먹다 ⇒ 빵을 먹고 있다. **ppangeul meokda** ⇒ **ppangeul meokgo itda**
to eat bread ⇒ am/is/are eating bread.

태권도를 배우다 ⇒ 태권도를 배우고 있다.

taegwondoreul baeuda ⇒ **taegwondoreul baeugo itda**
to learn taekwondo ⇒ am/is/are learning taekwondo.

피아노를 치다 ⇒ 피아노를 치고 있다. **pianoreul chida** ⇒ **pianoreul chigo itda**
to play piano ⇒ am/is/are playing piano.

explanation | Converting to the V-고 있다 form |

Remove the –다 suffix from the base form and attach –고 있다 in its place.

explanation | 지금과 요즘 now and these days |

In the second example sentence on the previous page, you can see an example of 지금, which is attached to verb stems to signify that the activity is going on at the moment of speaking.

예) ○○○ 씨, 지금 뭐 해요?
    저는 지금 커피를 마시고 있어요.

요즘 is attached to verb stems as well but signifies that the activity has been going on recently. This is similar to the English phrase "these days."

예) ○○○ 씨, 요즘 뭐 해요?
    저는 요즘 기타를 배우고 있어요.

03 다 V da V

Finished V-ing

다 V is used to show that the subject of the verb has finished doing the activity.

커피를 마시다 ⇒ 커피를 다 마셨어요. **keopireul masida ⇒ keopireul da masyeosseoyo**
to drink coffee ⇒ I finished drinking coffee.

책을 읽다 ⇒ 책을 다 읽었어요. **chaegeul ikda ⇒ chaegeul da ilgeosseoyo**
to read a book ⇒ I finished reading the book.

숙제를 하다 ⇒ 숙제를 다 했어요. **sukjereul hada ⇒ sukjereul da haesseoyo**
to do one's homework ⇒ I finished doing my homework.

| **Exercise** | Fill in the blanks. You can find the answers on page 274.

Base Form	-(으)세요 –(eu)seyo *V present tense (honorific)*	**Base Form**	V-고 있어요 V–go isseoyo *am/is/are V-ing*
영화를 보다 **yeonghwareul boda** *to watch a movie*	영화를 보세요	커피를 마시다 **keopireul masida** *to drink coffee*	커피를 마시고 있어요
편지를 쓰다 **pyeonjireul sseuda** *to write a letter*		음악을 듣다 **eumageul deutda** *to listen to music*	
숙제하다 **sukjehada** *to do one's homework*	숙제하세요	요리하다 **yorihada** *to cook*	
책을 읽다 **chaegeul ikda** *to read a book*	책을 읽으세요	와인을 마시다 **waineul masida** *to drink wine*	
사진을 찍다 **sajineul jjikda** *to take a photo*		춤을 추다 **chumeul chuda** *to dance*	
자다/주무시다 **jada/jumusida** *to sleep*	주무세요	기타를 배우다 **gitareul baeuda** *to learn guitar*	
마시다/드시다 **masida/deusida** *to eat*	드세요	그림을 그리다 **geurimeul geurida** *to draw a picture*	

Conversation Practice 회화 연습

| 01 | 어머니도 백화점에 가세요 .
eomeonido baekwajeome gaseyo | My mother also goes to the
department store. |

Use the example sentences to guide you as you practice. Find model sentences on page 274.

저
어머니
백화점에
가다

다이애나: 저는 백화점에 가요.
jeoneun baekwajeome gayo
I go to the department store.

어머니도 백화점에 가세요.
eomeonido baekwajeome gaseyo
My mother also goes to the department store.

저
아버지
점심을 먹다

가: 저는 점심을 먹어요.

아버지도 _____ .

저
어머니
기타를
배우다

가: _____

_____ .

동생
아버지
방에 있다

가: _____

_____ .

저
책을 읽다
어머니
신문을 읽다

가: _____

_____ .

02 영화를 보세요 ?   **yeonghwareul boseyo**   **Do you watch movies?**

Use the example sentences to guide you as you practice. Find model sentences on page 274.

영화를
보다 X

책을 읽다 ✓

이준기: 다이애나 씨, 영화를 보세요?
daiaena ssi, yeonghwareul boseyo
Diana, do you watch movies?

다이애나: 아니요, 저는 영화를 안 봐요.
aniyo, jeoneun yeonghwareul an bwayo
No, I don't watch movies.

책을 읽어요. **chaegeul ilgeoyo** *I read books.*

오늘,
삼겹살을
먹다 ✓

가: 오늘 삼겹살을 드세요?

나: 네, _____ 을 먹어요.

저녁,
텔레비전을
보다 ✓

가: _____ ?

나: _____ .

주말,
설악산에
가다 ✓

가: _____ ?

나: _____ .

등산을
하다 X
수영을
하다 ✓

가: _____ ?

나: _____ .

_____ .

03 지금 커피를 마시고 있어요.
jigeum keopireul masigo isseoyo

I'm drinking coffee now.

Use the example sentences to guide you as you practice. Find model sentences on page 274.

커피를
마시다

이준기: 마스미 씨, 지금 뭘 하고 있어요?
masumi ssi, jigeum mwol hago isseoyo
Masumi, what are you doing now?

다이애나: 저는 지금 커피를 마시고 있어요.
jeoneun jigeum keopireul masigo isseoyo
I'm drinking coffee now.

신문을
읽다

가: 지금 뭘 하고 있어요?

나: 저는 지금 _____ 고 있어요.

버스를
기다리다

가: _____?

나: _____.

골프를
치다

가: _____?

나: _____.

영화를
보다

가: _____?

나: _____.

04 영화를 다 봤어요 ?
yeonghwareul da bwasseoyo

Did you finish watching the movie?

Use the example sentences to guide you as you practice. Find model sentences on page 274.

영화를
보다 X

이준기: 다이애나 씨, 영화를 다 봤어요?
daiaena ssi, yeonghwareul da bwasseoyo
Diana, did you finish watching the movie?

다이애나: 아니요, 아직 보고 있어요.
aniyo, ajik bogo isseoyo *No, I'm still watching it.*

그림을
그리다 X

가: 그림을 다 그렸어요?

나: 아니요, 아직 _____ .

커피를
마시다 X

가: _____ ?

나: _____ .

밥을
먹다 X

가: _____ ?

나: _____ .

숙제하다 X

가: _____ ?

나: _____ .

05 기타를 배우고 있어요.   **gitareul baeugo isseoyo**   **I'm learning the guitar.**

Use the example sentences to guide you as you practice. Find model sentences on page 274.

기타를
배우다

이준기: 다이애나 씨, 요즘 뭐 해요?
daiaena ssi, yojeum mwo haeyo
Diana, what are you doing these days?

다이애나: 저는 요즘 기타를 배우고 있어요.
jeoneun yojeum gitareul baeugo isseoyo
I'm learning the guitar these days.

중국어를
배우다

가: 요즘 뭐 해요?

나: 저는 요즘 _____ 있어요.

태권도를
배우다

가: _____ ?

나: _____ .

피아노를
가르치다

가: _____ ?

나: _____ .

영어를
가르치다

가: _____ ?

나: _____ .

ONLINE
AUDIO
02:34

Listening Practice 1　듣기 연습 1

01 행동 1　hwaldong 1　　　　　　　　　　**Activities1**

Look at the picture, and complete the sentences describing what each person is doing. Find model sentences on page 261.

마스미 씨는 리리 씨하고 같이 이야기하고 있어요.

1. 퍼디 씨는 ＿＿＿＿＿＿＿＿＿＿＿＿＿＿＿＿＿＿＿＿＿ .

2. 이준기 씨는 ＿＿＿＿＿＿＿＿＿＿＿＿＿＿＿＿＿＿＿＿ .

3. 왕샤위 씨는 ＿＿＿＿＿＿＿＿＿＿＿＿＿＿＿＿＿＿＿＿ .

4. 최지영 씨는 ＿＿＿＿＿＿＿＿＿＿＿＿＿＿＿＿＿＿＿＿ .

5. 다이애나 씨하고 벤슨 씨는 ＿＿＿＿＿＿＿＿＿＿＿＿＿ .

6. 로베르토 씨는 ＿＿＿＿＿＿＿＿＿＿＿＿＿＿＿＿＿＿＿ .

7. 비비엔 씨는 ＿＿＿＿＿＿＿＿＿＿＿＿＿＿＿＿＿＿＿＿ .

ONLINE
AUDIO
04:43

Listening Practice 2 듣기 연습 2

02 행동 2 hwaldong 2   **Activities 2**

Look at the picture, and complete the sentences describing what each person is doing. Find model sentences on page 261.

여기는 우리 하숙집이에요. 이 사람들은 모두 제 친구들이에요.

1. 리리 씨는 지금 _____ .

2. 마스미 씨는 지금 _____ .

3. 퍼디 씨는 지금 _____ .

4. 로이 씨는 지금 _____ .

5. 다이애나 씨는 지금 _____ .

6. 비비엔 씨는 지금 _____ .

7. 벤슨 씨는 지금 _____ .

ONLINE
AUDIO
06:50

Talking with Lee Joon-gi 이준기와 이야기하기

생활 습관 묻기 Asking questions about lifestyle

Try having a conversation with Lee Joon-gi as you listen to the audio. You can find a translation of this conversation on page 265. Write your own conversation in the box below, following this model.

이준기　다이애나 씨, 아침에 운동하세요?
daiaena ssi, achime undonghaseyo

다이애나　네, 저는 아침에 운동해요.
ne, jeoneun achime undonghaeyo

이준기　다이애나 씨, 담배를 피우세요?
daiaena ssi, dambaereul piuseyo

다이애나　아니요, 저는 담배를 안 피워요.
aniyo, jeoneun dambaereul an piwoyo

이준기　그럼, 요즘 한국 드라마는 보세요?
**geureom, yojeum hanguk
deuramaneun boseyo**

다이애나　네, 요즘 한국 드라마를 보고
있어요.
ne, yojeum hanguk deuramareul bogo isseoyo

▼
그럼 is a shortened form of 그러면. In the spoken Korean language, 그럼 is preferred.

가　＿＿＿＿＿ 씨,＿＿＿＿＿＿＿?

나　네, ＿＿＿＿＿＿＿＿＿.

가　＿＿＿＿＿ 씨,＿＿＿＿＿＿＿?

나　아니요, ＿＿＿＿＿＿＿＿.

가　그럼, ＿＿＿＿＿＿＿＿?

나　네, ＿＿＿＿＿＿＿＿＿.

Places 장소

도서관
doseogwan
library

학교
hakgyo
school

교회
gyohoe
church

식당
sikdang
restaurant

명동
myeongdong
Myeongdong

인사동
insadong
Insadong

이태원
itaewon
Itaewon

대학로
daehangno
Daehangno

영화관
yeonghwagwan
movie theater

은행
eunhaeng
bank

병원
byeongwon
hospital

커피숍
keopisyop
coffee shop

롯데월드
rotdewoldeu
Lotte World

백화점
baekwajeom
department store

광화문
gwanghwamun
Gwanghwamun

제주도
jejudo
Jeju Island

산
san
mountain

바다
bada
sea

온천
oncheon
spa

공원
gongwon
park

남대문 시장
namdaemun sijang
Namdaemun Market

대학교
daehakgyo
university/college

세탁소
setakso
laundromat

슈퍼마켓
syupeomaket
supermarket

신촌
sinchon
Sinchon

우체국
ucheguk
post office

일본
ilbon
Japan

민속촌
minsokchon
folk village

지하철
jihacheol
subway

출입국관리소
churipgukgwalliso
Immigration Office

편의점
pyeonuijeom
convenience store

호주
hoju
Australia

How Can I Get to Gyeongbokgung?

경복궁까지 어떻게 가요?

Lesson Goals

Situation
Using public
transportation
Vocabulary
Public transportation
Places
Traffic
Grammar
Verbs: command
form

ONLINE
AUDIO
00:10

최지영 choejiyeong	스테파니 씨, 이번 주말에 시간이 있으세요? **seutepani ssi, ibeon jumare sigani isseuseyo** *Stephanie, are you free this weekend?*	

스테파니
seutepani
네, 있어요. 왜요? **ne, isseoyo. waeyo**
Yes, I am. Why?

최지영
choejiyeong
그럼, 이번 주말에 같이 경복궁에 갈까요?
**geureom, ibeon jumare gachi gyeongbokgunge
galkkayo**
*Would you like go to Gyeongbokgung with me
this weekend?*

스테파니
seutepani
네, 좋아요. **ne, joayo**
Okay, that sounds good.

그런데 학교에서 경복궁까지 어떻게 가요?
**geureonde hakgyoeseo gyeongbokgungkkaji
eotteoke gayo**
By the way, how can I get to Gyeongbokgung from school?

최지영
choejiyeong
한남역에서 중앙선을 타세요.
hannamyeogeseo jungangseoneul taseyo
Take the Jungang line at Hannam subway station.

그리고 옥수역에서 3호선으로 갈아타세요.
geurigo oksuyeogeseo samhoseoneuro garataseyo
Then, take line Number 3 at Oksu Station.

그리고 경복궁역에서 내리세요.
geurigo gyeongbokgungeseo naeriseyo
And get off at Gyeongbokgung Station.

스테파니
seutepani
네, 알겠습니다. **ne, algetseumnida**
Okay. I get it.

Korea has a very well-
developed subway system.
Seoul has nine different
subway lines that connect
most parts of the city,
and there are a few more
lines that are connected to
suburban areas such as
Bundang and Incheon. Each
subway line has a different
color and each station has
an identification number so
that even a foreigner visiting
Seoul for the first time can
use it easily.

ONLINE
AUDIO
01:41

Vocabulary and Expressions 어휘와 표현

01 교통수단 gyotong sudan   Transportation

비행기 〔비행기〕 **bihaenggi** *airplane*

기차 〔기차〕 **gicha** *train*

지하철 〔지하철〕 **jihacheol**
  subway

KTX〔케이티엑스〕 **KTX keitiekseu**
  Korea Train Express

자전거 〔자전거〕 **jajeongeo** *bicycle*

시내버스 〔시:내버스〕 **sinaebeoseu** *local bus*
  (1, 2, 3, 4, 5, 6, 7, 8, 9)호선
  〔일호선／이:호선／삼호선／사:호선／오:호선／육호선／칠호선／팔호선／구호선〕
  hoseon *line no.(1, 2, 3, 4, 5, 6, 7, 8, 9)*
  1 호선 〔일호선〕 **ilhoseon** *line 1*

택시 〔택씨〕 **taeksi** *taxi*

배 〔배〕 **bae** *ship/boat*

고속버스 〔고속뻐스〕 **gosokbeoseu**
  express bus

오토바이 〔오토바이〕 **otobai**
  motorcycle

02 장소 jangso   Places

서울역 〔서울력〕 **seouryeok** *Seoul Station*

박물관 〔방물관〕 **bangmulgwan** *museum*

사당역 〔사당녁〕 **sadangyeok**
  Sadang Station

복도 〔복또〕 **bokdo** *corridor*

잔디밭 〔잔디받〕 **jandibat** *lawn*

사무실 〔사:무실〕 **samusil**
  office

03 교통 표지 gyotong pyoji   Traffic

신호등 〔신호등〕 **sinhodeung** *traffic signal*

횡단보도 〔횡단보도〕 **hoengdanbodo** *crosswalk*

버스 정류장 〔버스정뉴장〕 **beoseu jeongnyujang** *bus station*

04 동사 12 교통수단 dongsa sibi gyotongsudan — Verbs 12 Transportation

타다 〔타다〕 **tada** *to get on (a vehicle)*

갈아타다 〔가라타다〕 **garatada** *to transit*

내리다 〔내리다〕 **naerida** *get off/out of vehicle*

들어가다 〔드러가다〕 **deureogada** *to enter*

들어오다 〔드러오다〕 **deureooda** *to come in*

05 기타 gita — Other useful vocabulary

떠들다 〔떠:들다〕 **tteodeulda** *to talk loudly*

세탁하다 〔세:타카다〕 **setakada** *to wash clothes*

어떻게 가요? 〔어떠케가요〕 **eotteoke gayo** *how can I get to?*

늦다 〔늗따〕 **neutda** *late*

뛰다 〔뛰다〕 **ttwida** *to jump/run*

발 음 규 칙 Pronunciation Rules

Aspiration (Pronouncing consonants with a burst of air) 격음화

Before or after ㅎ, the consonants ㄱ, ㄷ, ㅂ and ㅈ combine with the ㅎ and become the aspirated consonants ㅋ, ㅌ, ㅍ and ㅊ.

$$어떻게 \Rightarrow 〔어떠케〕$$
$$ㅎ + ㄱ \Rightarrow ㅋ$$

하얗고 하:야코 **hayako** *white and*

파랗게 파:라케 **parake** *blue*

Grammar 문법

01 V-(으)세요 V-(eu)seyo

V, please

최지영 씨, 일어나세요. **choejiyeong ssi, ireonaseyo** *Jiyoung, get up, please.*

스테파니 씨, 두 번 읽으세요. **seutepani ssi, du beon ilgeuseyo**
Stephanie, read it twice, please.

이준기 씨, 케이크를 만드세요. **ijungi ssi, keikeureul mandeuseyo**
Joon-gi, please make a cake.

*먹다, 마시다 ⇒ 드시다　　*자다 ⇒ 주무시다

explanation | The command form |

This has the same conversion rule as –(으)세요 that is covered in Lesson 14, page 231. This is a suffix used for the polite command form.

When the last syllable of the stem does NOT have a final consonant:
가다 → 가다 + 세요 → 가세요

When the last syllable of the stem has a final consonant:
읽다 → 읽다 + 으세요 → 읽으세요

When the last syllable of the stem has the final consonant ㄹ:
만들다 → 만들다 + 세요 → 만드세요

| **Exercise** | Fill in the blanks. You can find the answers on page 275.

Base Form	-(으)세요 **-(eu)seyo** *V, please*		-(으)세요 **-(eu)seyo** *V, please*
가다 **gada** *to go*	가세요	영화를 보다 **yeonghwareul boda** *to watch a movie*	
오다 **oda** *to come*		타다 **tada** *to get on*	

02 V – 지 마세요 V–ji maseyo

Simply attach the suffix – 지 마세요. to the stem. This form is used to ask someone not to do something in a polite manner.

교실에서 담배를 피우지 마세요. **gyosireseo dambaereul piuji maseyo**
Don't smoke in the classroom, please.

이 의자에 앉지 마세요. **i uijae anji maseyo** *Don't sit on this chair, please.*

학생에게 술을 팔지 마세요. **haksaengege sureul palji maseyo**
Don't sell alcohol to students, please.

explanation | The negative command form |

The suffix – 지 마세요 is attached to the stem regardless of whether there is a final consonant on the last syllable of the stem or not.

When the last syllable of the stem does NOT have a final consonant:
보다→보다 + 지 마세요 → 보지 마세요

When the last syllable of the stem has a final consonant:
읽다→읽다 + 지 마세요 → 읽지 마세요

| **Exercise** | Fill in the blanks. You can find the answers on page 275.

Base Form	-지 마세요 –ji maseyo *Don't V, please*	Base Form	-지 마세요 –ji maseyo *Don't V, please*
가다 **gada** *to go*	가지 마세요	김치를 먹다 **gimchireul meokda** *to eat kimchi*	
담배를 피우다 **dambaereul piuda** *to smoke*		기다리다 **gidarida** *to wait*	

03 N(으)로 갈아타다 N(eu)ro garatada Transfer to N

When the last syllable of a noun does not have a final consonant or has the consonant ㄹ, then the suffix 로 is attached to the stem. But if it has a final consonant, then －으로 is attached. For example, you can say 3호선으로 and 버스로 and 지하철로.

3호선으로 갈아타세요. **samhoseoneuro garataseyo** *Transfer to line 3, please.*

402번 버스로 갈아타세요. **sabaegibeon beoseuro garataseyo**
Transfer to the 402 bus, please.

5호선 지하철로 갈아타세요. **ohoseon jihacheollo garataseyo**
Transfer to subway line 5, please.

시청에서 1호선으로 갈아타세요. **sicheongeseo ilhoseoneuro garataseyo**
Transfer to line 1 at City Hall Station, please.

| **Exercise** | Fill in the blanks. You can find the answers on page 275.

Base Form	N(으)로 갈아타다 **N(eu)ro garatada** *Transfer to N*
지하철 3호선 **jihacheol samhoseon** *subway line 3*	지하철 3호선으로 갈아타다 **jihacheol samhoseoneuro garatada** *transfer to subway line 3*
6000번 버스 **yukcheonbeon beoseu** *6000 bus*	
시청역에서 버스로 **sicheongyeogeseo beoseuro** *to a bus at City Hall Station*	
신촌에서 버스로 **sinchoneseo beoseuro** *to a bus at Sinchon*	
강남역에서 지하철로 **gangnamyeogeseo jihacheollo** *to the subway at Gangnam Station*	

Conversation Practice 회화 연습

01 경복궁에 어떻게 가요?
gyeongbokgunge eotteoke gayo

How can I get to Gyeongbokgung?

Use the example sentences to guide you as you practice. Find model sentences on page 275.

경복궁
학교 앞
버스 정류장
402번 버스
타다

가: 실례지만, 경복궁에 어떻게 가요?
sillyejiman, gyeongbokgunge eotteoke gayo
Excuse me, but how do I get to Gyeongbokgung?

나: 학교 앞 버스 정류장에서 402 번버스를 타세요.
hakgyo ap beoseu jeongnyujangeseo sabaegibeon beoseureul taseyo
Please take the 402 bus at the bus stop in front of the school.

가: 네, 알겠습니다. 감사합니다.
ne, algetseumnida *Okay. I get it.*
감사합니다. **gamsahamnida** *Thank you.*

신촌
시청역
2호선
갈아타다

가: 실례지만, 신촌에 어떻게 가요?
나: _____ .
가: 네, 알겠습니다. 감사합니다.

인사동
3호선 안국역
내리다

가: _____ ?
나: _____ .
가: _____ .

인천공항
한국대학교 앞
공항버스
타다

가: _____ ?
나: _____ .
가: _____ .

이태원
3호선 약수역
6호선
갈아타다

가: _____ ?
나: _____ .
가: _____ .

02 1호선을 타세요. **ilhoseoneul taseyo** **Take line 1**

Use the example sentences to guide you as you practice. Find model sentences on page 275.

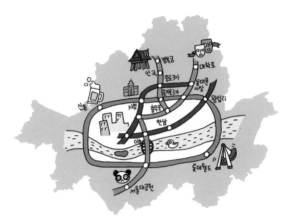

경복궁

시청 1호선
종로 3가 3
호선
경복궁

스테파니: 실례합니다. 시청역에서 경복궁까지 어떻게 가요?
sillyehamnida. sicheongyeogeseo gyeongbokgungkkaji eotteoke gayo *Excuse me. How do I get to Gyeongbokgung from City Hall Station?*

최지영: 시청역에서 1호선을 타세요. 그리고 종로 3가역에서 3호선으로 갈아타세요. 그리고 경복궁에서 내리세요.
sicheongyeogeseo ilhoseoneul taseyo. geurigo jongno samgayeogeseo samhoseoneuro garataseyo. geurigo gyeongbokgungeseo naeriseyo
Take line 1 at City Hall Station. Then, transfer to line 3 at Jongno 3-ga Station. Then, get off at Gyeongbokgung.

스테파니: 고맙습니다. **gomapseumnida** *Thank you.*

롯데월드

경복궁 3호선
을지로 3가
2호선
롯데월드

가: _____ ?
나: _____ .
_____ .
가: _____ .

안 국

시울대공원
4호선
충무로 3호선
안국

가: _____ ?
나: _____ .
_____ .
가: _____ .

03 교실에서 담배를 피우지 마세요 .
gyosireseo dambaereul piuji maseyo **Don't smoke in the classroom.**

Use the example sentences to guide you as you practice. Find model sentences on page 275.

 교실
담배를
피우다

가: 어! 로이 씨, 교실에서 담배를 피우지 마세요.
eo! roi ssi, gyosireseo dambaereul piuji maseyo
Oh! Roy, don't smoke in the classroom, please.

나: 아이고, 죄송합니다.
aigo, joesonghamnida
Oh, I'm sorry.

  교실
영어를 하다

가: 어! _____ .
나: 아이고, 죄송합니다.

  영화관
전화를 하다

가: _____ .
나: _____ .

  박물관
사진을 찍다

가: _____ .
나: _____ .

 공원
잔디밭에
들어가다

가: _____ .
나: _____ .

ONLINE
AUDIO
03:48

Listening Practice 듣기 연습

01 금지 표현하기   **geumji pyohyeonhagi**   **Negative command form**

Listen carefully to the audio, write the number of each activity mentioned, then make sentences, following the example below. You can find the answers on page 261.

최지영: 앗! 로이 씨, 교실에서 담배를 피우지 마세요.
　　　　at! roi ssi, gyosireseo dambaereul piuji maseyo
　　　　Oh my! Roy, don't smoke in the classroom, please.

로이: 아이고, 죄송합니다.
　　　aigo, joesonghamnida *Oh, I'm sorry.*

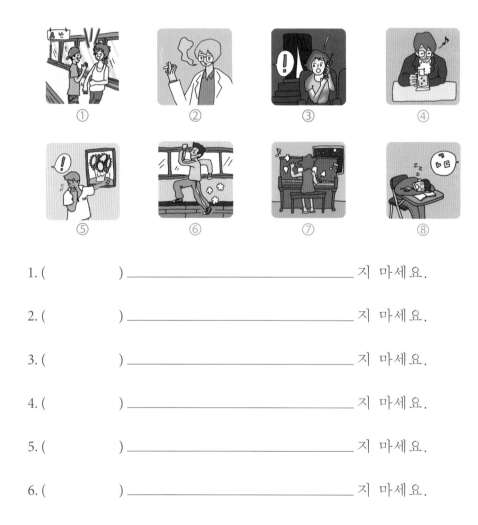

1. (　　　　　) ＿＿＿＿＿＿＿＿＿＿＿＿＿＿＿＿지 마세요.

2. (　　　　　) ＿＿＿＿＿＿＿＿＿＿＿＿＿＿＿＿지 마세요.

3. (　　　　　) ＿＿＿＿＿＿＿＿＿＿＿＿＿＿＿＿지 마세요.

4. (　　　　　) ＿＿＿＿＿＿＿＿＿＿＿＿＿＿＿＿지 마세요.

5. (　　　　　) ＿＿＿＿＿＿＿＿＿＿＿＿＿＿＿＿지 마세요.

6. (　　　　　) ＿＿＿＿＿＿＿＿＿＿＿＿＿＿＿＿지 마세요.

ONLINE
AUDIO
06:49

Talking with Lee Joon-gi 이준기와 이야기하기

스테파니 씨 하숙집의 규칙 The rules at Stephanie's boarding house

Read the rules at the boarding house where Stephanie stays, then make a list of rules that you could apply at the place where you live.

1. 아침 7시에 일어나세요.
2. 아침에 일어나면 청소하세요.
3. 밤에는 큰 소리로 떠들지 마세요.
4. 방에서 술을 마시지 마세요.
5. 담배는 밖에서 피우세요.
6. 식사 시간에 늦지 마세요.
7. 밤에 세탁하지 마세요.
8. 밤 12시까지 들어오세요.

| 우리 집의 규칙 | House Rules

1. _____

2. _____

3. _____

4. _____

5. _____

6. _____

7. _____

8. _____

Commands 금지와 명령의 표현

실내에서 담배를 피우지 마세요
sillaeeseo dambaereul piuji maseyo

No smoking indoors.

잔디밭에 들어가지 마세요
jandibate deureogaji maseyo

Keep off the grass.

작품에 손대지 마세요
jakpume sondaeji maseyo

Please don't touch the artwork.

이곳에 앉지 마세요
igose anji maseyo

Please don't sit here.

이곳에 주차하지 마세요
igose juchahaji maseyo

No parking.

본체 위에 물건을 올려놓지 마세요
bonche wie mulgeoneul ollyeonochi maseyo

Don't put objects on the computer.

폰 전원을 꺼 주세요
pon jeonwoneul kkeo juseyo

Please turn off your phone.

휴지는 휴지통에 버려 주세요
hyujineun hyujitonge beoryeo juseyo

Please throw trash in the garbage can.

한 줄로 서 주세요
han jullo seo juseyo

Please form a single line.

노약자에게 자리를 양보해 주세요
noyakjaege jarireul yangbohae juseyo

Please yield this seat for senior citizens.

APPENDIX

Translation of Dialogues
Answer Keys for Listening Practice
Translation of Talking with Lee Joon-gi
Answers to the Exercises
Index

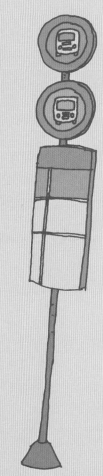

Answer Key for Listening Practice

Lesson 4: online audio file 03:53

01 날짜 받아쓰기 1

1. 가 : 오늘은 며칠이에요?
   나 : 오늘은 3월 10일(삼월 십일)이에요.
2. 가 : 오늘은 며칠이에요?
   나 : 오늘은 6월 6일(유월 육일)이에요.
3. 가 : 오늘은 며칠이에요?
   나 : 오늘은 11월 30일(십일월 삼십일)이에요.

02 날짜 받아쓰기 2

1. 가 : 로이 씨의, 생일이 언제예요?
   나 : 제 생일은 10월 10일(시월 십일)이에요.
2. 가 : 비비엔 씨, 시험이 언제예요?
   나 : 시험은 9월 18일(구월 십팔일)이에요.
3. 가 : 인터뷰가 언제예요?
   나 : 인터뷰는 6월 5일(유월 오일)이에요.

03 요일 받아쓰기

1. 가 : 내일은 무슨 요일이에요?
   나 : 내일은 화요일이에요.
2. 가 : 내일은 무슨 요일이에요?
   나 : 내일은 목요일이에요.
3. 가 : 내일은 무슨 요일이에요?
   나 : 내일은 금요일이에요.

Lesson 5: online audio file 02:45

01 시간 묻고 답하기

1. 가 : 실례지만, 지금 몇 시예요?
   나 : 지금 2시 30분(두 시 삼십 분, 두 시 반)
   이에요.
   가 : 감사합니다.
2. 가 : 실례지만, 지금 몇 시예요?
   나 : 지금 5시 25분(다섯 시 이십오 분)이에요.
   가 : 감사합니다.
3. 가 : 실례지만, 지금 몇 시예요?
   나 : 지금 8시 5분 전(여덟 시 오 분 전)이에요.
   가 : 감사합니다.

4. 가 : 실례지만, 지금 몇 시예요?
   나 : 지금 10시 40분(열 시 사십 분)이에요.
   가 : 감사합니다.

02 영업 시간 묻고 답하기

1. 가 : 실례지만, 은행은 몇 시부터 몇 시까지예요?
   나 : 은행 시간은 9시부터 4시(아홉 시부터 네 시)까지예요.
   가 : 고맙습니다.
2. 가 : 실례지만, 백화점은 몇 시부터 몇 시까지예요?
   나 : 백화점은 10시 30분(열 시 삼십 분, 열 시 반)부터 7시 30분(일곱 시 삼십 분, 일곱 시 반)까지예요.
   가 : 고맙습니다.
3. 가 : 실례지만, 도서관은 몇 시부터 몇 시까지예요?
   나 : 도서관은 새벽 5시부터 밤 12시(다섯 시부터 밤 열두 시)까지예요.
   가 : 고맙습니다.
4. 가 : 실례지만, 편의점은 몇 시부터 몇 시까지예요?
   나 : 편의점은 24시간(이십사 시간)이에요.
   가 : 고맙습니다.

Lesson 6: online audio file 04:15

01 장소 찾기

1. 가 : 실례합니다, 은행이 어디에 있어요?
   나 : 은행은 병원하고 백화점 사이에 있어요.
   가 : 고맙습니다.
2. 가 : 실례합니다, 과일 가게가 어디에 있어요?
   나 : 과일 가게는 공원 앞에 있어요.
   가 : 고맙습니다.
3. 가 : 실례합니다, 식당이 어디에 있어요?
   나 : 식당은 슈퍼마켓 옆에 있어요.
   가 : 고맙습니다.

4. 가 : 실례합니다, 슈퍼마켓이 어디에 있어요?
   나 : 슈퍼마켓은 과일 가게하고 식당 사이에 있어요.
   가 : 고맙습니다.
5. 가 : 실례합니다. 병원이 어디에 있어요?
   나 : 병원은 은행 옆에 있어요.
   가 : 고맙습니다.
6. 가 : 실례합니다, 주유소가 어디에 있어요?
   나 : 주유소는 영화관 옆에 있어요.
   가 : 고맙습니다.

Lesson 8: online audio file 02:57

01 주말 활동 묻기

1. (③, ⑥)
   가 : 로이 씨, 주말에 무엇을 합니까?
   나 : 저는 주말에 쇼핑을 하고 영화를 봅니다.
2. (①, ⑧)
   가 : 퍼디 씨, 주말에 무엇을 합니까?
   나 : 저는 주말에 요리하고 청소합니다.
3. (⑤, ⑦)
   가 : 다이애나 씨, 주말에 무엇을 합니까?
   나 : 저는 주말에 인터넷을 하고 노래를 합니다.
4. (④, ⑥)
   가 : 로베르토 씨, 주말에 무엇을 합니까?
   나 : 저는 주말에 커피를 마시고 영화를 봅니다.

Lesson 10: online audio file 03:18

01 주말 활동 묻기

1. (⑧, ⑤)
   가 : 비비엔 씨, 주말에 뭐 해요?
   나 : 종로에서 영화를 보고 맥주를 마셔요.
2. (②, ③)
   가 : 스테파니 씨, 주말에 뭐 해요?
   나 : 롯데월드에서 바이킹을 타고 롤러코스터를 타요.

3. (④, ⑨)
   가 : 퍼디 씨, 주말에 뭐 해요?
   나 : 대학로에서 연극을 보고 밥을 먹어요.
4. (⑦, ⑥)
   가 : 다이애나 씨, 주말에 뭐 해요?
   나 : 집에서 그림을 그리고 요리를 해요.

Lesson 11: online audio file 02:13

01 하루 일과 묻기

1. (①, ⑧)
   가 : 최지영 씨, 아침에 일어나서 뭐 해요?
   나 : 저는 아침에 일어나서 운동하고 신문을 읽어요.
2. (⑤, ⑥)
   가 : 리리 씨, 저녁에 집에 가서 뭐 해요?
   나 : 저는 집에 가서 요리하고 커피를 마셔요.
3. (③, ④)
   가 : 로베르토 씨, 학교에 가서 뭐 해요?
   나 : 저는 학교에 가서 그림을 그리고 인터넷을 해요.
4. (②, ⑥)
   가 : 마스미 씨, 보통 친구를 만나서 뭐 해요?
   나 : 저는 친구를 만나서 쇼핑하고 커피를 마셔요.

Lesson 12: online audio file 03:23

01 지난 일 묻기

1. (⑥, ⑨)
   가 : 벤슨 씨, 지난 주말에 무엇을 했어요?
   나 : 저는 지난 주말에 친구하고 같이 맥주를 마시고 노래했어요.
2. (②, ⑦)
   가 : 다이애나 씨, 지난 주말에 무엇을 했어요?
   나 : 저는 지난 주말에 등산하고 친구 집에 갔어요.

3. (①, ⑥)

가 : 로이 씨, 지난 주말에 무엇을 했어요?

나 : 저는 지난 주말에 골프를 치고 맥주를 마셨어요.

4. (⑧, ⑤)

가 : 퍼디 씨, 지난 주말에 무엇을 했어요?

나 : 저는 지난 주말에 태권도를 하고 잤어요.

Lesson 13: online audio file 02:16

01 방학 계획 묻기

1. (⑤, ⑧)

가 : 리리 씨, 방학을 하면 뭐 해요?

나 : 저는 방학을 하면 태권도를 하고 피아노를 쳐요.

2. (②, ③)

가 : 퍼디 씨, 방학을 하면 뭐 해요?

나 : 저는 방학을 하면 등산을 하고 골프를 쳐요.

3. (④, ⑨)

가 : 로베르토 씨, 방학을 하면 뭐 해요?

나 : 저는 방학을 하면 친구를 만나고 여행을 해요.

4. (⑥, ⑦)

가 : 마스미 씨, 방학을 하면 뭐 해요?

나 : 저는 방학을 하면 유럽에 가고 사진을 찍어요.

Lesson 14: online audio file 02:34

01 친구들의 행동에 대해 말하기 1

1. 퍼디 씨는 맥주를 마시고 있어요.
2. 이준기 씨는 스테파니 씨의 사진을 찍고 있어요.
3. 왕샤위 씨는 책을 읽고 있어요.
4. 최지영 씨는 잠을 자고 있어요.
5. 다이애나 씨하고 벤슨 씨는 아이스크림을 먹고 있어요.
6. 로베르토 씨는 콜라를 마시고 있어요.
7. 비비엔 씨는 기타를 치고 있어요.

02 친구들의 행동에 대해 말하기 2

1. 리리 씨는 지금 사과를 먹고 있어요.
2. 마스미 씨는 지금 일본 카레를 만들고 있어요.
3. 퍼디 씨는 지금 텔레비전을 보고 있어요.
4. 로이 씨는 지금 음악을 듣고 있어요.
5. 다이애나 씨는 지금 책을 읽고 있어요.
6. 비비엔 씨는 지금 커피를 마시고 있어요.
7. 벤슨 씨는 지금 잠을 자고 있어요.

Lesson 15: online audio file 03:48

01 금지 표현하기

1. (③)

가 : 어! 스테파니 씨, 여기서 전화를 하지 마세요.

나 : 아이고, 죄송합니다.

2. (⑦)

가 : 어! 리리 씨, 밤에 피아노를 치지 마세요.

나 : 아이고, 죄송합니다.

3. (⑤)

가 : 앗! 퍼디 씨, 그림을 만지지 마세요.

나 : 아이고, 죄송합니다.

4. (⑧)

가 : 앗! 왕샤위 씨, 수업 시간에 자지 마세요.

나 : 아이고, 죄송합니다.

5. (④)

가 : 앗! 로베르토 씨, 맥주를 마시지 마세요.

나 : 아이고, 죄송합니다.

6. (⑥)

가 : 앗! 벤슨 씨, 복도에서 뛰지 마세요.

나 : 아이고, 죄송합니다.

Translation of Talking with Lee Joon-gi

Lesson 1 Introducing yourself, page 58

Lee Joon-gi
Hello.
My name is Lee Joon-gi.
I am Korean.
I am a movie actor.
My hobby is taekwondo.
Nice to meet you.

Vivien
Hello.
My name is Vivien.
I am German.
I am a student.
My hobby is watching movies.
Nice to meet you.

Lesson 2 Asking the names of objects, page 71

Joon-gi: Is this a watch?
Stephanie: Yes, it is a watch.
Joon-gi: What is that?
Stephanie: This is a computer.
Joon-gi: Is that a telephone card?
Stephanie: No, that is not a telephone card.
It is a transportation card.

Lesson 3 Shopping, page 87

Clerk: Welcome. What would you like?
Joon-gi: Ma'am, what is the price of this apple?
Clerk: It is 500 won for one.
Joon-gi: What is the price of the bunch of bananas?
Clerk: It is 2,000 won per bunch.
Joon-gi: I would like two apples and two bunches of bananas.

Clerk: Here you are. The total is 5,000 won.
Joon-gi: Goodbye.
Clerk: Thank you. Goodbye.

Lesson 4 Asking about dates, days of the week and birthdays, page 102

Joon-gi: Vivien, What is the date today?
Vivien: Today is June 20.
Joon-gi: Is today Monday?
Vivien: Yes, today is Monday.
Joon-gi: Well then, when is your birthday?
Vivien: My birthday is October 9.
Joon-gi: Really? October 9 is Hangul Day.
Vivien: Oh, I see.

Lesson 5 Talking about business hours, page 115

Lili: Excuse me, but what time is it now?
Joon-gi: It is 2:45.
Lili: What are the bank's business hours?
Joon-gi: The bank is open from 9AM until 4PM
Lili: What are the business hours of Dongdaemun Market?
Joon-gi: Dongdaemun Market is open from 5PM until 5AM
Lili: Thank you.

Lesson 6 Asking questions about famous places, page 128

Joon-gi: Stephanie, where is the Opera House?
Stephanie: The Opera House is in Sydney.
Joon-gi: Where are the pyramids?
Stephanie: The pyramids are in Egypt.
Joon-gi: Is the Eiffel Tower in Germany?
Stephanie: No, the Eiffel Tower is in France.
Joon-gi: Thank you.

Lesson 7 Asking about someone's schedule, pages 140–141

Joon-gi: Diana, what are you doing now?

Diana: I am reading a book.

Joon-gi: Diana, what are you doing tomorrow?

Diana: I am watching a movie tomorrow.

Joon-gi: So, what are you doing this weekend?

Diana: I am hanging out with my friends this weekend.

Monday	Studying Chinese
Tuesday	Studying Chinese
Wednesday	Working on a movie
Thursday	Reading books
Friday	Studying Chinese
Saturday/Sunday	Meeting friends

I study Chinese on Mondays and Tuesdays.

I also study Chinese on Fridays.

I don't study Chinese on Wednesdays. I shoot movies.

I read books on Thursdays.

And I meet friends at the weekend.

Lesson 8 Asking and answering questions about the weekend, page 152

Joon-gi: Jiyoung, where are you going this weekend?

Jiyoung: I am going to Gwanghwamun this weekend.

Joon-gi: What are you going to do in Gwanghwamun?

Jiyoung: I am going to go to an exhibition and have some coffee. Joon-gi, where are you going this weekend?

Joon-gi: I am going to Sinchon this weekend.

Jiyoung: What are you going to do in Sinchon?

Joon-gi: I am going to buy a bag and go for a meal.

Lesson 9 Asking about the weather and impressions of Korea, page 166

Joon-gi: Wangshaowei, what country are you from?

Wangshaowei: I am from China.

Joon-gi: What is the weather like in China at the moment?

Wangshaowei: It is nice and cool. What is the weather like in Korea these days?

Joon-gi: It is warm and pleasant. How is your Korean study going and how do you like your Korean teacher?

Wangshaowei: Studying Korean is difficult but interesting, and my Korean teacher is fun and kind.

Lesson 10 Asking about your friend's daily routine, page 183

Joon-gi: Lili, what are you doing today?

Lili: I am studying Korean today.

Joon-gi: Where do you study Korean?

Lili: I study Korean in the library. Joon-gi, what are you doing today?

Joon-gi: I am going to Yeouido.

Lili: What are you going to do in Yeouido?

Joon-gi: There is a film shooting at a TV station.

Lesson 11 Asking about your friend's every-day schedule, page 195

Benson: Joon-gi, what do you usually do when you get up?

Joon-gi: In the morning, I work out in the park. Afterwards, I take a shower and make breakfast for myself.

Benson: What do you usually do at the weekend?

Joon-gi: I study Thai with my Thai friend. Afterwards, I come back home, go over my weekly schedule, and go to bed. Benson, what do you usually do at the weekend?

Benson: I usually go see a movie and meet my friends.

Lesson 12 Talking about what you did at the weekend, page 210–211

Joon-gi: Vivien, what did you do last weekend?

Vivien: I went shopping with my friend.

Joon-gi: Where did you go shopping?

Vivien: I went to Myeongdong.
Joon-gi, what did you do last weekend?

Joon-gi: I did some exercise last weekend.

Vivien: What kind of exercise did you do?

Joon-gi: I practiced taekwondo.

May 5, Sunny
Yesterday, the weather was very nice.
My teacher and friends came to visit my house.

Vivien came with her boyfriend.
We had some Spanish and Chinese food and some Japanese tea.
Vivien and Roberto sang songs.
Roy sang songs from Hong Kong.
It was really fun.

Lesson 13 Talking about plans, page 225

Joon-gi: Masumi, do you want to go to Gyeongbokgung this weekend?

Masumi: Sure, that would be great.

Joon-gi: Shall we take the bus or the subway?

Masumi: Let's take the subway. Joon-gi, what kind of food would you like to have for lunch?

Joon-gi: Let's have bibimbap.

Masumi: Okay, that sounds good.

Lesson 14 Asking questions about lifestyle, page 241

Joon-gi: Diana, do you exercise in the morning?

Diana: Yes, I do.

Joon-gi: Diana, do you smoke?

Diana: No, I don't smoke.

Joon-gi: Are you watching Korean dramas these days?

Diana: Yes, I am watching Korean dramas these days.

Lesson 15 The rules at Stephanie's boarding house, page 255

1. Get up at 7AM.
2. Clean your room in the morning.
3. Don't talk loudly at night.
4. Don't drink alcohol in your room.
5. Don't smoke in your room.
6. Don't be late for meals.
7. Don't use the washing machine at night.
8. Get home before midnight.

Answers to the Exercises

Lesson 1

P. 54

나 : 로베르토
가 : 이름이 무엇입니까?
나 : 제 이름은 리리입니다.
가 : 이름이 무엇입니까?
나 : 제 이름은 퍼디입니다.
가 : 이름이 무엇입니까?
나 : 제 이름은 마스미입니다.

P. 55

나 : 홍콩
가 : 어느 나라 사람입니까?
나 : 저는 중국 사람입니다.
가 : 어느 나라 사람입니까?
나 : 저는 일본 사람입니다.
가 : 어느 나라 사람입니까?
나 : 저는 필리핀 사람입니다.

P. 56

나 : 의사
가 : 왕샤위 씨 직업이 무엇입니까?
나 : 제 직업은 경찰관입니다.
가 : 마스미 씨 직업이 무엇입니까?
나 : 제 직업은 요리사입니다.
가 : 퍼디 씨 직업이 무엇입니까?
나 : 제 직업은 학생입니다.

P. 57

나 : 요리
가 : 취미가 무엇입니까?
나 : 제 취미는 축구입니다.
가 : 취미가 무엇입니까?
나 : 제 취미는 독서입니다.
가 : 취미가 무엇입니까?
나 : 제 취미는 태권도입니다.

Lesson 2

P. 67

시계입니까?/시계가 아닙니다
떡볶이가 아닙니다
김밥입니까?/김밥이 아닙니다
폰입니다/폰이 아닙니다

P. 68

나 : 지갑
가 : 이것은 무엇입니까?
나 : 그것은 안경입니다.
가 : 이것은 무엇입니까?
나 : 그것은 구두입니다.
가 : 이것은 무엇입니까?
나 : 그것은 전화카드입니다.

P. 69

나 : 비빔밥
가 : 이것은 치약입니까?
나 : 네, 그것은 치약입니다.
가 : 이것은 비누입니까?
나 : 네, 그것은 비누입니다.
가 : 이것은 샴푸입니까?
나 : 네, 그것은 샴푸입니다.

P. 70

나 : 비빔밥이/삼계탕
가 : 이것은 불고기입니까?
나 : 아니요, 불고기가 아닙니다.
　　그것은 자장면입니다.
가 : 이것은 비누입니까?
나 : 아니요, 비누가 아닙니다.
　　그것은 수건입니다.
가 : 이것은 숟가락입니까?
나 : 아니요, 숟가락이 아닙니다.
　　그것은 젓가락입니다.

Lesson 3

P. 80
커피하고 콜라
햄하고 통조림
바나나하고 수박
건전지하고 폰
밥하고 계란

P. 81
포도예요
바나나예요/바나나가 아니에요
폰이에요
오백 원이 아니에요

P. 84
가 : 이것은 건전지예요?
나 : 네, 그것은 건전지예요.
가 : 그것은 배예요?
나 : 아니요, 그것은 배가 아니에요. 사과예요.
가 : 저것은 과자예요?
나 : 아니요, 저것은 과자가 아니에요.
　　빵이에요.

P. 85
나 : 사이다 세 병/맥주 두 병
가 : 뭘 드릴까요?
나 : 돼지고기 일 킬로그램하고, 닭고기 한 마리
　　주세요.
가 : 뭘 드릴까요?
나 : 계란 열 개하고, 캔 커피 다섯 개하고,
　　화장지 여섯 개 주세요.
가 : 뭘 드릴까요?
나 : 형광등 한 개하고, 휴지 일곱 개하고,
　　바나나 한 송이 주세요.

P. 86
가 : 바나나는/한 송이
나 : 바나나는/한 송이/이천 원
가 : 이 콜라는 한 병에 얼마예요?
나 : 그 콜라는 한 병에 육백 원이에요.
가 : 그 소고기는 일 킬로그램에 얼마예요?

나 : 이 소고기는 일 킬로그램에 만 이천
　　원이에요.
가 : 그 생선은 한 마리에 얼마예요?
나 : 이 생선은 한 마리에 삼천오백 원이에요.

Lesson 4

P. 96
6월 6일 (유월 육일)이에요
7월 7일 (칠월 칠일)이에요
8월 15일 (팔월 십오일)이에요
9월 30일 (구월 삼십일)이에요
10월 5일 (시월 오일)이에요

P. 97
나 : 2월 18일 (이월 십팔일)
가 : 오늘은 며칠이에요?
나 : 오늘은 10월 9일 (시월 구일)이에요.
가 : 내일은 며칠이에요?
나 : 내일은 4월 10일 (사월 십일)이에요.
가 : 모레는 며칠이에요?
나 : 모레는 11월 11일 (십일월 십일일)이에요.

P. 98
나 : 10월 20일 (시월 이십일)
가 : 수료식이 언제예요?
나 : 수료식은 12월 28일 (십이월 이십팔일)이에요.
가 : 방학이 언제예요?
나 : 방학은 7월 23일 (칠월 이십삼일)이에요.
가 : 오리엔테이션이 언제예요?
나 : 오리엔테이션은 2월 27일 (이월 이십칠일)이
　　에요.

P. 99
나 : 화요일
가 : 모레는 무슨 요일이에요?
나 : 모레는 수요일이에요.
가 : 7월 3일 (칠월 삼일)은 무슨 요일이에요?
나 : 7월 3일 (칠월 삼일)은 일요일이에요.
가 : 오늘은 무슨 요일이에요?
나 : 오늘은 토요일이에요.

Lesson 5

P. 112
나 : 9시(아홉 시)
가 : 실례지만, 지금 몇 시예요?
나 : 지금 12시 30분(열두 시 반, 열두 시 삼십 분)
　　이에요.
가 : 고맙습니다.
가 : 실례지만, 지금 몇 시예요?
나 : 지금 4시 15분(네 시 십오 분)이에요.
가: 고맙습니다.
가 : 실례지만, 지금 몇 시예요?
나 : 지금 8시 50분(여덟 시 오십 분, 아홉 시
　　십 분 전) 이에요.
가 : 고맙습니다.

P. 113
가 : 우체국은
나 : 우체국은/9시부터 6시까지
　　(아홉 시부터 여섯 시까지)
가 : 실례지만 은행은 몇 시부터 몇 시까지예요?
나 : 은행은 9시부터 4시까지
　　(아홉 시부터 네 시까지)예요.
가 : 고맙습니다.
가 : 출입국관리소는 몇 시부터 몇 시까지예요?
나 : 출입국관리소는 9시부터 5시까지
　　(아홉 시부터 다섯 시까지)예요.
가 : 고맙습니다.
가 : 실례지만 병원은 몇 시부터 몇 시까지예요?
나 : 병원은 24시간(이십사 시간)이에요.
가 : 고맙습니다.

Lesson 6

P. 121
(오른쪽/아래)(밑)
(앞)(뒤)(밖)
(사이)

P. 122
가 : 화장실이
나 : 화장실은/매점 앞
가 : 실례합니다. 계단이 어디에 있어요?
나 : 계단은 엘리베이터 옆(오른쪽)에 있어요.
가 : 감사합니다.
가 : 실례합니다. 휴지통이 어디에 있어요?
나 : 휴지통은 책상 옆(오른쪽)에 있어요.
가 : 감사합니다.
가 : 실례합니다. 구두가 어디에 있어요?
나 : 구두는 가방 앞에 있어요.
가 : 감사합니다.

P. 123
가 : 세탁소가
나 : 세탁소는/편의점 옆(편의점 오른쪽)
가 : 실례합니다. 은행이 어디에 있어요?
나 : 은행은 주유소와 도서관 사이(주유소 옆/
　　주유소 오른쪽/도서관 옆/도서관 왼쪽)에
　　있어요.
가 : 감사합니다.
가 : 실례합니다. 꽃 가게가 어디에 있어요?
나 : 꽃 가게는 주유소 왼쪽(주유소 옆)에 있어요.
가 : 감사합니다.
가 : 실례합니다. 주유소는 어디에 있어요?
나 : 주유소는 꽃 가게 오른쪽(은행 왼쪽/꽃
　　가게와 은행 사이/꽃 가게 옆/은행 옆)에
　　있어요.
가 : 감사합니다.

P. 124
가 : 비비엔 씨 뒤에 퍼디 씨가 있어요?
나 : 네, 비비엔 씨 뒤에 피디 씨가 있어요.
가 : 책상 위에 컴퓨터가 있어요?
나 : 네, 책상 위에 컴퓨터가 있어요.
가 : 가방 안에 옷이 있어요?
나 : 네, 가방 안에 옷이 있어요.

P. 125

가 : 냉장고가
나 : 냉장고는/3층
가 : 실례합니다. 화장실이 몇 층에 있어요?
나 : 화장실은 2층에 있어요.
가 : 감사합니다.
가 : 실례합니다. 지갑이 몇 층에 있어요?
나 : 지갑은 1층에 있어요.
가 : 감사합니다.
가 : 실례합니다. 주차장이 몇 층에 있어요?
나 : 주차장은 B2, 3층에 있어요.
가 : 감사합니다.

Lesson 7

P. 136

배우지 않습니다
마십니까?
씁니다/쓰지 않습니다
만납니까?/만나지 않습니다
먹습니다

P. 137

가 : 로이 씨
나 : 지금 맥주를 마십니다.
가 : 비비엔 씨, 지금 무엇을 합니까?
나 : 저는 지금 바나나를 먹습니다.
가 : 왕샤위 씨, 지금 무엇을 합니까?
나 : 저는 지금 음악을 듣습니다.
가 : 퍼디 씨, 지금 무엇을 합니까?
나 : 저는 지금 요리를 합니다.

P. 138

나 : 주말에 친구를 만납니다.
가 : 언제 청소를 합니까?
나 : 저는 아침에 청소를 합니다.
가 : 언제 책을 읽습니까?
나 : 저는 잠자기 전에 책을 읽습니다.
가 : 언제 영화를 봅니까?
나 : 저는 토요일, 일요일에 영화를 봅니다.

P. 139

가 : 이준기 씨, 오늘 피자를 먹습니까?
나 : 네, 피자를 먹습니다.
가 : 벤슨 씨, 오늘 책을 읽습니까?
나 : 아니요, 책을 읽지 않습니다. 텔레비전을 봅니다.
가 : 왕샤위 씨, 오늘 영화를 봅니까?
나 : 아니요, 영화를 보지 않습니다. 음악을 듣습니다.

Lesson 8

P. 147

책을 읽고 편지를 씁니다
텔레비전을 보고 잠을 잡니다
밥을 먹고 영화를 봅니다
친구를 만나고 도서관에 갑니다
커피를 마시고 음악을 듣습니다
백화점에 가고 쇼핑합니다

P. 148

가 : 최지영
나 : 명동
가 : 리리 씨, 어디에 갑니까?
나 : 저는 교회에 갑니다.
가 : 마스미 씨, 어디에 갑니까?
나 : 저는 백화점에 갑니다.
가 : 왕샤위 씨, 어디에 갑니까?
나 : 저는 식당에 갑니다.

P. 149

나 : 학교/한국어를 가르칩니다.
가 : 어디에서 친구를 만납니까?
나 : 저는 명동에서 친구를 만납니다.
가 : 어디에서 비빔밥을 먹습니까?
나 : 저는 식당에서 비빔밥을 먹습니다.
가 : 어디에서 책을 읽습니까?
나 : 저는 도서관에서 책을 읽습니다.

P. 150

나 : 오늘 오후/텔레비전을 보/편지를 씁니다.

가 : 오늘 오후에 무엇을 합니까?

나 : 저는 오늘 오후에 명동에서 영화를 보고
　　친구를 만납니다.

가 : 일요일에 무엇을 합니까?

나 : 저는 일요일에 공원에서 운동하고
　　그림을 그립니다.

가 : 내일 무엇을 합니까?

나 : 저는 내일 신문을 읽고 커피를 마십니다.

Lesson 9

P. 162

덥지 않습니다

춥습니다

시원하지 않습니다

비가 오지 않습니다

눈이 내립니다

P. 163

나 : 호주는 날씨가 덥습니다.

가 : 일본은 날씨가 어떻습니까?

나 : 일본은 날씨가 덥고 비가 옵니다.

가 : 홍콩은 날씨가 어떻습니까?

나 : 홍콩은 날씨가 시원합니다.

가 : 제주도는 날씨가 어떻습니까?

나 : 제주도는 날씨가 따뜻합니다.

P. 164

나 : 김치는 맵지만 맛있습니다.

가 : 한국 음식은 어떻습니까?

나 : 한국 음식은 맛있지만 비쌉니다.

가 : 지하철은 어떻습니까?

나 : 지하철은 빠르지만 복잡합니다.

가 : 한국어 공부는 어떻습니까?

나 : 한국어 공부는 어렵지만 재미있습니다.

P. 165

나 : 맵지 않습니다. 맛있습니다.

가 : 만들기는 어렵습니까?

나 : 아니요, 만들기는 어렵지 않습니다. 쉽습니
　　다.

가 : 버스는 사람이 적습니까?

나 : 아니요, 버스는 사람이 적지 않습니다. 많습
　　니다.

가 : 백화점은 쌉니까?

나 : 아니요, 백화점은 싸지 않습니다. 비쌉니다.

Lesson 10

P. 178

만나요/안 만나요/만나지 않아요

와요/안 와요/오지 않아요

봐요/안 봐요/보지 않아요

앉아요/안 앉아요/앉지 않아요

서요/안 서요/서지 않아요

배워요/안 배워요/배우지 않아요

먹어요/안 먹어요/먹지 않아요

그려요/안 그려요/그리지 않아요

가르쳐요/안 가르쳐요/가르치지 않아요

마셔요/안 마셔요/마시지 않아요

요리해요/요리 안 해요/요리하지 않아요

청소해요/청소 안 해요/청소하지 않아요

추워요/안 추워요/춥지 않아요

더워요/안 더워요/덥지 않아요

P. 179

가 : 퍼디 씨, 어디에 가요?

나 : 민속촌에 가요.

가 : 퍼디 씨, 민속촌에 가요?

나 : 아니요, 민속촌에 안 가요. 롯데월드에 가요.

가 : 퍼디 씨, 강남에 가요?

나 : 아니요, 강남에 안 가요. 신촌에 가요.

P. 180

나 : 롯데월드에서 바이킹을 타요.

가 : 오늘 뭐 해요?

나 : 인사동에서 전통차를 마셔요.

가 : 오늘 뭐 해요?

나 : 저는 공원에서 그림을 그려요.

가 : 오늘 뭐 해요?

나 : 저는 강남에서 떡볶이를 먹고 쇼핑을 해요.

P. 181

나 : 영화를 안 봐요. 친구를 만나요.

가 : 학교에서 한국어를 공부해요?

나 : 아니요, 저는 한국어를 공부 안 해요.
영어를 가르쳐요.

가 : 집에서 텔레비전을 봐요?

나 : 아니요, 저는 텔레비전을 안 봐요. 청소해요.

가 : 롯데월드에서 바이킹을 타요?

나 : 아니요, 바이킹을 안 타요. 롤러코스터를
타요.

Lesson 11

P. 190

가 : 아침에 일어나서 보통

나 : 아침에 일어나서 신문을 읽어요.

가 : 아침에 일어나서 보통 뭐 해요?

나 : 저는 아침에 일어나서 청소해요.

가 : 아침에 일어나서 보통 뭐 해요?

나 : 저는 아침에 일어나서 샤워해요.

가 : 아침에 일어나서 보통 뭐 해요?

나 : 저는 아침에 일어나서 밥을 먹어요.

P. 191

가 : 학교에 가서 보통

나 : 학교에 가서 친구를 만나요.

가 : 동대문시장에 가서 보통 뭐 해요?

나 : 저는 동대문시장에 가서 옷을 사요.

가 : 이태원에 가서 보통 뭐 해요?

나 : 저는 이태원에 가서 맥주를 마셔요.

가 : 인사동에 가서 보통 뭐 해요?

나 : 저는 인사동에 가서 선물을 사요.

P. 192

가 : 친구를 만나서 보통

나 : 친구를 만나서 커피를 마셔요.

가 : 친구를 만나서 보통 뭐 해요?

나 : 저는 친구를 만나서 영화를 봐요.

가 : 이준기 씨를 만나서 보통 뭐 해요?

나 : 저는 이준기 씨를 만나서 피자를 먹어요.

가 : 로이 씨를 만나서 보통 뭐 해요?

나 : 저는 로이 씨를 만나서 놀이 기구를 타요.

P. 193

가 : 요리해서

나 : 요리해서 친구와 같이 먹어요.

가 : 김치를 만들어서 뭐 해요?

나 : 저는 김치를 만들어서 친구에게 줘요.

가 : 스파게티를 만들어서 뭐 해요?

나 : 저는 스파게티를 만들어서 친구와 같이
먹어요.

가 : 편지를 써서 뭐 해요?

나 : 저는 편지를 써서 친구에게 보내요.

P. 196

① 아픕니다/아파요

② 예쁘지 않습니다/안 예뻐요

③ 예쁘지만/예뻐서

④ 기쁩니다/기뻐요

⑤ 기쁘고/기쁘지 않아요

⑥ 기쁘지만/기뻐서

⑦ 쓰지 않습니다/안 써요

Lesson 12

P. 204

안 만났어요

안 왔어요/오지 않았어요

보지 않았어요

앉았어요

배웠어요/안 배웠어요

읽었어요/안 읽었어요

그렸어요/그리지 않았어요

P. 205

나 : 지난 주말에 도서관에 갔어요.
가 : 지난 주말에 어디에 갔어요?
나 : 저는 지난 주말에 설악산에 갔어요.
가 : 지난 주말에 어디에 갔어요?
나 : 저는 지난 주말에 온천에 갔어요.
가 : 지난 주말에 어디에 갔어요?
나 : 저는 지난 주말에 놀이동산에 갔어요.

P. 206

나 : 도서관/백화점에 갔어요.
가 : 지난 주말에 설악산에 갔어요?
나 : 아니요, 저는 설악산에 안 갔어요. 온천에 갔
　　어요.
가 : 지난 주말에 바다에 갔어요?
나 : 아니요, 저는 바다에 안 갔어요. 산에 갔어요.
가 : 지난 주말에 부산에 갔어요?
나 : 아니요, 저는 부산에 안 갔어요. 제주도에
　　갔어요.

P. 207

나 : 저는 어제 영화관에서 영화를 보고 술을 마셨
　　어요.
가 : 어제 무엇을 했어요?
나 : 저는 어제 집에서 텔레비전을 보고 청소했어
　　요.
가 : 지난 주말에 무엇을 했어요?
나 : 저는 지난 주말에 명동에서 피자를 먹고
　　쇼핑을 했어요.
가 : 지난 주말에 무엇을 했어요?
나 : 저는 지난 주말에 이태원에서 술을 마시고
　　춤을 추었어요.

P. 208

나 : 영화/친구를 만났어요.
가 : 어제 도서관에서 책을 읽었어요?
나 : 아니요, 저는 책을 안 읽었어요. 인터넷을
　　했어요.
가 : 어제 집에서 피아노를 쳤어요?
나 : 아니요, 저는 피아노를 안 쳤어요. 기타를
　　쳤어요.

가 : 지난 주말에 등산을 했어요?
나 : 아니요, 저는 등산을 안 했어요. 골프를
　　쳤어요.

Lesson 13

P. 217

볼까요?
만날까요?
마실까요?

P. 218

봅시다
만납시다
마십시다

P. 219

수업이 끝나면
시간이 있으면
시간이 없으면

P. 220

나 : 점심을 먹읍시다.
가 : 오늘 저녁에 술을 마실까요?
나 : 네, 좋아요. 술을 마십시다.
가 : 이번 주말에 온천에 갈까요?
나 : 네, 좋아요. 온천에 갑시다.
가 : 내일 농구를 할까요?
나 : 네, 좋아요. 농구를 합시다.

P. 221

가 : 골프를 할까요? 수영을 할까요?
가 : 오늘 점심을 먹읍시다.
　　비빔밥을 먹을까요? 비빔국수를 먹을까요?
나 : 비빔국수를 먹읍시다.
가 : 금요일에 영화를 봅시다.
　　007을 볼까요? 타이타닉을 볼까요?
나 : 타이타닉을 봅시다.
가 : 주말에 여행을 갑시다.
　　스케이트를 탈까요? 스키를 탈까요?
나 : 스키를 탑시다.

P. 222

나 : 저는 수업이 끝나면 친구를 만나요.
가 : 친구를 만나면 뭐 해요?
나 : 저는 친구를 만나면 농구를 해요.
가 : 집에 가면 뭐 해요?
나 : 저는 집에 가면 텔레비전을 봐요.
가 : 인사동에 가면 뭐 해요?
나 : 저는 인사동에 가면 전통차를 마셔요.

P. 223

나 : 저는 집에 안 가요. 도서관에 가요.
가 : 아침에 일어나면 신문을 읽어요?
나 : 아니요, 저는 신문을 안 읽어요. 커피를
　　마셔요.
가 : 시간이 있으면 영화를 봐요?
나 : 아니요, 저는 영화를 안 봐요. 경복궁에 가요.
가 : 수업이 끝나면 숙제해요?
나 : 아니요, 저는 숙제 안 해요. 명동에 가요.

Lesson 14

P. 233

편지를 쓰세요
사진을 찍으세요
음악을 듣고 있어요
요리하고 있어요
와인을 마시고 있어요
춤을 추고 있어요
기타를 배우고 있어요
그림을 그리고 있어요

P. 234

가 : 점심을 드세요.
가 : 저는 기타를 배워요. 어머니도 기타를
　　배우세요.
가 : 동생은 방에 있어요. 아버지도 방에 계세요.
가 : 저는 책을 읽어요. 어머니도 신문을 읽으세
　　요.

P. 235

나 : 저는 삼겹살
가 : 저녁에 텔레비전을 보세요?
나 : 네, 저는 텔레비전을 봐요.
가 : 주말에 설악산에 가세요?
나 : 네, 저는 설악산에 가요.
가 : 등산을 하세요?
나 : 아니요, 저는 등산을 안 해요. 수영을 해요.

P. 236

나 : 신문을 읽
가 : 지금 뭘 하고 있어요?
나 : 저는 지금 버스를 기다리고 있어요.
가 : 지금 뭘 하고 있어요?
나 : 저는 지금 골프를 치고 있어요.
가 : 지금 뭘 하고 있어요?
나 : 저는 지금 영화를 보고 있어요.

P. 237

나 : 그리고 있어요.
가 : 커피를 다 마셨어요?
나 : 아니요, 아직 마시고 있어요.
가 : 밥을 다 먹었어요?
나 : 아니요, 아직 먹고 있어요.
가 : 숙제 다 했어요?
나 : 아니요, 아직 하고 있어요.

P. 238

나 : 중국어를 배우고
가 : 요즘 뭐 해요?
나 : 저는 요즘 태권도를 배우고 있어요.
가 : 요즘 뭐 해요?
나 : 저는 요즘 피아노를 가르치고 있어요.
가 : 요즘 뭐 해요?
나 : 저는 요즘 영어를 가르치고 있어요.

Lesson 15

P. 248

오세요

영화를 보세요

타세요

P. 249

담배를 피우지 마세요

김치를 먹지 마세요

기다리지 마세요

P. 250

6000번 버스로 갈아타다

시청역에서 버스로 갈아타다

신촌에서 버스로 갈아타다

강남역에서 지하철로 갈아타다

P. 251

나 : 시청역에서 2호선으로 갈아타세요.

가 : 실례지만, 인사동에 어떻게 가요?

나 : 3호선 안국역에서 내리세요.

가 : 네, 알겠습니다. 감사합니다.

가 : 실례지만, 인천 공항에 어떻게 가요?

나 : 한국대학교 앞에서 공항버스를 타세요.

가 : 네, 알겠습니다. 감사합니다.

가 : 실례지만, 이태원에 어떻게 가요?

나 : 3호선 약수역에서 6호선으로 갈아타세요.

가 : 네, 알겠습니다. 감사합니다.

P. 252

가 : 실례합니다.

경복궁에서 롯데월드까지 어떻게 가요?

나 : 경복궁역에서 3호선을 타세요.

그리고 을지로 3가역에서 2호선으로

갈아타세요.

그리고 롯데월드역에서 내리세요.

가 : 고맙습니다.

가 : 서울대공원(역)에서 안국(역)까지 어떻게

가요?

나 : 서울대공원역에서 4호선을 타세요.

그리고 충무로역에서 3호선으로 갈아타세요.

그리고 안국역에서 내리세요.

가 : 고맙습니다.

P. 253

가 : 교실에서 영어를 하지 마세요.

가 : 어! 영화관에서 전화를 하지 마세요.

나 : 아이고, 죄송합니다.

가 : 어! 박물관에서 사진을 찍지 마세요.

나 : 아이고, 죄송합니다.

가 : 어! 공원에서 잔디밭에 들어가지 마세요.

나 : 아이고, 죄송합니다.

Vocabulary Index

그림을 그리다 **geurimeul geurida** *to draw a picture*

그저께 **geujeokke** *the day before yesterday*

근처 **geuncheo** *in the vicinity*

금요일 **geumyoil** *Friday*

금지 **geumji** *prohibition*

기다리다 **gidarida** *to wait*

기쁘다 **gippeuda** *happy*

기차 **gicha** *train*

기타 **gita** *others*

기타를 치다 **gitareul chida** *to play the guitar*

길다 **gilda** *long*

김밥 **gimbap** *gimbap*

김치 **gimchi** *kimchi*

김치찌개 **gimchijjigae** *kimchi stew*

까치 **kkachi** *magpie*

깎다 **kkakda** *to cut*

깨끗하다 **kkaekkeutada** *clean*

꼬리 **kkori** *tail*

꼬마 **kkoma** *kid*

꽃 **kkot** *flower*

꽃 가게 **kkot gage** *flower shop*

끝나다 **kkeunnada** *to finish*

나 **na** *I/my/me*

나가다 **nagada** *to go out*

나라 **nara** *country*

나무 **namu** *tree*

나비 **nabi** *butterfly*

나쁘다 **nappeuda** *bad*

나이아가라 폭포 **niagara pokpo** *Niagara Falls*

낚시 **naksi** *fishing*

날 **nal** *day*

날씨 **nalssi** *weather*

날짜 **naljja** *date*

남녁 **namnyeok** *the south*

남대문 시장 **namdaemun sijang** *Namdaemun Market*

낫 **nat** *sickle*

낮 **nat** *daytime*

낮다 **natda** *low*

내년 **naenyeon** *next year*

내리다 **naerida** *to alight (from a vehicle)*

내일 **naeil** *tomorrow*

내일 만나요 **naeil mannayo** *see you tomorrow*

냉면 **naengmyeon** *naengmyeon noodles*

냉장고 **naengjanggo** *refrigerator*

넓다 **neolda** *wide*

네 **ne** *yes*

넷 **net** *four*

년 **nyeon** *year*

노래 **norae** *song*

노래하다 **noraehada** *to sing a song*

노루 **noru** *roe deer*

놀이 기구 **nori gigu** *ride*

놀이동산 **noridongsan** *amusement park*

농구를 하다 **nonggureul hada** *to play basketball*

누나 **nuna** *older sister (term used by men)*

눈 **nun** *snow*

눈 **nun** *eye*

눈이 내리다 **nuni naerida** *snow falls*

느리다 **neurida** *slow*

늦다 **neutda** *late*

다녀오겠습니다 **danyeoogetseumnida**
    I'm leaving, see you later (polite)

다녀오세요 **danyeooseyo** *see you later (polite)*

다리 **dari** *leg/bridge*

다섯 **daseot** *five*

다음 달 **daeum dal** *next month*

다음 주 **daeum ju** *next week*

달 **dal** *month/moon*

달다 **dalda** *sweet*

달력 **dallyeok** *calendar*

달리다 **dallida** *to run*

닭고기 **dakgogi** *chicken (meat)*

담배를 피우다 **dambaereul piuda** *to smoke a cigarette*

대학교 **daehakgyo** *university*

대학로 **daehangno** *Daehangno (road)*

더럽다 **deoreopda** *dirty*

덥다 **deopda** *hot*

도서관 **doseogwan** *library*

도토리 **dotori** *acorn*

독서 **dokseo** *reading books*

독일 **dogil** *Germany*

돈 **don** *money*

동네 **dongne** *town*

동대문 시장 **dongdaemun sijang** *Dongdaemun Market*

돼지 **dwaeji** *pig*

돼지고기 **dwaejigogi** *pork*

된장찌개 **doenjangjjigae** *doenjang stew*

두부 **dubu** *tofu*

둘 **dul** *two*

뒤 **dwi** *behind*

드라마 **deurama** *drama*

드시다 **deusida** *to eat (polite)*

듣다 **deutda** *to listen to/to hear*

들어가다 **deureogada** *to enter*

들어오다 **deureooda** *to come in*

등산을 하다 **deungsaneul hada** *to go hiking*

따다 **ttada** *to pick (from a plant)*

따뜻하다 **ttatteutada** *warm*

딸기 **ttalgi** *strawberry*

때 **ttae** *time*

떠나다 **tteonada** *to leave*

떠들다 **tteodeulda** *to talk loudly*

떡볶이 **tteokbokki** *tteokbokki (rice cake)*

또 만나요 **tto mannayo** *see you again*

뛰다 **ttwida** *to jump/to run*

뜨겁다 **tteugeopda** *hot*

뜨다 **tteuda** *to float*

띠 **tti** *belt*

라디오 **radio** *radio*

라면 **ramyeon** *noodles*

러시아 **reosia** *Russia*

롤러코스터를 타다 **rolleokoseuteoreul tada** *to ride a roller coaster*

롯데월드 **rotdewoldeu** *Lotte World*

린스 **rinseu** *hair conditioner*

마리 **mari** *counter for animals*

마시다 **masida** *to drink*

마흔 **maheun** *forty*

만 **man** *ten thousand*

만나다 **mannada** *to meet*

만나서 반갑습니다 **mannaseo bangapseumnida** *nice to meet you*

만두 **mandu** *dumplings*

만들다 **mandeulda** *to make something*

만지다 **manjida** *to touch*

많다 **manta** *many*

맏이 **maji** *eldest child*

맏형 **matyeong** *eldest brother*

맑다 **makda** *sunny*

맛없다 **madeopda** *not tasty*

맛있다 **masitda** *delicious*

맞은편 **majeunpyeon** *across from*

매일 **maeil** *every day*

맥주 **maekju** *beer*

맥주를 마시다 **maekjureul masida** *to have a beer*

맵다 **maepda** *spicy*

머리 **meori** *head*

먹다 **meokda** *to eat*

멀다 **meolda** *far*

멋있다 **meositda** *gorgeous/fancy*

멕시코 **meksiko** *Mexico*

며칠 **myeochil** *a few days*

명동 **myeongdong** *Myeongdong (district)*

몇 년 **myeot nyeon** *a few years*

몇 월 **myeot wol** *what month?*

몇 층 **myeot cheung** *which floor?*

모두 **modu** *all/total/altogether*

모레 **more** *the day after tomorrow*

모자 **moja** *hat*

목요일 **mogyoil** *Thursday*

몫 **mok** *quotient*

몸 **mom** *body*

몽골 **monggol** *Mongolia*

무 **mu** *radish*

무겁다 **mugeopda** *heavy*

무릎 **mureup** *knee*

무엇 / 뭐 **mueot/mwo** *what*

문 **mun** *door*

문어 **muneo** *octopus*

묻다 **mutda** *to ask*

물 **mul** *water*

물건 **mulgeon** *object*

뭘 (= 무엇을) **mwol** (= **mueoseul**) *what (object)*

미국 **miguk** *USA*

미안합니다 **mianhamnida** *I am sorry/I apologize*

미역국 **miyeokguk** *miyeokguk (seaweed soup)*

미용실 **miyongsil** *hairdresser's*

민속촌 **minsokchon** *folk village*

믿는다 **minneunda** *to trust/to believe in*

밑 **mit** *underneath*

ㅂ

바 **ba** *bar*

바꾸다 **bakkuda** *to change*

바나나 **banana** *banana*

바다 **bada** *sea*

바쁘다 **bappeuda** *busy*

바이킹을 타다 **baikingeul tada** *to ride the pirate ship*

박물관 **bangmulgwan** *museum*

밖 **bak** *outside*

반 **ban** *half*

발 **bal** *foot*

밝다 **bakda** *bright*

밟다 **babpda** *to step on*

밤 **bam** *night*

밥 **bap** *rice*

방 **bang** *room*

방송국 **bangsongguk** *broadcasting company*

방학 (방학하다) **banghak(banghakada)** *to have a school holiday*

밭 **bat** *field*

배 **bae** *pear*

배 **bae** *ship*

배우다 **baeuda** *to learn*

백 **baek** *one hundred*

백만 **baengman** *one million*

백화점 **baekwajeom** *department store*

버스 정류장 **beoseu jeongnyujang** *bus stop*

버찌 **beojji** *cherry*

번개가 치다 **beongaega chida** *lightning strikes*

벚 **beot** *cherry blossom*

베트남 **beteunam** *Vietnam*

벽 **byeok** *wall*

병 **byeong** *bottle*

병원 **byeongwon** *hospital*

보내다 **bonaeda** *to send*

보다 **boda** *to see*

보통 **botong** *usually*

복도 **bokdo** *corridor*

복잡하다 **bokjapada** *crowded/complicated*

볼링을 치다 **bollingeul chida** *to bowl*

부부 **bubu** *husband and wife*

부산 **busan** *Busan*

부엌 **bueok** *kitchen*

북한산 **bukansan** *Mt. Bukhan*

분 **bun** *minute*

불고기 **bulgogi** *bulgogi*

불친절하다 **bulchinjeolhada** *unkind*

불편하다 **bulpyeonhada** *inconvenient*

브라질 **beurajil** *Brazil*

비가 내리다 **biga naerida** *it's raining*

비누 **binu** *soap*

비빔국수 **bibimguksu** *bibimguksu (spicy noodles)*

비빔밥 **bibimbap** *bibimbap*

비싸다 **bissada** *expensive*

비행기 **bihaenggi** *airplane*

빗 **bit** *comb*

빛 **bit** *light*

빠르다 **ppareuda** *fast*

빵 **ppang** *bread*

뽀뽀 **ppoppo** *kiss*

뿌리 **ppuri** *root*

사 **sa** *four*

사과 **sagwa** *apple*

사다 **sada** *to buy*

사당역 **sadangyeok** *Sadang Station*

사무실 **samusil** *office*

사물 **samul** *object*

사십 **sasip** *forty*

사월 **sawol** *April*

사이 **sai** *between*

사이다 **saida** *lemon-lime soda*

사일 **sail** *4th day (of a month)*

사진을 찍다 **sajineul jjikda** *to take (a picture)*

산 **san** *mountain*

살다 **salda** *to live*

삶 **sam** *life*

삼 **sam** *three*

삼겹살 **samgyeopsal** *pork belly*

삼계탕 **samgyetang** *ginseng chicken soup*

삼십 **samsip** *thirty*

삼월 **samwol** *March*

새 **sae** *bird*

생선 **saengseon** *fish*

생일 **saengnil** *birthday*

생일 축하합니다 **saengnil chukahamnida** *happy birthday*

생활필수품 **saenghwalpilsupum** *daily necessities*

샤워하다 **syawohada** *to take a shower*

샴푸 **syampu** *shampoo*

서다 **seoda** *to stand*

서른 **seorun** *thirty*

서울대공원 **seouldaegongwon** *Seoul Grand Park*

서울랜드 **seoullaendeu** *Seoul Land*

서울역 **seouryeok** *Seoul Station*

선물 (선물하다) **seonmul (seonmulhada)**
  to buy a present

선생님 **seonsaengnim** *teacher*

설악산 **seoraksan** *Mt. Seorak*

세계 **segye** *world*

세수하다 **sesuhada** *to wash one's face*

세탁소 **setakso** *laundromat*

세탁하다 **setakada** *to wash clothes*

셋 **set** *three*

소 **so** *cow*

소고기 **sogogi** *beef*

소나무 **sonamu** *pine tree*

소주 **soju** *soju*

속 **sok** *inside*

송이 **songi** *counter for flowers*

쇼핑하다 **syopinghada** *to shop*

수건 **sugeon** *towel*

수고 **sugo** *effort*

수료식 **suryosik** *graduation ceremony*

수박 **subak** *watermelon*

수세미 **susemi** *dish sponge*

수업 **sueop** *class*

수영 (수영하다) **suyeong (suyeonghada)** *to swim*

수요일 **suyoil** *Wednesday*

숙제 (숙제하다) **sukje (sukjehada)**
  to do one's homework

숟가락 **sutgarak** *spoon*

술을 마시다 **sureul masida** *to drink alcohol*

숲 **sup** *forest*

쉬다 **swida** *to take a break*

쉰 **swin** *fifty*

쉽다 **swipda** *easy*

슈퍼마켓 (슈퍼) **syupeomaket (syupeo)** *supermarket*

스물 **seumul** *twenty*

스케이트를 타다 **seukeiteureul tada** *to skate*

스키를 타다 **seukireul tada** *to ski*

스파게티 **seupageti** *spaghetti*

스페인 **seupein** *Spain*

스피커 **seupikeo** *speaker*

슬프다 **seulpeuda** *sad*

시 **si** *o'clock*

시간 **sigan** *hour*

시간이 없다 **sigani eopda** *to have no free time*

시간이 있다 **sigani itda** *to have some free time*

시계 **sigye** *watch/clock*

시내버스 **sinaebeoseu** *local bus*

시다 **sida** *sour*

시원하다 **siwonhada** *pleasantly cool*

시월 **siwol** *October*

시험 **siheom** *test/quiz/exam*

식당 **sikdang** *restaurant*

식품 **sikpum** *foods*

신문 **sinmun** *newspaper*

신문을 읽다 **sinmuneul ikda** *to read the newspaper*

신촌 **sinchon** *Sinchon (district)*

신호등 **sinhodeung** *traffic signal*

실례지만 **sillyejiman** *excuse me, but…*

실례합니다 **sillyehamnida** *excuse me*

싫다 **silta** *to dislike*

심리 **simni** *psychology*

십 **sip** *ten*

십만 **simman** *one hundred thousand*

십이월 **sibiwol** *December*

십일월 **sibirwol** *November*

싱겁다 **singgeopda** *bland*

싸다 **ssada** *inexpensive*

쌀쌀하다 **ssalssalhada** *chilly (weather)*

쏘다 **ssoda** *to shoot*

쓰다 **sseuda** *to write*

쓰다 (맛) **sseuda(mat)** *bitter*

쓰러지다 **sseureojida** *to fall down*

아가씨 **agassi** *(unmarried) young woman*

아래 **arae** *below/underneath*

아버지 **abeoji** *father*

아빠 **appa** *dad*

아우 **au** *younger brother/sister*

아이 **ai** *kid*

아저씨 **ajeossi** *Mister, Uncle*

아주머니 **ajumeoni** *(married) middle-aged woman (polite)*

아직 **ajik** *yet*

아침 **achim** *morning*

아파트 **apateu** *apartment*

아홉 **ahop** *nine*

아프리카 **apeurika** *Africa*

안 **an** *inside*

안개가 끼다 **angaega kkida** *to fog*

안경 **angyeong** *glasses*

안녕하세요 **annyeonghaseyo** *hello*

안녕하십니까 **annyeonghasimnikka** *hello*

안녕히 가세요 **annyeonghi gaseyo** *goodbye*

안녕히 계세요 **annyeonghi gyeseyo** *goodbye*

안녕히 주무세요 **annyeonghi jumuseyo** *good night (polite)*

앉다 **anda** *to sit/to take a seat*

앉히다 **alda** *to seat someone*

알다 **alda** *to know*

알래스카 **allaeseuka** *Alaska*

앞 **ap** *front*

앞마당 **ammadang** *front yard*

애 **ae** *shortened form of* 아이 **ai** *child*

야구 **yagu** *baseball*

약 **yak** *medicine*

약속 **yaksok** *promise/appointment*

얘기 **yaegi** *shortened form of* 이야기 **iyagi** *story/talk*

어 ? **eo?** *uh?*

어둡다 **eodupda** *dark*

어디 **eodi** *where*

어떻다 **eotteota** *how*

어렵다 **eoryeopda** *difficult*

어머니 **eomeoni** *mother*

어서 오세요 **eoseo oseyo** *welcome (greeting)*

어제 **eoje** *yesterday*

언제 **eonje** *when*

엄마 **eomma** *mom*

에버랜드 **ebeoraendeu** *Everland*

에스컬레이터 **eseukeolleiteo** *escalator*

엘리베이터 **ellibeiteo** *elevator*

여덟 **yeodeol** *eight*

여섯 **yeoseot** *six*

여의도 **yeouido** *Yeouido*

여행 (여행하다) **yeohaeng (yeohaenghada)** *to travel*

연극을 보다 **yeongeugeul boda** *to watch a play*

열 **yeol** *ten*

염려 **yeomnyeo** *worry*

영어 책 **yeongeo chaek** *English book*

영화 **yeonghwa** *movie*

영화 감상 **yeonghwa gamsang** *movie watching*

영화관 **yeonghwagwan** *movie theater*

영화를 보다 **yeonghwareul boda** *to watch a movie*

영화배우 **yeonghwabaeu** *movie actor/actress*

영화 촬영 **yeonghwa chwaryeong** *movie shooting*

옆 **yeop** *side*

예쁘다 **yeppeuda** *pretty*

예순 **yesun** *sixty*

예의 **yeui** *courtesy*

오 **o** *five*

오늘 **oneul** *today*

오다 **oda** *to come*

오랜만이에요 **oraenmanieyo** *long time no see*

오른쪽 **oreunjjok** *right side*

오리 **ori** *duck*

오리엔테이션 **orienteisyeon** *orientation*

오십 **osip** *fifty*

오월 **owol** *May*

오이 **oi** *cucumber*

오전 **ojeon** *AM*

오천 원 **ocheon won** *five thousand won*

오토바이 **otobai** *motorcycle*

오후 **ohu** *PM*

온천 **oncheon** *spa*

올해 **olhae** *this year*

옷을 사다 **oseul sada** *to buy clothes*

와인 **wain** *wine*

왕의 남자 **wangui namja** *The King and the Clown (movie)*

왜 **wae** *why*

외곬 **oegol** *narrow-mindedness*

외투 **oetu** *coat*

왼쪽 **oenjjok** *left side*

요리 (요리하다) **yori (yorihada)** *to cook*

요리사 **yorisa** *chef/cook*

요일 **yoil** *days of the week*

요즘 **yojeum** *these days*

우리 **uri** *we/our/us*

우리 동네 **uri dongne** *our neighborhood/our town*

우유 **uyu** *milk*

우체국 **ucheguk** *post office*

우표 **upyo** *postage stamp*

운동 (운동하다) **undong (undonghada)** *to exercise*

운전하다 **unjeonhada** *to drive (a car)*

원 **won** *won (Korean currency)*

월요일 **woryoil** *Monday*

위 **wi** *above*

유럽 **yureop** *Europe*

유명 **yumyeong** *fame*

유월 **yuwol** *June*

육 **yuk** *six*

육십 **yuksip** *sixty*

은행 **eunhaeng** *bank*

음식 이름 **eumsik ireum** *names of food*

음악 감상 **eumak gamsang** *listening to music*

음악을 듣다 **eumageul deutda** *to listen to music*

의미 **uimi** *meaning*

의사 **uisa** *doctor*

의자 **uija** *chair*

이 **i** *two*

이름 **ireum** *name*

이번 달 **ibeon dal** *this month*

이번 주 **ibeon ju** *this week*

이십 **isip** *twenty*

이야기하다 **iyagihada** *to talk*

이월 **iwol** *February*

이집트 **ijipteu** *Egypt*

이탈리아 **itallia** *Italy*

이태원 **itaewon** *Itaewon (district)*

인사 **insa** *greeting*

인사동 **insadong** *Insadong (district)*

인터넷 (인터넷하다) **inteonet (inteonetada)** *(to surf) the Internet*

인터뷰 **inteobyu** *interview*

일 **il** *one/day*

일곱 **ilgop** *seven*

일과 **ilgwa** *daily activities*

일본 **ilbon** *Japan*

일본 사람 **ilbon saram** *Japanese person*

일상생활 **ilsangsaenghwal** *everyday life*

일어나다 **ireonada** *to wake up/to get up*

일요일 **iryoil** *Sunday*

일월 **irwol** *January*

일정 **iljeong** *schedule*

일흔 **ilheun** *seventy*

읽다 **ikda** *to read*

입학 **ipak** *entrance into a school*

있다 **itda** *to be/to exist*

잎 **ip** *leaf*

자 **ja** *ruler*

자기소개 **jagisogae** *self-introduction*

자다 **jada** *to sleep*

자장면 **jajangmyeon** *jajangmyeon (noodle dish)*

자전거를 타다 **jajeongeoreul tada** *to ride a bicycle*

작년 **jangnyeon** *last year*

작다 **jakda** *small*

잔디밭 **jandibat** *lawn*

잘 다녀와 **jal danyeowa** *see you later*

잘 먹겠습니다 **jal meokgetseumnida** *thanks for the meal (before meal)*

잘 먹었습니다 **jal meokgetseumnida** *thanks for the meal (after meal)*

잠을 자다 **jameul jada** *to sleep*

장소 **jangso** *place*

재미없다 **jaemieopda** *boring*

재미있다 **jaemiitda** *interesting/fun*

저 **jeo** *that*

저녁 **jeoryeok** *evening*

적다 **jeokda** *few/little*

전 **jeon** *before*

전시회 **jeonsihoe** *exhibition*

전통차를 마시다 **jeontongchareul masida** *to have a traditional tea*

전화를 하다 (걸다) **jeonhwareul hada (geolda)** *to make (a phone call)*

전화카드 **jeonhwakadeu** *telephone card*

젊다 **jeomda** *young*

점심 **jeomisim** *lunch/lunchtime*

점심을 먹다 **jeomsimeul meokda** *to have lunch*

젓가락 **jeotgarak** *chopsticks*

정류장 **jeongnyujang** *(bus/train) stop*

정리하다 **jeongnihada** *to go over/arrange*

정오 **jeongo** *noon*

제주도 **jejudo** *Jeju Island*

좁다 **jopda** *narrow*

좋다 **jota** *good*

죄송합니다 **joesonghamnida** *I am sorry (polite)*

주 **ju** *week*

주다 **juda** *to give*

주말 **jumal** *weekend*

주말 잘 보내세요 **jumal jal bonaeseyo**
have a good weekend (polite)

주말 잘 지내세요 **jumal jal jinaeseyo**
have a good weekend (polite)

주무시다 **jumusida** *to sleep (polite)*

주세요 **juseyo** *give it to me, please (I will take it)*

주스 **juseu** *juice*

주유소 **juyuso** *gas station*

주차장 **juchajang** *parking lot*

중국 **jungguk** *China*

중국 사람 **jungguk saram** *Chinese person*

중국집 **junggukjip** *Chinese restaurant*

지갑 **jigap** *wallet*

지금 **jigeum** *now*

지난달 **jinandal** *last month*

지난 일 **jinan il** *something that belongs to the past*

지난주 **jinanju** *last week*

지난 주말 **jinan jumal** *last weekend*

지도 **jido** *map*

지하 **jiha** *basement*

지하철 **jihacheol** *subway*

직업 **jigeop** *occupation*

집 **jip** *house*

짜다 **jjada** *salty*

짧다 **jjalda** *short*

쯤 **jjeum** *around/approximately*

찌개 **jjigae** *Korean stew*

찌르다 **jjireuda** *to poke*

ㅊ

차 **cha** *car*

차갑다 **chagapda** *cold*

창문 **changmun** *window*

채소 **chaeso** *vegetable*

책 **chaek** *book*

책상 **chaeksang** *desk*

책을 읽다 **chaegeul ikda** *to read books*

천 **cheon** *one thousand*

천둥이 치다 **cheondungi chida** *to thunder*

천만에요 **cheonmaneyo** *you're welcome*

천 원 **cheon won** *one thousand won*

청소하다 **cheongsohada** *to clean*

초 **cho** *second*

촬영 **chwaryeong** *filming*

최고 **choego** *best*

축구 **chukgu** *soccer*

축하합니다 **chukahamnida** *congratulations (formal)*

출입국관리소 **churipgukgwalliso** *Immigration Office*

춤을 추다 **chumeul chuda** *to dance*

춥다 **chupda** *cold*

취미 **chwimi** *hobby*

층 **cheung** *floor (of a building)*

치마 **chima** *skirt*

치약 **chiyak** *toothpaste*

친구를 만나다 **chingureul mannada** *to meet friends*

친절하다 **chinjeolhada** *kind*

칠 **chil** *seven*

칠십 **chilsip** *seventy*

칠월 **chirwol** *July*

칫솔 **chitsol** *toothbrush*

 ㅋ

카메라 **kamera** *camera*

카푸치노 **kapuchino** *cappuccino*

칼국수 **kalguksu** *kalguksu (noodle dish)*

캄보디아 **kambodia** *Cambodia*

캐나다 **kaenada** *Canada*

캔 커피 **kaen keopi** *canned coffee*

커피 **keopi** *coffee*

커피를 마시다 **keopireul masida** *to have some coffee*

커피숍 **keopisyop** *coffee shop*

컴퓨터 **keompyuteo** *computer*

컵 **keop** *cup*

컵 라면 **keop ramyeon** *cup noodles*

케냐 **kenya** *Kenya*

코 **ko** *nose*

코트디부아르 **koteudibuareu** *Côte d'Ivoire*

콜라 **kolla** *coke*

크다 **keuda** *big*

키 **ki** *height*

킬로그램 **killogeuraem** *kilogram*

타다 **tada** *to get on/to ride*

타이타닉 **taitanik** *the Titanic*

타조 **tajo** *ostrich*

태권도 **taegwondo** *taekwondo*

태권도장 **taegwondojang** *taekwondo studio/gym*

택시 **taeksi** *taxi*

테니스를 치다 **teniseureul chida** *to play tennis*

테니스장 **teniseujang** *tennis court*

텔레비전 **tellebijeon** *television*

텔레비전을 보다 **tellebijeoneul boda** *to watch TV*

토끼 **tokki** *rabbit*

토요일 **toyoil** *Saturday*

통조림 **tongjorim** *canned food*

투수 **tusu** *pitcher*

파 **pa** *leek*

파도 **pado** *wave*

파티를 하다 **patireul hada** *to have a party*

팔 (숫자) **pal (sutja)** *eight*

팔 (신체) **pal (sinche)** *arm*

팔다 **palda** *to sell*

팔십 **palsip** *eighty*

팔월 **parwol** *August*

편리하다 **pyeollihada** *convenient*

편의점 **pyeonuijeom** *convenience store*

편지를 쓰다 **pyeonjireul sseuda** *to write a letter*

포도 **podo** *grape*

폰 **pon** *phone*

프랑스 **peurangseu** *France*

피아노를 치다 **pianoreul chida** *to play the piano*

필리핀 **pillipin** *Philippines*

하나 **hana** *one*

하마 **hama** *hippo*

학교 **hakgyo** *school*

학년 **hangnyeon** *school year, grade*

학생 **haksaeng** *student*

학생 식당 **haksaeng sikdang** *student cafeteria*

한국 **hanguk** *Korea*

한국 드라마 **hanguk deurama** *Korean drama*

한국 사람 **hanguk saram** *Korean person*

한국어 **hangugeo** *Korean*

한국어를 가르치다 **hangugeoreul gareuchida** *to teach Korean*

한국어 수업 **hangugeo sueop** *Korean class*

한국어 책 **hangugeo chaek** *Korean book*

한국 음식 **hanguk eumsik** *Korean food*

한글 **Hangul** *Hangul*

한글날 **Hangullal** *Hangul Commemoration Day*

한남동 **hannamdong** *Hannam-dong (district)*

한잔하다 **hanjanhada** *to have a drink*

해 **hae** *year*

해 (태양) **hae (taeyang)** *sun*

해돋이 **haedoji** *sunrise*

햄 **haem** *ham*

허리 **heori** *waist*

현관 **hyeongwan** *the front door*

형광등 **hyeonggwangdeung** *light*

호떡 **hotteok** *hotteok (pancake)*

호수 **hosu** *lake*

호주 **hoju** *Australia*

호프 **hopeu** *pub*

혼자 **honja** *alone*

홍콩 **hongkong** *Hong Kong*

화가 **hwaga** *painter*

화요일 **hwayoil** *Tuesday*

화장실 **hwajangsil** *bathroom/restroom/toilet*

화장지 (티슈) **hwajangji (tisyu)** *toilet paper (tissue)*

회사 **hoesa** *corporation*

회의 **hoeui** *conference*

횡단보도 **hoengdanbodo** *crosswalk*

휴지 **hyuji** *trash*

휴지통 **hyujitong** *garbage can*

흐리다 **heurida** *cloudy*

히읗 **hieut** *the letter* ㅎ

● 기타 **gita others**

007 **gonggongchil** *007*

KTX **keitiekseu** *Korea Train Express*

"Books to Span the East and West"

Tuttle Publishing was founded in 1832 in the small New England town of Rutland, Vermont [USA]. Our core values remain as strong today as they were then—to publish best-in-class books which bring people together one page at a time. In 1948, we established a publishing office in Japan—and Tuttle is now a leader in publishing English-language books about the arts, languages and cultures of Asia. The world has become a much smaller place today and Asia's economic and cultural influence has grown. Yet the need for meaningful dialogue and information about this diverse region has never been greater. Over the past seven decades, Tuttle has published thousands of books on subjects ranging from martial arts and paper crafts to language learning and literature—and our talented authors, illustrators, designers and photographers have won many prestigious awards. We welcome you to explore the wealth of information available on Asia at **www.tuttlepublishing.com**.

Published by Tuttle Publishing, an imprint of Periplus Editions (HK) Ltd.

www.tuttlepublishing.com

이준기와 함께하는 안녕하세요 한국어 1
Copyright © Maribooks, 2010.
Originally published in Korea by Maribooks.
English translation rights arranged with Maribooks in care of Danny Hong Agency, Seoul.

English translation copyright © 2023 Periplus Editions (HK) Ltd.

Library of Congress Control Number: 2023944617

ISBN 978-0-8048-5620-1

TUTTLE PUBLISHING® is a registered trademark of Tuttle Publishing, a division of Periplus Editions (HK) Ltd.

Distributed by

North America, Latin America & Europe
Tuttle Publishing
364 Innovation Drive
North Clarendon,
VT 05759-9436 U.S.A.
Tel: 1 (802) 773-8930; Fax: 1 (802) 773-6993
info@tuttlepublishing.com
www.tuttlepublishing.com

Asia Pacific
Berkeley Books Pte. Ltd.
3 Kallang Sector #04-01
Singapore 349278
Tel: (65) 6741-2178; Fax: (65) 6741-2179
inquiries@periplus.com.sg
www.tuttlepublishing.com

25 24 23 23   5 4 3 2 1
Printed in China   2308EP